THE SELECTED LETTERS OF

HENRY JAMES

Great Letters Series

THE
SELECTED LETTERS OF
HENRY JAMES

EDITED WITH AN INTRODUCTION BY
LEON EDEL

FARRAR, STRAUS AND GIROUX

NEW YORK

First printing, 1955

Copyright 1955 by Leon Edel
Library of Congress catalog card number 55:11183
Manufactured in the United States of America
American Book–Stratford Press, Inc., New York
ISBN 0-374-52743-1

For DONALD BRIEN

A NOTE ON THE TEXT

In this volume are printed some hundred and twenty of the
thousands of letters written by Henry James. One half of those
given here appear for the first time. Obviously a selection so
limited from a correspondence so vast imposes a particular
responsibility upon the editor. For every letter chosen, fifty—
or a hundred—others might have been substituted, any one of
them conveying the tone, the style, the very atmosphere invariably evoked by James's vigorous epistolary pen.

It seemed profitless, therefore, to attempt to select "the best,"
or the "most representative," the "most friendly" or "most literary" of the novelist's letters. The letters were nearly all friendly
and certainly all were literary. The logic imposed upon the
editor was simply that of gathering as good a bouquet as possible out of a very large garden, and of trying to find a generous
number of samples of each kind of flower. In other words, once
the categories had been established, it became a question of discovering those letters that would best illustrate them. Readers
of this volume must not look, therefore, for letters to one or
another of James's friends or for certain famous letters already
in print. What they are being offered here, in a sense, is a
kind of guide to the different types of James letters—and some
suggestions as to how they should be read.

The letters selected have been taken from a variety of

sources: a few from the first and largest collection, edited by Percy Lubbock in two volumes in 1920; others are gathered from scattered volumes of memoirs, long out of print, appendices to diverse books, articles in periodicals and such collections as Elizabeth Robins's *Theatre and Friendship* or the *Letters to A. C. Benson* which appeared in small editions and are no longer available. The letters here published for the first time are drawn from various manuscript collections and private sources enumerated in the acknowledgment.

James did not, on the whole, tend to be brief in his correspondence. Many of his letters in print exist therefor in truncated form. One, written from Paris to his brother William, was published piecemeal in three different volumes—Lubbock printed one section, Ralph Barton Perry used another in his life of William James, and F. O. Matthiessen printed still another portion in his anthology of James family writings. The letter has been re-assembled and collated with the original manuscript and is given here in its entirety for the first time. Most of the letters in the present volume were copied from the manuscript and are given without abridgement. Those taken from other sources, without the opportunity of collation with the original, appear to contain some excisions, but these are few in number.

James wrote his letters rapidly and abbreviated certain words, writing &, and wh. for *which,* etc. These words have been written out in full here as a convenience to the reader. Otherwise the original text has been carefully followed.

L. E.

ACKNOWLEDGMENT

I am deeply indebted to Mr. William James of Cambridge, nephew of the novelist, for the generous access he has continued to give me to his uncle's papers. I owe also a special debt of gratitude to Mary James Vaux, daughter of Robertson James, for making available to me a considerable body of family documents.

Much of the hitherto unpublished material included in this volume comes from collections in various libraries, former correspondents of Henry James, and private collections. I wish to express thanks to the following who supplied such material or who provided information of use to me in the selection and editing of the letters:

F. B. Adams Jr. librarian of the Morgan Library; the late Lady Alexander; C. Waller Barrett; Miss Theodora Bosanquet; Donald G. Brien; Earl Daniels; the late Lucien Daudet; Daphne Du Maurier; the late Lady Forbes-Robertson; John Frost of the New York University Library; Donald Gallup of the Yale Collection of American Literature; William M. Gibson of New York University; Miss Virginia Harlow; Rupert Hart-Davis; William A. Jackson, librarian of the Houghton Library at Harvard; Miss Carolyn E. Jakeman of the Houghton Library; the late Edna Kenton; Rev. John LaFarge S.J.; Harold M. Landon; Dan H. Laurence of Hofstra College; the late Urbain Mengin;

ACKNOWLEDGMENT

Burgess Noakes; Simon Nowell-Smith, Librarian of the London Library; the late Elizabeth Robins; John K. Reeves of Skidmore College; Christopher St. John; the late G. Bernard Shaw; Norman Holmes Pearson of Yale; the late Jocelyn Persse; Miss Florence Pertz; the estate of William Roughead; Miss Ethel Sands; Robert M. Taylor; the late Allan Wade; Miss Dorothy Ward; Carl J. Weber of Colby College; Herbert F. West of Dartmouth College.

Collections of the Library of Congress, the British Museum, the National Library of Scotland, the New York Public Library, the Brotherton Library of the University of Leeds, the Princeton University Library, the Baker Library of Dartmouth College and the libraries of Johns Hopkins University and Colby College were consulted, as were the archives of Macmillan & Co. Ltd. and William Blackwood & Sons. On all sides I have been shown the greatest courtesy and given the fullest assistance in my task.

L. E.

CONTENTS

INTRODUCTION

IN the novels and stories of Henry James letters are usually burned. "I have done the great thing," says Miss Tina after she has put the precious Aspern papers, one by one, into the kitchen fire. It is the "great thing;" it is also "the real right thing" in the world of Henry James—silence, privacy, anonymity. In his personal notebooks the novelist jotted down on March 26, 1892: "The idea of the *responsibility* of destruction—the destruction of papers, letters, records, etc. connected with the private and personal history of some great and honoured name." Thus, Peter Baron, coming upon the letters of Sir Dominick Ferrand in the secret compartment of an old desk, withholds them from prying hands. There was a secret compartment in Henry James's desk at Lamb House but no letters were found in it—only a prescription for eye-glasses and a gout remedy. And this was not surprising. The rules of his fiction ruled his life.

One day, during the last years, James built a large bonfire in his Lamb House garden and piled upon it the accumulated correspondence of four decades. The irony implicit in this act could have been the theme of still another Henry James story. Like Dickens, who had built a similar fire at Gad's Hill, the American novelist warmed his hands by blazing letters written not by him but by others *to him*. And like Dickens he could have exclaimed: "Would to God every letter *I* have ever written was on that pile." But this was not to be. James might destroy the letters of his contemporaries; he could not touch the match of privacy to the thousands he had himself written for more than fifty years on both sides of the Atlantic. These were always treasured for their ornate expression of the amenities of friendship, or because of the abundance of feeling that was poured into them or, above all, because they represented the over-flow of a great creativity, the rich surplus of Henry James's genius. It might be conservatively estimated that seven thousand are extant and every year more turn up. Even when James admonished his correspondents "Burn this, *burn, burn,*" (although what was to be burned was nothing more than a harmless anecdote) they did not respect his wishes. Perhaps in asking for destruction he put a premium on his words: the request was almost an incentive to preservation; it tended to make what he had written assume an importance he had never intended in writing his letter.

Not all persons, indeed, were ideally capable of the "great thing" and James himself had faltered before the Lamb House bonfire. He held out a handful of cherished letters. In a number of instances he saved one trivial letter from each correspondent —as if to preserve one little part of them from complete obliteration. From these little snippets of letters we can deduce to a degree the pattern of James's destruction. But each relic serves also as an unintended mockery: it tells us that there were other letters which we will never see, that in this given case or that there has been a victory for the private life.

Early in his career, James wrote in a review of Hawthorne's notebooks that the artist can only blame himself for any personal papers that survive him. Nevertheless he recognized the need of the historian and the biographer for more letters and documents than he can ever use. He accepted the fortuitous circumstances that had preserved the letters of Balzac, Sainte-Beuve, Flaubert, and indeed wrote lengthy and fascinated articles about them. But in reviewing the Balzac correspondence he could not suppress the feeling that he had "broken open a cabinet or rummaged an old desk." In later years, however much he might protest at the way in which George Sand's life was stripped bare by the publication of her love letters, he nevertheless read them with the same mixture of curiosity and perturbation. Did not such posthumous relics simplify unduly the biographer's task? Could not a more equal battle be arranged between the artist who wishes to remain locked in the "invulnerable granite" of his art and the biographer who seeks to wrest from him every secret of his life? Every paper burned, James wrote, forces the biographer to confront the work itself. There could be an even more effective coercion—that of "every letter unanswered."

This was genuinely to disarm posterity. It offered it the silence of the tomb, the eloquence of the art. By the same stroke it devaluated all letters that had been answered. It was perhaps Henry James's way of implying that the really important letters of his life—the intimate letters—were never written and that all others were perhaps a necessary, but carefully-worded, residue.

I

The residue, if one can apply such a word to so huge a quantity of letters, nevertheless offers us a few distinct loopholes through which we may come closer to Henry James. Certain facts are there from which others may be deduced; for the letters of a great writer, even when they are written with extreme caution, are still projected from the same mind and set upon paper by the same pen that produced the work's "invulnerable granite." Henry James could, and doubtless did, withhold his personal life from many of his letters. He could not, however, inhibit his artist's nature. His pen invariably ran away from him to indulge its fluent self, to express the generosity and warmth of his friendship, to throw out ideas, prejudices, opinions, in gossamer phrases or sonorous sentences. Long before the end, it had become second nature with him to clothe the innocuous small-change of letter-writing in the vestments of literature. Such letters may signify little and sometimes indeed, by their very volume, they degenerate into mere sound. They are still touched, however, by the mind and the imagination that fathered them. Henry James was incapable of offering a thought without pinning a flower in its button-hole and the reverse of this was that he could disguise the absence of thought by a shameless gilding of his verbal lilies. "When I lay down the mercenary pen my fingers ache too much to grasp the sentimental one," he wrote to one of his correspondents. He did, however, grasp the sentimental one at the end of a day's work, or sometimes at the beginning, to dash off in his large racing hand a dozen or more letters. When today we sometimes recover the full dozen we can see the way in which the well-minted epistolary phrase is often made to serve over and over on the given occasion. Yet each letter remains good and vivid talk addressed to a particular ear. He could assume a knightly attitude:

> I envy you the sweet labor of feathering your nest at Bellosguardo [he is writing to his friend Lizzie Boott] and if I were an angel, would pluck the softest plumes from my own wings to upholster your own peculiar corner. But I am not an angel; I am only a poor tired letter-writer (this is the sixth letter I've written this morning,) who however thinks *you* an angel.

He could issue, late in life, a gentle summons:

> Dearest Jocelyn, If you are miraculously able to come—on the 7th and to sit through my twaddle, to feel you beautifully

[xvi]

there will give all the pleasure in life and be an immense support, to your all-affectionate old Henry James.

Or he could accept an invitation with the ponderous humor of an Olympian:

Dearest Clare, You should have heard the peal of strident laughter with which I greeted—and treated—your question of whether I shall really turn up on Friday next; a question so solemnly and so sacredly settled in the affirmative, an intention so ardently cherished, a prospect so fondly caressed . . .

or give his correspondent the broad descriptive strokes of

I was lifted over the wide sea in the great smooth huge kind Mauretania as if I had been carried in a gigantic grandmother's bosom and the gentle giantess had made but one mighty stride of it from land to land . . .

This virtuosity of the mail-box, and in later years of the telegram, makes James's social correspondence seem like a glistening spider-web of amiability. Taken by themselves, these letters offer us the affectionate, the chatty, friendly side of the novelist. They tell us little about his art and indeed very little about the man who wrote them save that he possessed a verbal magic which he liked to wrap around friends and acquaintances the better to tie them—by these colored threads—to his lonely writing table; or that he was overgenerous of his valuable time. Unfortunately too many of the James letters in print are of this particular type and their very abundance has produced an impression of a greater epistolary evasiveness and artificiality than is actually the case. Hardly any of the novelist's business letters have been published and too few of those dealing with the craft of fiction as he practiced it.

II

Every letter unanswered. Some letters—particularly in a trans-Atlantic correspondence—can not be left unanswered, especially when editorial projects and literary reputations have to be discussed and matters of payment and copyright settled. James's "working letters" are the reverse of his social letters. It is true that he is often sociable in them, especially when he is dealing with an old and devoted friend who happens also to be an editor, like William Dean Howells. Otherwise he is brief and very much to the point—the point being always for James, money. The business letters here published for the first time reveal a side of James never before fully disclosed: the Henry James of the market place, a professional writer driving his bargains and conducting his financial affairs with an airy majesty that brooks no contradictions and makes few compromises, in an era when writers could dictate their terms, and contracts were signed by informal letter-pledge. "I have no right to let it be anything but a pure money question," James says to Howells in 1874 when he is offering him *Roderick Hudson*. In 1876 it is "the money question solely that has to determine me" in the disposal of *The American* and that same year he tells Whitelaw Reid of the *Tribune* that he cannot write that newspaper's kind of reportage "especially for the money" they are paying him. In 1884 he asks $500 an instalment for the serial rights of *The Princess Casamassima* (but settles for less), and one of his prime motives in his attempt to write for the stage is to earn more money than his books bring in. These letters are shrewd and practical: their money-hauntedness would not be questioned in any professional correspondence but might be in this instance because of the legend that James did not really have to live by his pen. The truth was, however, that he did. He had early demonstrated that he could earn his way by his writing. He did not like to appeal to his father for funds especially since the family income was heavily drained by the needs of the younger sons and the invalid daughter. Writing was the key to the freedom which Henry cherished, and he was practical enough to sell to the best market, and artist enough to feel that the world could never pay him sufficiently for what he had to offer. Indeed when he finally inherited his share of his father's estate, at forty, his affairs had so prospered that he turned over his annual income entirely to his sister and continued to make his way by his profession. His scale of living was modest and comfortable; his extravagances were his London clubs and his continental travels; but the journeys too were usually turned into literary capital. He wrote almost daily—novels, tales, articles, book reviews, drama criticism, literary portraits, travel pieces— seldom turning down an assignment which would yield him a handsome fee. *"Make the pot boil,"* he counselled a young artist, *"at any price, as the only real basis of freedom and sanity."* And he underlined his words. Again, he explained that the "the potboiler . . . represents, in the lives of all artists, some of the most beautiful things ever done by them." One has only to read his letter to Sir Frederick Macmillan rejecting the offer of an advance sum for *The Tragic Muse* which he deemed insufficient, to see how adroitly and resolutely the novelist held his ground in his particular business world.

This Balzacian money-side of Henry James is to be found in one section of his professional correspondence. The other is his expression of that pride of craft which was so strong in the writers of the last century. Side by side with the problems of the literary market we find James's pronouncements on the art of fiction, his fight for international copyright, his forthright statement against the censorship of plays, his insistence upon the writer's need for absolute freedom to express himself without dictation from self-appointed moralists and politicians. James had a strong sense of belonging to a dedicated order, the fraternity of letters. That fraternity demanded loyalty, unity, protection against the Philistines, devotion to one's fellows. His loyalty was illustrated by the promptness with which he participated in the bestowing of honors upon his literary peers and the generosity he showed in helping his fellow-writers when they were visited by misfortune. It was Henry James who, on learning that Stephen Crane's hours were numbered, slipped a check for fifty pounds into a letter to Mrs. Crane suggesting that she cash it without saying another word. "I've money, moreover I care . . ."

III

The early letters of Henry James, largely to his family, are pictorial and documentary, as if the future novelist were seeking to capture and retain the fleeting hours of his youth upon the pages of his correspondence—his impressions of Italy, his emotions and "vibrations" on discovering the world of art, his feelings about European manners and the American vision of them. These were the letters that the writer's father proudly read to Emerson and Charles Eliot Norton sent to his friend John Ruskin. The later letters, those written to his contemporaries and particularly to his fellow-craftsmen, belong to the intercourse of first-rate minds, although ideas in general are not discussed in them. The concrete is preferred to the general and the abstract. "I regard the march of history," James wrote to Norton, "very much as a man placed astride of a locomotive, without knowledge of help, would regard the progress of that vehicle. To stick on, somehow, and even to enjoy the scenery as we pass, is the sum of my aspirations." He might have added that he wanted also to leave some record of the adventure of sticking on and of such of the scenery as caught his fancy. Henry James's mind was not given to high flights on great universal themes; his was not the allegorizing mind, or the mind that seeks mystical or recondite symbols to express itself. His letters to his contemporaries contain a fund of ironic wisdom and only passing talk of the passions and illusions of his art, the whole "creative mystery" to which he was ever loyal. His point of view is always aesthetic and he sketches those ideas that will emerge, full-blown, in the late prefaces on the art of fiction, *his* fiction, and what was to be learned from his particular practice of it. He looks always at experience as a rational being and with a deep fund of feeling understands the helplessness of man before the wear and tear of life. Death he can accept, and does with a compassion and tenderness that make of some of his letters of condolence beautiful prose elegies. A striking example of this is his tribute to Mrs. Procter who had known all the great poets of her century: "She was a kind of window in the past—now it's closed there is so much less air." Or the words with which he describes, to her daughter, the funeral of Fanny Kemble and sums up her life:

> I am conscious of a strange bareness and a kind of evening chill as it were in the air, as if some great object that had filled it for long had left an emptiness—from displacement— to all the senses.

The letters of James's "middle years"—that is from the 1870's to the 1890's—are on the whole terse and lively, reflecting the boundless energy of a man leading a life of movement, preoccupied with his work, his goals always within view. During these years he uses half sheets for his correspondence, as if to indicate that he has little time and can confine himself only to polite brevity. But after 1895, as he settles down to dictating directly to the typewriter and moves from London to Rye, in Sussex, his correspondence undergoes a significant change. Now there are long, lonely evenings in the quiet town near the salt flats, the great marsh and the roaring sea. Sometimes wintry storms rage, the wind howls down the old chimneys of Lamb House and James, secure from the driving rain, can talk endlessly by his bright fireside to his old friends. By day he dictates; by night he returns to the use of his pen. Now he writes on the full sheet, giving himself the latitude of his leisure. He himself described the essential characteristics of the letters of his later years to his old Venetian friend, Mrs. Daniel Curtis:

> I seem to myself to do nothing now but wallow in the apologetic. When I am not apologizing for delayed letters I am doing the conciliatory for writing them in Remingtonese. Most often I am doing both at once—that is pleading guilty to deplorable lapses in the very accents of the machine which is now definitely supplanting my no longer at all manageable or controllable, though at the same time essentially peaceful and innocuous fist. I can't say it's as long as it's broad—I mean the question of the dictated letter; it has all the air, thanks to the cloud of explanations in which it moves, of becoming ever so much longer.

The letters did become longer and more intricate in expression. The late style, with its euphemisms, parentheses, inflections, ornate metaphors, nuanced impressions, cadenced sentences, was carried over from the novels into the letterwriting. Friends of James have said that the best of these late letters sound like the very talk of the novelist during his hours of ease at Rye. Sometimes the letters seem rather tired and perfunctory, for correspondence cannot always be kept up at the pitch of art. And sometimes the sentences, in their orotundity, sound as if James has strayed into a maze of his own making and is more concerned with creeping out of it by a show of ingenuity than in completing the letter. John Singer Sargent, reading them with the eye of a painter, felt he was "watching the evolution of a bird of paradise in a tropical jungle." On the other hand, Harold Laski, reading them with the eye of a social theorist, wrote to Mr. Justice Holmes "these letters make me vomit." And while these extremes of feeling tell us more about the readers of the letters than the letters themselves, they show perhaps that the correspondence of Henry James is capable of evoking strong emotions, mixed though they may be. Neither Sargent's descriptive view, nor Laski's revulsion, took account sufficiently of the fact that these were letters not intended for their eyes. They belonged, in reality, to two lives only—James's and the person he was addressing. The reading of the correspondence of great men is, after all, a socially acceptable form of eavesdropping, and we must always remember that the voice we hear is speaking in another room—and not to us.

What becomes clear when we have listened to James's voice for a long time is that it has many inflections and tones, suited in each case to the person he is addressing. He is often at his most syrupy when writing to a mere acquaintance; tartness and bluntness were reserved for his intimates. Yet even when he is doing something as perfunctory as explaining to an invited guest how to make his way from Charing Cross to Ashford, there to change for the train to Rye, and assuring him that he will be met by the host himself at the station and marched up the cobbled hill to Lamb House, he is spinning his routine ritual as part of the elaborate web he wove around his relationships with men and women. The visitors to Rye were numerous and the ritual was usually the same: yet each instance had its particular variations and stemmed from James's overwhelming need to mould and structure life, to give form and meaning to all experience, to create the order that made for calm and security.

All his friends have testified to the outpouring of affection they received from him during these visits. The friendly embrace, the pat on the shoulder, were ways of putting himself into a reassuring relation with them and we can discern a similar tendency in his letters. These often began and ended, as one of the novelist's nephews was to remark, "by enveloping the person addressed in some kind of affectionate hug." It was fraternal when he was addressing his illustrious colleagues; intimate when he spoke to such London friends as Rhoda Broughton or Lucy Clifford; paternal when from benign old age he saluted the bright young men of letters and of society—the Hugh Walpoles and Jocelyn Persses—who sparkled then with promises of achievement, literary and social, the fading of which James did not live to see. In the letters the affection sometimes becomes coyness, or is surrounded with too many smothering metaphors; but it has its spontaneous side as well, the same kind of spontaneity James showed once when, receiving a visit from Bernard Shaw at Lamb House, he rushed across the lawn to plant a kiss in the best Gallic manner, on both his cheeks as if he were awarding him the Legion of Honor. Shaw told this story many years later in a tone of dewy amazement. Amazement it well might be, for James by this demonstration of feeling for a playwright he liked, also broke through the Shavian incapacity to communicate with people save across a brilliant wall of words.

IV

Henry James, of course, had his own brilliant wall of words. It was reserved in particular for those letters in which he was called upon to play his role as a celebrity, acknowledge uninvited gifts, or show an interest in books written by anxious novelists who sought a word, a sign, a nod, from the Master. Such intrusions into his private life were handled by James with artful efficiency. He resorted invariably to verbal ambiguity and ironic shadings. It was an encircling process by which he managed to be candid while relying on the vanity of his correspondents to read only that which would please them. In writing to close friends James did not resort to such indirection: there is no damning with faint praise, for instance, when he tells Hugh Walpole that his new novel suffers from a "vast formless featherbediness." Other letters show James characteristically structuring the situation: he praises where he can use a series of cushion-words which will surround the expression of the truth or act as an immediate palliative to the administered shock. Sometimes the cushion-words neutralized the criticism to such a degree that the correspondent tended to overlook the real significance of what was being said. An outstanding example is to be found in certain of the letters to Mrs. Humphry Ward which, despite their sharp and direct critical content, she judged to be so flattering that she reproduced them in later prefaces—much to James's embarrassment. For the cushioning process James had his special phrase. It was the "mere twaddle of graciousness." A key to the process is to be found in the letter which James wrote to Sarah Orne Jewett who had sent him her historical novel, *The Tory Lover*. The novelist begins by politely circling round what he wants to say: but for once he grows weary of the attempt to marshal soft words. We can see it happening as he writes. He thanks Miss Jewett for her "charming" and "generous" present. He tells her he has read the book with an "earnest, a pensive, a liberal—yes a benevolent attention." The word "benevolent" might pass unnoticed but it is already a hint that he has had to invoke generosity in the process of his reading. He promptly softens this ambiguity by speaking of the "charming touch, tact and taste" and then just as promptly adds the nullifying ". . . of this ingenious exercise." Then suddenly he throws away all the cushions ". . . how little I am in sympathy with experiments of its general (to my sense) misguided stamp."

> There I am!—yet I don't do you the outrage, as a fellow craftsman and a woman of genius and courage, to suppose you not as conscious as I am myself of all that, in these questions of art and truth and sincerity, is beyond the mere twaddle of graciousness.

This letter, then, teaches us how to read James's letters. It also suggests that we must take very seriously his repeated warning that he demands attentive reading, for each word is used to particular ends. There are, for example, letters in which James speaks of writers and painters as "clever" and this might seem like praise until we discover that the novelist put little store in cleverness. It was his way often of dismissing mere surface competence devoid of deeper intelligence and feeling.

A particularly deceptive instance of the "mere twaddle" is the famous letter to Walter Berry, printed by Lubbock, in which James thanks him for the gift of an elaborately-wrought leather dressing case designed for more ardent and less sedentary travellers than the novelist. Never once is this elaborate object mentioned in the letter. James piles pyramid upon pyramid of satiric description of the role it is destined to play in his life, "the tawny lion, portentous creature, in my path."

I can't get past him, I can't get round him, and on the other hand he stands glaring at me, refusing to give way and practically blocking all my future. I can't live with him, you see; because I can't live *up* to him. His claims, his pretensions, his dimensions, his assumptions and consumptions, above all the manner in which he causes every surrounding object (on my poor premises or within my poor range) to tell a dingy or deplorable tale—all this makes him the very scourge of my life, the very blot on my scutcheon.

What James is saying in this elegant banter—which was highly pleasing to the recipient—is that he wishes Berry had never dumped on him the glittering, glazed, polished, expensive but quite useless object. It has "got me down forever" and "it makes me feel so awkward and graceless and poor." Euphemism is piled upon euphemism; the very thickness of the gilding takes on meaning for us. But it never occurred to Berry that he had received from James anything but a brilliant and whimsical letter of thanks.

The same kind of banter was extended to the telegrams James indited to his friends. The brevity of this form was a challenge to ingenuity and he liked nothing better than to pack adverbial politeness into a succinct message. "Intensely though respectfully deprecate social attendance at station. Elegant choice of cabs." Such badinage was cherished with the longer letters.

V

Comparatively few of the hundreds of letters Henry James wrote to his family—his parents, his brothers, his sister, his beloved Aunt Kate—have been given to the world. The best of them are very long and usually only excerpts have been published. A series of fragments appeared in the two volumes of James's letters published in 1920; a goodly number can be

found in Ralph Barton Perry's life of William James, and excerpts are included in the Matthiessen anthology of James
family writings. It would take many volumes to give them in
their entirety. The early letters to the parents are the travel
letters to which I have already alluded. Then, as he journeyed
in the exercise of his profession, the letters become a regular
chronicle of life in London, Rome, Paris. Many are filled with
business details, since for a few years, both Henry James the
elder and his wife acted informally as their son's agents in
America, receiving cheques from the magazines and taking care
of immediate publication problems that required quick decisions and impersonal correspondence.

After the death of the parents, the principal correspondence
is between Henry and his elder brother William. For the next
thirty years the trans-Atlantic exchanges between the philosopher and the novelist continued with a warmth and consistency
that reveals to the full the singular bonds of mind and heart
that united them. Family loyalties and family feeling among the
Jameses were strong, and in a group so articulate, found high
expression in the letters they exchanged. In these letters no
subterfuges were needed, no irony, no cushion-words. The letters are less a chronicle of daily life than a reflection upon the
unfolding world, a quick, sympathetic play of ideas between the
two, occasional comments upon current events and such personal family matters as had to be discussed. William's letters
contain also blunt critiques of Henry's works to which the
novelist replied sometimes cheerfully and sometimes with a
helpless shrug.

Taken as a whole, it might be said that Henry James's correspondence is the oddest of any man of letters of his time. While
letters tend to be many things to many men, James's, preserved in their abundance, take on all the complexities of his

personality and all the refinements of his relationships with his fellow-men. And since many of the letters were conceived as art they can, legitimately—even though we eavesdrop in reading them—consider them as corollary to some of his work. Too many of them have been read at their face value and out of the context of his life. They must be seen in all their points of attachment to the novelist's daily experience—and if this is true, in a measure, of the letters of any writer, we must nevertheless insist upon its importance here because of the multiplicity of James's points of attachment. Yet if one were to seek some common denominator for the great majority of them, it would be to see them as reflecting James's singular devotion to his aesthetic beliefs: art was supreme for him and even when it dealt with gross realities, there was the beauty inherent in the imaginative process that created it. What he is saying always is that the artist must live in his world, and by live he meant *see*, be *aware*, feel: and be addicted to the expression of truth about it. He must be proud of his virtuosity and jealous of his prerogatives, passionate in his pride and proud of his passions. Above all he must be kind, generous, warm. "You are really too savage with your painters and poets and dilettanti," he says in a letter to Vernon Lee: "*life* is less criminal, less obnoxious, less objectionable, less crude, more *bon enfant*, more mixed and casual, and even in its most offensive manifestations, more *pardonable*, than the unholy circle with which you have surrounded your heroine."

Here spoke the Henry James who refused ever to set himself up as a judge of his fellows and who wanted to see the *comédie humaine* in its many-sidedness. This note of compassion is to be found even in the most ornate of his letters. It is the human warmth of his epistolary art that undoubtedly impelled his numerous correspondents to tie up the thick bundles of his letters and put them aside instead of allowing the match of time to consume them. Thus preserved for us, they constitute a great literary heritage, to be cherished, read, understood.

Leon Edel

New York University

JAMES FAMILY AND
OTHER CORRESPONDENTS

ABBEY, EDWIN AUSTIN (1852-1911), painter and illustrator whose "Quest of the Holy Grail" murals are in the Boston Public Library.

ADAMS, HENRY (1838-1918), historian, author of *Mont-St. Michel and Chartres* and *The Education of Henry Adams*.

ALDRICH, THOMAS BAILEY (1836-1907), author, editor of the *Atlantic Monthly* from 1881 to 1890.

ALEXANDER, SIR GEORGE (1858-1918), popular London actor-manager at the turn of the century who produced James's *Guy Domville*.

ARCHER, WILLIAM (1856-1924), drama critic and playwright, English translator of Ibsen.

ASQUITH, H. H., Earl of Oxford and Asquith (1852-1928), British prime minister from 1908 to 1916.

BESANT, SIR WALTER (1836-1901), a minor Victorian novelist and historian.

BOOTT, ELIZABETH (DUVENECK) (1846-1888), wife of the artist Frank Duveneck. She served as model for Pansy, in James's *The Portrait of a Lady*.

BROUGHTON, RHODA (1840-1920), English novelist and close friend of Henry James for many years.

BURNETT, FRANCES HODGSON (1849-1924), Anglo-American novelist, author of *Little Lord Fauntleroy*.

BYNNER, WITTER (1881-   ), American author and poet.

CLIFFORD, MRS. W. K. (? -1929), widow of a famous mathematician, novelist and dramatist, an intimate friend of Henry James.

CONRAD, JOSEPH (1857-1924), Polish mariner who left the sea to become an English novelist.

DALY, AUGUSTIN (1838-1899), American playwright and theatre manager.

DAUDET, ALPHONSE (1840-1897), French novelist. James translated his *Port Tarascon* into English.

DU MAURIER, GEORGE (1834-1896), illustrator and cartoonist, author of *Trilby*.

FORD, FORD MADOX (HUEFFER) (1873-1935), novelist, author of *Henry James: A Critical Study* (1913).

ELLIOTT, GERTRUDE (1871-1940), later Lady Forbes-Robertson, American actress, sister of Maxine Elliott.

FULLERTON, W. MORTON (1865-1952), American journalist distinguished for his work for the *Times* of London and his editorials on American politics in *Le Figaro*.

GARDNER, ISABELLA STEWART (1840-1924), Wealthy American art lover who built Fenway Court in Boston.

GARLAND, HAMLIN (1860-1940), American novelist of the Middle Border.

GODKIN, EDWIN LAWRENCE (1831-1902), founder and editor of the *Nation;* one of the first editors to publish Henry James.

GOSSE, SIR EDMUND (1849-1928), author, translator, critic, librarian of the House of Lords and intimate of Henry James particularly during his London years.

HERRICK, ROBERT (1868-1938), Chicago novelist and teacher.

HOLMES, JUSTICE OLIVER WENDELL (1841-1935), son of Oliver Wendell Holmes, associate justice of the Supreme Court 1902 to 1932.

HOWELLS, WILLIAM DEAN (1837-1920), novelist, editor of the *Atlantic Monthly* 1871-1881 and a life-long friend of Henry James.

JAMES, ALICE (1848-1892), sister of the novelist, whose journal was published in 1934.

JAMES, HENRY, SR. (1811-1882), father of Henry and William James, writer and lecturer, author of *The Secret of Swedenborg*.

JAMES, MARY WALSH (1810-1882) mother of William and Henry James.

JAMES, ROBERTSON (1846-1910), youngest brother of Henry James.

JAMES, WILLIAM (1842-1910), elder brother of the novelist, philosopher and psychologist.

JEWETT, SARAH ORNE (1849-1909), American author known for her studies of New England life.

KEMBLE, FRANCES ANNE (1809-1893), member of the famous Kemble family of actors, generally known as Fanny Kemble, famous in her later years for her Shakespearian readings.

LA FARGE, JOHN (1835-1910), painter, distinguished for his work in stained glass, an early friend and mentor of the novelist.

LEE, VERNON (1856-1935), pseudonym of Violet Paget, English essayist and novelist.

LINTON, ELIZA LYNN (1822-1898), Victorian novelist.

LOWELL, JAMES RUSSELL (1819-1891), poet, essayist and editor; U.S. minister in England 1880-1885.

MACMILLAN, SIR FREDERICK (1851-1936), member of the firm of Macmillan & Co. publishers, elected its chairman in 1898.

NORRIS, WILLIAM EDWARD (1847-1925), English novelist.

NORTON, CHARLES ELIOT (1827-1908), co-editor of the *North American Review* 1864-1868, professor of history of art at Harvard 1873-1898 and translator of Dante.

NORTON, GRACE (1834-1926), sister of Charles Eliot Norton and Cambridge friend of the novelist to whom James wrote some of his finest letters.

PENNELL, JOSEPH (1857-1926), illustrator, etcher and lithographer; illustrator of several of James's volumes of travel.

PERRY, THOMAS SERGEANT (1845-1928) editor and critic, Newport school-mate and lifelong friend of Henry James.

REID, WHITELAW (1837-1912), editor of the New York *Tribune* 1872-1905, ambassador to Britain 1905-1912.

RITCHIE, ANNE THACKERAY (1837-1919), elder daughter of W. M. Thackeray, and author of a number of novels.

ROBINS, ELIZABETH (1865-1952), American actress famous for the creation of Ibsen roles in England. Played the role of Mme. de Cintré in James's dramatization of *The American*.

SCUDDER, HORACE ELISHA (1838-1902), editor of the *Atlantic Monthly* 1890-1898.

SHAW, G. BERNARD (1856-1950), Irish dramatist, critic, novelist.

SHORTER, CLEMENT KING (1858-1926), English author and journalist, editor of the *London Illustrated News* 1891-1900.

SMALLEY, GEORGE WASHBURN (1833-1916), American journalist. European correspondent of the New York *Tribune* 1866-1895.

STEPHEN, SIR LESLIE (1832-1904), English writer and editor, published "Daisy Miller" in the *Cornhill Magazine* thereby launching Henry James in England.

STEVENSON, ROBERT LOUIS (1850-1894), poet, essayist, novelist.

TERRY, DAME ELLEN (1848-1928), Noted English actress for whom James wrote a one act play later known as *The High Bid*.

WALPOLE, SIR HUGH (1884-1941), novelist and friend of Henry James during the last eight years of the novelist's life.

WELLS, HERBERT GEORGE (1866-1946), English novelist, sociologist, historian and Utopian.

WHARTON, EDITH (1862-1937), American novelist, friend of James's last years.

THE SELECTED LETTERS OF
HENRY JAMES

I

YOUTH, FAMILY, FRIENDS

FROM his earliest years Henry James had a vision of life on two
continents. He learned as a boy to look at Europe with observant
American eyes; and being observant could discern also how the
Europeans looked at America. Thoughtful, bookish, full of
high spirits and an unusual degree of curiosity, he came to be as
much at home in London and Paris as in New York and Boston.
He was born on April 15, 1843, a stone's throw from Washington
Square, at No. 21 Washington Place, where today the Brown
Building of New York University stands. His father, after whom
he was named, was the son of a prosperous Albany merchant and
banker, who had immigrated from Ireland just after the American Revolution. The elder Henry James rebelled against the
Calvinism of his Albany father, and in a search for a less de-
manding Deity discovered Swedenborg's visions of the "cor-
respondences" between earthly effects and heavenly causes. In
the writings of Swedenborg the senior Henry found the peace
and guidance he had sought. He devoted his life to spreading
his gospel.

Having been exposed to strict disciplines in childhood, the
father gave his own children—four boys and a girl—free rein.
His eldest son, William, became a philosopher; his second son

[3]

a novelist; the two younger sons, Garth Wilkinson (Wilky) and Robertson (Bob) fought in the Civil War and then pushed westward with the railway. The daughter, Alice, was nervous, highstrung, with a keen mind and pen. Her journal published in 1934 showed her to be an acute observer and commentator on the life she watched from her perpetual sick-room.

Henry was taken abroad by his parents when he was six months old. He emerged from the nursery in Windsor, England and was not quite three when the family returned to Albany and New York. His boyhood was spent in an assortment of private schools and in the streets, in and around Fifth Avenue, between 14th Street and the Square. His mother, Mary Walsh James, was a woman of considerable strength of character, worshipped by her husband, devoutly loved by her children. The atmosphere of the home tended to be almost excessively "permissive." In his old age the novelist wondered whether he had not been allowed to flounder too much: but he concluded that it was this very process—involving to a degree paternal laxities and maternal discipline—that endowed him with the capacity to formulate his own standards and muddle out the world around him for himself. Throughout his creative career he was to believe that the greatest good was individual freedom—freedom from involvements with others, freedom from the destructive character human relationships can sometimes assume—a kind of sovereignty of the spirit. Relationships among people as well as manners, customs, social codes, came to be at the center of his fictional explorations.

When Henry was twelve the father took his family abroad (in 1855) and for three years the children were schooled by tutors and governesses in Geneva, London, Paris and finally Boulogne-sur-mer. Through these years Henry was a constant reader of fiction—English, French and American—and his view

[4]

of life came to be colored by the imaginative experiences gained from the printed pages of literature. In this way he is, perhaps, a supreme example of a writer who wrote alike from a literary saturation—which can become a very important part of the individual creative consciousness—and from life itself, which in his case was often an extension of what he had read in his books.

The stages of his advance into his career were leisurely and virtually without interruption. In 1858 the family returned from Europe for a year at Newport. This gave Henry a new sense of his homeland. The following year found him in Geneva, and his life there is reflected in the first letters given here, written to his Newport friend Thomas Sergeant Perry. Thereafter the James family settled in Newport where, during the Civil War, a prolonged illness confirmed the young writer in his sedentary habits. In 1862 he briefly attempted to follow courses at the Harvard Law School; however he was already writing articles and short stories. From 1864—his twenty-first year—he was a writer whose work, at first anonymous but later signed, began consistently to appear in various American journals. During the next half century he practiced his craft largely in England, and became the very considerable figure in the Anglo-American world of letters that he remains to this day, long after his death.

The letters which follow, to his family and the friends of his early days, show the young Henry at school in Geneva and Bonn; his meditations upon the future of American literature; his first adult journey to Europe in 1869-70 and his discovery of the world of painting; the death of his beloved cousin Minny Temple, who was to inspire James's *Portrait of a Lady* and *The Wings of the Dove,* and finally the beginning of his residence abroad in Paris and London, during which he made his name with *Roderick Hudson, The American,* and *Daisy Miller.*

To THOMAS SERGEANT PERRY

Geneva, 26 Jan. 1860

Dear Perry,

I received your letter about ten minutes ago, and behold me already answering it. Was such a pitch of virtue ever before attained? I had been expecting to hear from you for a long time and had intended to consecrate this afternoon which is Thursday and a holiday to writing to find out what had become of you, but I now have the pleasure of doing so with a mind relieved of all anxiety. I supposed you were established at the South by this time, and from your account of it you must be having a very jolly time. Nothing of moment has transpired in our family since I last wrote. Wilkie and Robby are still at boarding-school, Willie still at the Academy and I stillest at M. Rochettes. I am getting on very well there, and am studying very hard. I have never had a life of such routine as during the past three months. Every day is the same, and an account of one would be an account of all. I rise every day except Sunday at half-past six o'clock, break fast alone, go to school at eight, return at twelve, lunch, go back again at one, come home at five, dine and study till bed time. On Thursday I go to school at eight, home at twelve and stay for the rest of the day. After twelve I walk as I did today, read, look out of the window, or make the purchases for which I have no time on other days. This morning I wint [*sic*] with Willie to "the Junction" a place where the rivers Rhone and Arve meet, one of the deepest blue, and the other sluggish and muddy, and flow on side by side without their waters mingling. Sometimes I go along the borders of the Lake, sometimes out to see the boys at school and these are my perambulations. Perhaps you would like to know about my school. The building is wholly unlike that of the Berkeley Institute.[1] It is a dilapidated old stone house in the most triste quarter of the town. Scarcely a soul passes by it all day, and I do not remember to have seen a wheeled vehicle of any kind near it since I've been there. Beside it is the prison and opposite the Cathedral of St. Peter, in which Calvin used to preach. It seems to me that none but the most harmless and meekest men are incarcerated in the former building. While at my lesson in a class room which looks out on the door, I have once in a while seen an offender brought up to his doom. He marches along with handcuffs on his wrist, followed by a gendarme in "spick and span" uniform. The gendarme knocks on the door, which is opened by some internal spring, shoves in his charge, the door closes, the gendarme retraces his steps. What happens after the prisoner is inside I don't know, but as the only officer I have ever seen about the prison is a diminutive little porter with a most benign countenance, I am inclined to think that the most inoffensive subjects are sent to him to deal with. The Scholars are divided into what are here called Internes and externes. The former are the regular scholars who stay at the school all day take all their lessons there etc. I am one of these. The others are those who only come for certain lessons, which they recite and leave as soon as they've done so. There are about twenty of the Internes, and a dozen externes. The principal study of the school is mathematics, as it is intended to prepare young men to be Engineers, Architects &c. One can study other things though, if he wants. The School course is divided into three years, and I take the studies of the

[1] School run by Rev. W. C. Leverett which Henry James and T. S. Perry attended in Newport.

first year with Latin in addition, there being but two or three of the regular scholars who study Latin. They have most of them a pretty good knowledge of the classics though as in the schools here, where boys go till they are about fifteen and sixteen, those are the principal studies. I fully intended to study Greek when I came here, but I have not now the time. I shall commence it as soon as I possibly can. I needn't be discouraged; I read the other day of a man with a good knowledge of Greek who didn't begin to study it till he was forty-six years of age. In the first year with me there are four other fellows, three sixteen or seventeen, the other I think a little older. Two of them are Genevese, one is a Russian and the other an Englishman. He is the only one with whom I have been able to become the least bit friendly. He seems to be a nice sort of fellow, but as he is only an externe I do not see much of him. Of one of the Genevese I think I may say I never saw a more uninteresting individual, and of the other Genevese and the Russian that I have often seen more interesting. None of the other fellows have shown the least desire to make friends. When I first went there no one spoke to me, I had to commence every conversation myself. I think that if a Frenchman had come to Mr. Leverett's he would have been more hospitably received. The reason why I chose the School rather than any other was not because I was destined "à une carrière scientifique ou industrielle," but because it was the best *school* beside the Academy and the Gymnase neither of which I was prepared to enter. I might have had lessons at home, but I would have had no one to talk French with, and there were other causes for making that unsuitable. As for boarding in a Swiss family—which I told you of at Newport, that is a very good way to learn French, but I would have had to have learnt everything else elsewhere.

Here are five pages all about myself, but the reason I have

written so much is because I like nothing better than for you to write about your own manners and customs, and suppose that you have the same taste in regard to me.

How did you leave all the Newporters? Have you any correspondent there, to furnish you with news? You've no idea what pleasure I have in thinking about the old place. I remember every little detail about it as well as if I'd only seen it yesterday. What ever news you get about it I wish you would transmit it to us if you think it would interest us. You say you saw MacKaye,[2] the painter-philosopher before you left. When you see him again, though as he is in New-York your chances for doing so are not very great, I wish you would remember us kindly to him, and tell him that we shall never forget him. As for LaFarge[3] we've heard nothing from him yet although Willie wrote to him a long time ago.

Sunday 29th

This has lain by from Thursday from [sic] today, I have had no time to take it up; in reading it over I think I have told you all there is to tell and in a very lugubrious manner. Please answer me soon, and our correspondence will perhaps be truly *voluminous*. Please also keep my letters, and I will yours, for I think it will be fun reading them over when we meet again. I had very little hope that my "insane" idea of your coming abroad would ever be realized, but I thought there was no harm in trying; you can do the next best thing, though, that is you can write as often as possible.

Yours very truly
Henry James.

2 Steele MacKaye (1842-94) actor, playwright, stage designer and producer, a boyhood friend of the Jameses at Newport.
3 John La Farge (1835-1910) artist and author, a close friend of Henry's at Newport.

P.S. I was completely overcome by the hope of a letter from your sister. If she does not keep her promise and speedily I will not answer for the consequences. Please remember us all to the Porters and to your mother and sisters. Willie sends his love to you, and so I am sure would Wilkie and Robby if they were to hum. [sic]

To THOMAS SERGEANT PERRY

> *Bonn am Rhein, Pruessen*
>
> *Sunday the fifth day of August 1860*

Number one hundred an ninety Bongasse The Fust of August: a Romance in 3 volumes. By 'Arry Jeames, alias G. P. R. author of the "beacon, beacon, beacon light" etc. Vol. I. Part I. Book I. Chap. I. The morning broke! High into the vast unclouded vault of Heving rode the Awb of Day, chasing before it the fleeting clouds that enshroud the slumbers of men. Nowhere shone it brighter than on thy banks O! lovely Rhine! The rippling wavelets of the noble river sparkled in its genial light, and the jew on the vine-leaves which clothe with a garment of sweetest verdure its fair encastled banks glittered with a rarer lustre than e'er did priceless diamond on a proud bewty's neck. It's golden rays slanted through the casement of an apartment whose furniture denoted a princeley wealth as did the appearance of its two occupants bespeak noble blood. Full on the upturned countenance of one of the latter glanced its rays as he lay enwrapped in slumber, on a luxurious couch in an attitude, wherein with the listless grace of the child was mingled somewhat of the sterner dignity of the man. Through the long lashes of his drooped eyes pierced the radiant glare, which though tempered by the rose-coloured hangings through which it was shed, still caused those lashes slowly to turn upwards and disclose a pair of eyes full at once of the liquid tenderness of the gazelle and the fierceness of the angered tiger. In sooth, ne'er was seen a nobler form than that of 'Enry James de Jeames or one which the most cunning sculptor might endeavour to imitate with less hope of success. Born of a race who counted their ancestors far back into the dim ages of chivalry he seemed to have been endowed by the Wizard Nature, both with the fiery indomitable spirit of those times and with their softer attributes of poesy and romance. Turning as he woke upon his couch, covered with the skin of a leopard, which he had killed with his own hands in the burning wastes of Arabia, where he had already served, young as he was under the crusading banner of Richard the Lion-heart, he stretched forth to a jewelled casked which lay at his bedside an arm in which the cerulean veins swelled like ivy creepers around a giant oak, and grasping a time piece more glittering with brilliants than an eastern monarch's diadem he, ... Nay—but a truce to this idiotic strain. This meaneth in plain English that your good friend Henry James Jr. Esquire was awakened by the sun at six o'clock on the morning of the first of August, that being so awakened he lept out of bed and made speed to don his accustomed *simple,* but SCRUPULOUSLY NEAT attire.

Now, ye, who demand a record of my humble doings prepare for no actions worthy to figure on history's storied page. If your appetite be for hairbreadth escapes and "exciting adventures by flood and field," you must apply elsewhere for wherewith to gratify it. *Some folks* may go trapessing about the country from *Rhode Island* to *Louisiana,* (indeed I might be more particular and say from *Newport* to *Oaklawn*), with a self-exploding gun on their shoulders, insinuating themselves into the society of their betters and frightening their lives out with *fibs* about their alligators, forsooth and their turtles, but I for my part, and

Heaven be thanked for it! have no such tastes and if I had would scorn to thrust them under the notice of other people in *forward letters* and make a *parade* and *show* of them! Some folks, I say, but far be it from me to make any insinuations or *mention any names* as Heaven knows I well might. Let him as the shoe fits wear it. It is to those who admire a life of *strict morality* such as *some one* I know cannot boast of that I now address myself.

As I said, bien cher ami, I rose at six o'clock on Wednesday morning from a bed which is shapen more like a bird's nest than a human one, being deeply hollow in the middle and rising to a tremendous height round the sides, thereby causing me to feel when I enter it as if I were stepping into a well. I then dressed. My washstand deserves a line but I know not unto what to liken it unless it be a refrigerator which indeed, it strongly resembles both in form colour and above all in odour, it having once on an emergency been perhaps applied to that use. Having dressed I awoke the dormant Wilkie who occupies a sort of baby's crib in the same room with me, and having received asseverate assurance of his immediate rising descended to breakfast. Breakfast is here a meal of no ceremony. It consists merely of bread and butter and coffee, which is placed upon the table at seven o'clock and lies there open to attack for about two hours, although toward nine, as you may imagine the coffee has begun to cool off. When I went down the doctor was eating and as people eat who are bereft of teeth, with his gums. Of course there were the usual salutations, the "Wie geht's?" and the everlasting "Haben Sie gut geschlafen?" which members of this family never fail to ask you even if your first meeting does not happen to be until dinner time. While we were engaged, the other young gents made their appearance, one by one, in a desperate hurry to gulp down their breakfast and escape being late for the Gymnasium which with the exception of two they all attend. I am afraid I did them injustice in my former letter. They are all bigger and older than I first thought them. They are almost a different race from boys of their own age at home. They have, if I may judge from these five specimens more book learning, but less general knowledge which comes from unrestrained reading and less of the quality which we call *smartness*. They have no sports, which I have yet found out, except swimming (in which however they excel); and they have very few books to read. They study naught else than Latin and Greek. Their only recreations are going to bathe in the Rhine and going for a walk. They seldom make any jokes themselves, though if you tell them one they do not seem incapable of enjoying it. Neither do they ever quarrel. Sometimes they have lively little discussions, but only raise their voices never their hands. All their ideas of America are taken from some German expurgated adaptations of Cooper's novels, the life therein depicted being as they imagine the life that we lead when at home. But if, on an average, these little fellows are not so acute or clever as their brothers at home, I think that they are infinitely more comely mannered. There are no *Cozzenses* among them. When I had finished breakfast, it being about half past seven, I went into the study. The study is the doctors library and the room where all the boys except Wilkie and I get their lessons. It is not a large room and there being bookshelves but on one side of it, the library is not extensive, and even such as it is it is not attractive. It has scarcely any but the Ancient Authors. In German there is nothing of any consequence but Goethe, Schiller, Lessing and Humboldt's Cosmos. In English there are several of Fielding's and Smollet's novels and a few old fashioned books picked up I suppose at some sale or second hand book-stall, though for what purpose, I am at loss to determine, as the Doctor does not read English with any degree of facility. I sat down to read till our room should be made ready for me to go in and set to work. I looked over an odd volume of the "British Chronicle," a lot of bound weekly newspapers of the time of Byron, Shelley, Tom Moore and Walter Scott and which I had discovered in a corner the night before. Then I finished the Letters of Lady M. W. Montague which I had commenced a few days before from curiosity and had continued from interest. By this time Wilkie had come down breakfasted, and the hand-maiden flaxen haired blue-eyed Anna had set our room to rights. This was about nine o'clock. We both went up and commenced study, which simply consists in translating German into English. I am now working at Schiller's play of *Maria Stuart,* which I like exceedingly, although I do get along so slowly with it. I am convinced that German may take its stand among the difficult languages of the earth. I shall consider myself fortunate if I am able, when I leave Bonn, to translate even the simplest things. I worked on ploddingly till dinner-time which is at one o'clock. Shall I tell you what we had for dinner? I took particular note on purpose. Primo, some tepid cabbage-soup, it's tepidity being the result of Fraulein Stamm's having poured it out almost a half an hour before we were called to dinner. (Fraulein Stamm is the sister of the Frau Doctorin—she sets the table and waits thereat) secundo—some boiled beef in rags and some excellent and greasy potatoes; tertio some Westphalia smoked ham and some black beans. Lastly some stewed cherries and tarts. Voilà. After dinner I went up stairs and set to work again, but had not been long occupied when Willie came in and told us that Mother proposed going to the Drachenfels, a mountain on the other side of the Rhine and commanded our attendance. This was cheerfully given. I went with Willie up to mothers lodgings. These are in a huge brick mansion built to imitate a feudal

castle, situated immediately on the flat shore of the Rhine, so as
that the water, I am told, sweeps in winter round its base. From
M.'s sitting room which has a fine big stone balcony overlook-
ing the river there is a lovely view. The Rhine is just here very
broad. On its opposite bank are some fertile meadows and green
hills called the Seven Mountains. The Drachenfels is one of
these. Mother, my Aunt, Willie, Wilkie, and Theodor the
Doctor's son whom we asked to come with us formed our party.
We took the steamboat for a place called Königswinter at the
foot of the mountain. On the boat were a lot of students from
the University here, who were going down the river to hold
what they call a *Commerz* i.e. to go into a room and swill beer
and wine with certain formalities and with emulative vigour
till an advanced hour in the morning. I saw one of these enter-
tainments in Switzerland and will tell you more about it when
I see you. They had already commenced their work with huge
ox-horns filled with Rhenish wine, and forced all the ladies on
board (the German ones at least) to assist them therein at intervals of about ten minutes. We walked up the Drachenfels (it is
not more than an hours ascent, with an excellent road), that is
we all walked except mother who had the aid, if aid it truly be,
of a donkey. On the top of the mountain, there stands a high
crag with a ruined castle on the top of *it,* in truly Rhenish
fashion. (Do you remember the picture in Brown and Robn.
of one of those gentlemen's preconception of the Rhine?) We
went for the prospect, but the weather being cloudy, we had no
prospect. We came home about eight o'clock, by the boat. I
went back to Mother's with her. I went up in the tower with
Alice, for the mansion can boast of a tower and a constellation
of turrets. Then I came back here with Wilkie. They had kept
our tea for us. It was composed of boiled potatoes, rolls, cold-
meat and stewed cherries, the "specialité" of this bill of fare. It

being past nine when we had done and almost ten before I had finished the account of our excursion delivered to the other members of the family in the study I did not get till late at the letter which I intended to write you. The consequence was that after commencing I decided to leave the continuation of it till the morrow, the morrow however Willie, Wilkie, Father and I went to Cologne which is about an hour's journey from Bonn by rail, and there in the contemplation of its manifold wonders we spent the whole day. On the following day Friday I left the letter purposely till to day when I could finish it without appropriating thereunto time which rightfully belonged to other things i.e. to *Maria Stuart* and the like.

At Cologne I saw several sights, foremost among which was the Cathedral, which is hardly a sight though, as while in it you seem rather to feel than to see it. I will reserve telling you about it till we get home as I am now in a hurry to close. Father, Mother and my Aunt and sister go to morrow to Paris there to remain until we sail, and I wish to give this to them to post there. I must therefore as they leave at seven A.M. be speedy for it is now near 7 P.M.

We were rather stunned at first by the thought of going home so soon, but now we have got accustomed to it. Father has written to Mr. Alf. Smith about a house in Newport. I have not the remotest idea of how I shall spend my time next winter. I don't wish to go back to Mr. Leverett, at least under the same conditions as before. I wish, although I've no doubt it is a very silly wish, that I were going to college. Although I have some prudential uneasiness about going back to Newport I have a delight of heart that stifles all such. The first thing on arriving I vote we go for a long walk to Lily Pond or Purgatory, or the Boat House. I can't find words to tell you how glad I shall be to see you. Remember me to all of those of whom you think I can say that with equal truth—that is say it to everyone I knew there—good bye. All send their love, I've no doubt, though they're not by to give it.

Believe me ever yr affectionate
Henry James Jr.

Wilkie begs to send this scrap of paper. You see he is also guilty of beacon-becon light-ism.

To HIS MOTHER

[*190*] *Bonngasse* [*Bonn*]
Tuesday Evening [*August 1860*]

My very dear Mother

We are going to see each other so soon that it seems hardly worth while to write, but I must do so in order not to appear less meritorious than Willie and Wilkie who are so free in their communications that I begin to suspect they simply despatch you blank sheets of paper, for what they can find to say about Bonn to fill so many pages is to me inconceivable—unless indeed they cover their epistles with protestations of love and admiration, which from occasional glimpses I have had of them seem to be in a tone much better suiting a young man who is writing a letter to his lady love than to his venerable mother.

The three last days, however, have been a little more eventful than for some time past. On Sunday Wilkie and I went to Rolandseck with the Humbards[1] "Kaffee trinken." It was a repetition of the performances, with a few alternations (for the better) which took place at Godesberg, the first Sunday we were here. There were about 800 people there all bent upon the same pleasure as ourselves and among them was an American lady

1 Henry James here mis-spells the name of Dr. Humpert at whose pension he was staying.

who shone with the beauty of an angel among the 700 hideous German women.

We spent all yesterday in Cologne. We were most of the time in the Cathedral. We also went to see the Collection of pictures which we visited on the previous occasion. I suppose you have been informed that we are not going to Strasbourg, (we think "le jeu ne vaut pas la chandelle").

This afternoon Wilkie and I went up to Howenzberg and were shewn the corpses and staircase.

The weather for the past three or four days has been very fine. I hope it will continue so until our journey's over. The doctor entertained thoughts of accompanying us to America but his lady gave symptoms of such dread and horror at the idea that he has relinquished it. She and Miss Stamm seem to think that it is the exception in going to America not to be drowned and assurances to the contrary are received with uplifted eyes and hands and raised eyes and incredulous "Ohs!" and "achs," and pious ejaculations. I wish we could take Madame Humbart to America with us as cook. She is by far the best one I ever saw. I wish you could come on and take a few lessons from her; I shall bring you a lot of receipts by which I shall expect you to profit next winter. I shall look for a *marked improvement* in the cookery department.

We have not heard from Robby for a long time; his last communication was merely an official announcement of his intention to enter a dry-goods store on his return to New York, where he would receive a comfortable salary of from $500 to $1000.

We are all in the enjoyment of excellent health. I don't know what is the matter with me, but I have not been able to study for a few days past so well as I had hitherto done.

To THOMAS SERGEANT PERRY [*1867*]

Please remember me most kindly to Father, Aunt Kate, and
my sister and believe me ever, Madam, your
most obedient humble servt.
HENRY JAMES Jr.

To THOMAS SERGEANT PERRY
Cambridge, September 20, 1867
Mon cher vieux Thomas:
J'ai là sous les yeux depuis hier ta gentille letter du 4 7bre.
Je fus bien aisé de te savoir de retour a Paris, que tu n'as sans
doute pas quitté. Je crois que tu ne regretteras jamais d'y avoir
passé une grosse partie de ton temps; car enfin, quoiqu'on en
dise, c'est une des merveilles de l'univers. On y apprend à
connaître les hommes et les choses, et pour peu qu'on soit par-
venu à y attraper le sentiment du *chez soi,* quelque genre de vie
qu l'on mène plus tard, on ne sera jamais un ignorant, un er-
mite—enfin un provincial.—Tu as depensé toute une page de ta
lettre à me parler de l'exposition.—Que le diable l'emporte, ⁻
cette maudite baraque! Nous en avons bien assez, même ici à
Cambridge. J'aurais bien mieux aimé que tu m'eusses parlé de
toi, que tu m'eusses donne de tes nouvelles intimes. (En voilà,
des imparfaits du subjonctif! Apres cela dira qui voudras que
je ne sais pas le Français!) Je me suis donné hier le plaisir
d'aller chez tes camarades, Storey et Stratton, recueillir de tes
nouvelles. Ces messiers ont été bien bien aimables, ils m'ont
fait part des lettres qu'ils ont reçues de toi pendant l'été. J'en ai
beaucoup ri, de ces lettres folles et charmantes. On ne peut
avoir plus d'esprit, ni une gaillardise de meilleur ton. Ah mon
cher, que je t'en porte envie, de tes courses et de tes aventures,
et de ton humeur Rabelaisiaque!—Decidément, je plante la mon
français: ou plutôt c'est lui qui me plante.—As I say, Storey and

To THOMAS SERGEANT PERRY [*1867*]

Stratton read me and lent me a large portion of your recent letters, beginning with a long one from Venice to the former. Many of your gibes of course I didn't understand, the context being absent. But I understood enough to enjoy the letters very much and to be able to congratulate you on your charming humour. (How detestable this *you* seems after using the Gallic *toi*!) Let me repeat in intelligible terms that I'm very glad to think of you as being as much as possible in Paris—city of my dreams! I feel as if it would count to my advantage in our future talks (and perhaps walks.) When a man has seen Paris somewhat attentively, he has seen (I suppose) the biggest achievement of civilization in a certain direction and he will always carry with him a certain little *reflet* of its splendour.—I had just been reading, when your letter came, Taine's *Graindorge,* of which you speak. It seems to me a truly remarkable book in the way of *writing* and description, but to lack very much the deeper sort of observation. As a writer—a man with a language, a vocabulary and a style, I enjoy Taine more almost than I do any one; but his philosophy of things strikes me as essentially superficial and as if subsisting in the most undignified subservience to his passion for description.—I have also read the last new Mondays of Sainte-Beuve[1] and always with increasing pleasure. Read in the 7th (I think) if you haven't already, an account of A. de Vigny. Truly, exquisite criticism can't further go.—Have you read *M. de Camours,* by Octave Feuillet?[2]—a sweet little story! Read by all means if you haven't (I assume that you have the time,) *Prosper Radoce,* by V. Cherbuliez. It's a work of extraordinary skill and power and I think takes the rag off all the French Romancers, save the illustrious G. Sand, *facile*

---

[1] Henry James reviewed a volume of Sainte-Beuve's *Portraits,* unsigned, in the *Nation* 4 June 1868.
[2] Reviewed by James, unsigned, in the *Nation,* 30 July, 1868.

princeps. I read recently, by the way, this lady's *Memoirs* a compact little work in ten volumes. It's all charming (if you are not too particular about the exact truth) but especially the two 1st volumes, containing a series of letters from her father, written during Napoleon's campaigns. I think they are the best letters I ever read. But you doubtless know the book.—In English I have read nothing new, except M. Arnold's *New Poems,* which of course you will see or have seen.—For real and exquisite pleasure read Morris' *Life and Death of Jason.*³ It's long but fascinating, and replete with genuine beauty.—There is nothing new of course in the universe of American letters—except the projected resuscitation of Putnam's Magazine. Great news, you see! We live over here in a thrilling atmosphere.—Well, I suppose there *are* thrills here; but they dont come from the booksellers not even from Ticknor & Fields, publishers of *Every Saturday.* I applaud your high resolves with regard to work, when you get home. You will always have my sympathy and co-operation.—Have you in view a particular office here at Harvard, for which you are particularly fitting yourself, or meaning so to do?—Upon this point, on which I have long felt a natural curiosity I have as yet failed to obtain satisfaction. Tell me all about it and unfold your mind to your devoted H.J. —I should think that by the time you get home you will have become tolerably well saturated with the French language and spirit; and if you contrive to do as much by the German, you will be a pretty wise man. There will remain the classical and the English. On the 1st I say nothing. *That* you will take care of; and I suppose you will study Latin and Greek by the aid of German and *vice-versa.* But the English literature and spirit is a thing which we tacitly assume that we know much more of than we actually do.—Don't you think so? Our vast literature

³ Reviewed by James, unsigned, in the *North American Review,* October, 1867.

and literary history is to most of us an unexplored field—
especially when we compare it to what the French is to the
French.—Deep in the timorous recesses of my being is a vague
desire to do for our dear old English letters and writers *something* of what Ste. Beuve and the best French critics have done
for theirs. For one of my calibre it is an arrogant hope. *Aussi*
I don't talk about it.—To enter upon any such career I should
hold it invaluable to spend two or three years on English soil
—face to face with the English landscape, English monuments
and English men and women.—At the thought of a study of this
kind, on a serious scale, and of possibly having the health and
time to pursue it, my eyes fill with heavenly tears and my heart
throbs with a divine courage.—But men don't accomplish valuable results [illegible], dear Sarge, and there will be nothing so
useful to me as the thought of having companions and a laborer
with whom I may exchange feelings and ideas. It is by this constant exchange and comparison, by the wear and tear of living
and talking and observing that works of art shape themselves
into completeness; and as artists and workers, we owe most to
those who bring to us most of human life.—When I say that I
should like to do as Ste. Beuve has done, I don't mean that I
should like to imitate him, or reproduce him in English: but
only that I should like to acquire something of his intelligence
and his patience and vigour. One feels—I feel at least, that he
is a man of the past, of a dead generation; and that we young
Americans are (without cant) men of the future. I feel that my
only chance for success as a critic is to let all the breezes of the
west blow through me at their will. We are Americans born—
il faut en prendre son parti. I look upon it as a great blessing;
and I think that to be an American is an excellent preparation
for culture. We have exquisite qualities as a race, and it seems
to me that we are ahead of the European races in the fact that

more than either of them we can deal freely with forms of civilization not our own, can pick and choose and assimilate and in short (aesthetically &c) claim our property wherever we find it. To have no national stamp has hitherto been a regret and a drawback, but I think it not unlikely that American writers may yet indicate that a vast intellectual fusion and synthesis of the various National tendencies of the world is the condition of more important achievements than any we have seen. We must of course have something of our own—something distinctive and homogeneous—and I take it that we shall find it in our moral consciousness, our unprecedented spiritual lightness and vigour. In this sense at least we shall have a national *cachet.*—I expect nothing great during your lifetime or mine perhaps; but my instincts quite agree with yours in looking to see something original and beautiful disengage itself from our ceaseless fermentation and turmoil. You see I am willing to leave it a matter of instinct. God speed the day.— But enough of "abstract speculation", marked as it is by a very concrete stupidity. I haven't a spark of your wit and humor, my boy, and I can't write amusing letters. Let me say, now while I think of it, that I was quite unaware until I heard it the other evening from Ben Pierce, of how serious your accident had been on Mt. Vesuvius. In writing to you after first hearing of it, I believe I didn't even speak of it. A 1000 pardons for my neglect. My poor dear fellow: accept all my retrospective commiseration. It must have been the very devil of an exasperation. And you carry a classic wound—a Vesuvius scar!—Ah why was I not there (i.e. at the hotel) to sponge your gory face, and to change your poultices?—Well, thank the Lord it was no worse. I always said so when we used to walk on the hanging rock at Newport.—I have used up my letter with nonentities, and have no space nor strength for sweet familiar talk. No news. The summer (like a civil young man in the horse car) is giving its seat to the mellow Autumn—the glorious, the grave, the divine. We are having October weather in September: *pourvu que ça dure.* This is *American* weather—worth all the asphaltic breezes of Paris.—I have been all summer in Cambridge—*sans découcher une seule nuit.* Tiens! mon français qui me retrouve! —It has been quite cool and comfortable, but "stiller than chiselled marble"—Vide Tennyson. I have a pleasant room with a big soft bed and good chairs, and with books and shirt-sleeves I found the time pass rapidly enough.—I'm sorry to hear you say that your plans may not agree with Willie's for the winter. I hope you may adjust them. You'll of course find it pleasant enough to be together; but I hope neither of you will sacrifice any thing to your serious interests. I should suppose of course that *you* will prefer Berlin. We are expecting daily to hear from W [illiam]. He wrote eight weeks ago that he was feeling much better: news which gladded my heart.—I haven't seen John [La Farge] all summer; but I heard from him yesterday.—Your sister[4] is again a mother: a little girl, and doing well. But this you will have heard. I draw to a close. My letter is long but not brilliant. I can't make 'em brilliant until some one or something makes me brilliant. A 100 thanks for the photos. [Edmond] About has a capital, dear face; and Sardou a highly refined and Parisian one.—By all means send your own and others. Write punctually.—Farewell, mon vieux, tout à toi.

H.J.

---

[4] T. S. Perry's sister had married John La Farge.

To WENDELL HOLMES

Waumbek House, Jefferson N.H.
July 29th [*1868*]

Dear Wendell—

I was on the point of writing to you last week, when I received a note from Wilky to the effect that he was coming up, and as I preferred not to have you here both at once I remained silent. But today Wilky writes that he will not come and I immediately revert to you. If you are still so disposed, my dear boy, come at your earliest convenience. I have now been here quite long enough to learn the long and short of the place and I have at least proved that it is habitable. At the present moment, I am sorry to say, it is very little more. The great charm and boast of Jefferson is its "view"—wherein, I assure you, you see many things; but this same view is now chronically obscured in a veil of putrid mist, or smoke, which reduces the land to the very flatness of our own clime. Nevertheless, it's tolerably cool; there are woods; there are women. Put two and two together. The woods are not vast; neither are the women; but they will perhaps hold you a week or so. Come therefore, as soon as you may, for in my heart of hearts, you are longed for. Morally, amid this vulgar crew, I am fast growing deaf and dumb, for want of use. I inhabit a great racketing roadside tavern, where I feel sadly remote and unfriended. Still I'm very contented. I loaf and lounge to the top of my bent and am not a bit better than any one else. . . .

Come as soon as you can, and write me, if your letter will precede you. I have lots of questions but I keep them. Farewell. If you disappoint me, you kill me—or rather, I kill you. Give my liveliest regards to your mother and sister, as well as your father and brother and believe me perpetually thine.

H. J. Jr.

P.S. Let me fairly get it off my conscience that it's mortally slow and stupid here. *Dixi;* now if you're bored, don't say I lied.

H. J. Jr.

To JOHN LA FARGE

Glion, Lake of Geneva
June 20 [*1869*]

My very dear John—
Your letter of June 3d was handed me last night, just at a moment when I was recording a silent oath that today and not a day later I should execute my long designed and oft-deferred letter to you. Truly, I have most earnestly been meaning to write to you. I felt the need of so doing: our parting in New York was so hurried and unsatisfactory that I wished to affix some sort of supplement or correction. Happily now, what I write may be a greeting rather than a farewell.

I am deeply delighted to hear that there is a prospect of your getting abroad this summer. Don't let it slip out of your hands. That your health has continued bad, I greatly regret, but I can't consider it an unmitigated curse, if it brings you to these parts. You must have pretty well satisfied yourself that homelife is not a remedy for your troubles, and the presumption is strong that a certain amount of Europe may be.—

As you see, I am already in Switzerland: in fact, I have been here for the past five weeks. I came directly to Geneva (giving but a day to Paris, and that to the Salon) and spent a month there: and then came up to this place which is at the other extreme of the lake, beyond Vevey, perched aloft on the mountainside, just above the Castle of Chillon. It is what they call a *hotel-pension:* a number of people, capital air, admirable scenery. Unhappily, the weather is bad, and seems determined to continue so. Heaven defend us from a rainy summer—no uncommon occurence here. My actual plans are vague; they are simply to continue in Switzerland as long as I can; but as I am not a regular tourist, I shall distribute my time between two or three places.—I enjoyed most acutely my stay in England. If you can only touch there, I think you will find it pay. Of people I saw very few, of course: and of places no vast number, but such of the latter as I did get a glimpse of, were awfully charming. I *did* see Rossetti, Charles Norton having conducted me to his studio—in the most delicious melancholy old house at Chelsea on the river. When I think what Englishmen *ought* to be, with such homes and haunts! Rossetti, however, does not shame his advantages. Personally he struck me as unattractive, poor man. I suppose he was horribly bored!—But his pictures, as I saw them in his room, I think decidedly strong. They were all large, fanciful portraits of women, of the type *que vous savez,* narrow, special, monotonous, but with lots of beauty and power. His chief inspiration and constant model is Mrs. William Morris (wife of the poet) whom I have seen, a woman of extraordinary beauty of a certain sort—a face, in fact, quite made to his hand. He has painted a dozen portraits of her—one, in particular, in a blue gown, with her hair down, pressing a lot of lilies against her breast—an almost great work.

I told him I was your intimate friend and he spoke very admiringly of three of your drawings he had seen.—I saw also some things of another man (tho' not himself), one Burne-Jones, a water-colorist and friend of Charles Norton. They are very literary, etc; but they have great merit. He does Circe preparing for the arrival of Ulysses—squeezing poison into a cauldron, with strange black beasts *dans les jambes:* thro' the openings of a sort of cloister you see the green salt ocean, with the Greek galleys blowing up to land. This last part is admirably painted.

I enjoyed vastly in London the National Gallery, which is a much finer collection than I supposed. They have just acquired a new Michael Angelo—Entombment of Christ—unfinished, but most interesting, as you may imagine. Then they have their great Titian—the Bacchus and Ariadne—a thing to go barefoot to see; as likewise his portrait of Ariosto. Ah, John! What a painter. For him, methinks, I'd give you all the rest I saw in the country (i.e. at Blenheim near Oxford and at Wilton House near Salisbury) some magnificent Vandykes. The great Wilton Vandyke (the Earl of Pembroke and family—an immense canvas) is I think worth a journey to contemplate. *A propos* of such things, I oughtn't to omit to say that I dined at Ruskin's with the Nortons. R. was very amiable, and showed his Turners. The latter is assuredly great: but if you wish to hold your own against exaggeration, go to see him at the National Gallery, where some thirty of his things stand adjoining the Old Masters. I think I prefer Claude. He had better taste, at any rate.—In England I saw a lot of cathedrals—which are good things to see; tho' to enjoy them properly, you mustn't take them quite as wholesale as I was obliged to do.—You ask my intentions for next winter. They are as yet indefinite and are not firmly fixed upon Paris. That is, I am thinking a little of Italy. If I give up Italy, however, of course I shall take up Paris. But I do most earnestly hope we shall be able to talk it over face-to-face. Of course, if you decide to come, you will lose no time. I wish greatly that your wife were to come with you. Short of that, I must hope that your visit, if it takes place, will really pave the way for her. Give her my love and tell her, persuasively, that if Europe does not wholly solve the problem of existence, it at least helps the flight of time—or beguiles its duration.

You give me no local or personal news, beyond that of your illness. I hope other matters are of a more cheerful complexion. I can hear nothing better than that you have sailed. If you determine to do so, write to me (Lombard, Odier & Cie, Geneva) and give your own address.

Meanwhile, till further news, farewell. *Portez vous mieux,* at least. Regards to J. Bancroft, if you see him. Most affectionate messages to your wife and youngsters and a bon voyage, if any, to yourself.

Always yours,
H. James

To JOHN LAFARGE

Venice, Hotel Barberi
September 21, 1869

My dear John—

Tho' I am tired with much writing, I must answer your letter of Aug. 26th without loss of time—in the hope that I may be able to say something to accelerate your coming abroad. I was very sorry your original plan had to be abandoned, and sorry again that your wife and children are not to come. I can't but agree with you tho', that if you are to come with full benefit, you should come without care. I can't help thinking that a six-months' or a year's stay here would do you great good. I speak from my own daily experience. As regards expense, I consider it on my own part as a species of investment, destined to yield later in life sufficient returns in the way of work to repay me. Can't you do the same? Of course the point is to raise ready money; and certainly it is better not to come than to come on such slender means that you have to be constantly pre-occupied, to the detriment of a free appreciation of things, with the money question. You are right, I think, in not particularly

[29]

caring to see any special country, and in longing generally for something European. Even if you only saw a portion of England, you would be richly rewarded. The more I see of the Continent, the more I value England. It is striking how as a mere place for sight-seeing—a home of the picturesque—she holds her own against Italy. It may be that I think so chiefly because my 1st stay was there, and my enjoyment enchanced by novelty. Nevertheless the only very violent wish I entertain with regard to my travels is that I may get three more months of England before my return.—Not, however, that Italy is not unspeakably fair and interesting—and Venice perfectly *Italianissima*. I extremely wish we were likely to meet and see some things together. Here, especially, one needs a companion and intellectual sympathy. Properly to see things you need to talk about them, and we should do much talking and seeing. I hope to be in Italy five or six months more: you might still get here. I have already eaten a good dish of the feast. I came over the Alps by Maggiore and Como, Milan, Pavia, Brescia, Verona and Vicenza; and I have been a week among these happy isles. I have seen a vast number of paintings, palaces and churches, and received far more "impressions" than I know what to do with. One needs a companion to help him to dispose of this troublesome baggage. Venice is quite the Venice of one's dreams, but it remains strangely the Venice of dreams more than of any appreciable reality. The mind is bothered with a constant sense of the exceptional character of the city: you can't quite reconcile it with common civilization. It's awfully sad, too, in its inexorable decay. Newport, by the way, is extremely like it in atmosphere and color; and the other afternoon, on the sands at the Lido, looking out over the dazzling Adriatic, I fancied I was standing on Easton's beach. Its treasures, of course, are innumerable, and I have seen but a small fraction. I have been haunting chiefly the ducal palace and the Academy, and putting off the churches. Tintoretto is omnipresent and well-nigh omnipotent. Titian I like less here than in London and elsewhere. He is strangely unequal. P. Veronese is great, and J. Bellini greater. Perfect felicity I find nowhere but in the manner of the ducal palace, and bits of other palaces on the Grand Canal. One thing strangely strikes me; viz. that if I were an *"artist"* all these immortal daubers would have anything but a directly discouraging effect upon me. On the contrary, they are full of their own peculiar compromises, poverties and *bêtises,* and are as far off from the absolute as Miss Jane Stuart. —I go hence to Florence, *via* Bologna, in about 10 days. I hope to remain some time at F., to see Rome and Naples and possibly have a glimpse of Sicily. I must stay my hand just now. I only wanted to let you know that if you find it possible to come within a short time, I should like well to do some travelling in your company. Offering counsel is repugnant to the discreet mind; yet I can't but say that I should predict serious good of your coming. Steady sight seeing is *extremely* fatiguing, but there is a way of taking it easy—such as I, theoretically, practise. I think of spending from March 15th to May 15th in France—(Paris, Normandy and Brittany), going during the next two months thro Belgium, Holland and the Rhine, and then going for three months to England.—I shall then either make up my mind to return (I [shall] have been here abroad about a year and eight months) or if I feel up to any serious reading shall make straight back to Dresden and spend the winter.[1] There you have my "line of march" as far as 'tis defined. But it's not in the least fixed.—I hope your wife and young ones are well, and that you've been having a decently entertaining

1 James did not carry out this plan. Illness forced him to return to America the following spring.

and comfortable summer. I wish I were hereditary possessor
of one of these old palazzi. I would make it over to you for a
year's occupancy. The gondola, by the way, is a thing divine.
Did you ever get my letter from Glion, in June? You don't
mention it. Thank Sargy for his good intentions in regard to
writing to me—infernal asphalti. Farewell. Let me hear from
you hopefully, and believe me yours always

H. James, jr.

The Nortons are to spend this winter in Florence.

To HIS MOTHER

Malvern, March 26, 1870

Dearest Mother,

I received this morning your letter with father's note, telling
me of Minny's death[1]—news more strong and painful than I
can find words to express. Your last mention of her condition
had been very far from preparing me for this. The event suggests such a host of thought[s] that it seems vain to attempt
to utter them. You can imagine all I feel. Minny seemed such
a breathing immortal reality that the mere statement of her
death conveys little meaning; really to comprehend it I must
wait—we must all wait—till time brings with it the poignant
sense of loss and irremediable absence. I have been spending
the morning letting the awakened swarm of old recollections
and associations flow into my mind—almost *enjoying* the exquisite pain they provoke. Wherever I turn in all the recent
years of my life I find Minny somehow present, directly or
indirectly—and with all that wonderful ethereal brightness of
presence which was so peculiarly her own. And now to sit down

---

[1] Mary (Minny) Temple, James's cousin, had died on March 8 at New
Rochelle, of tuberculosis.

to the idea of her death! As much as a human creature may, I fancy, she will survive in the unspeakably tender memory of her friends. No attitude of the heart seems tender and generous enough not to do her some unwilling hurt—now that she has melted away into such a dimmer image of sweetness and weakness! Oh dearest Mother! oh poor struggling suffering *dying* creature! But who complains that she's gone or would have her back to die more painfully? She certainly never seemed to have come into this world for her own happiness—as that of others—or as anything but as a sort of divine reminder and quickness—a transcendent protest against our acquiescence in its grossness. To have known her is certainly an immense gain, but who would have wished her to live longer on such a footing—unless he had felt within him (what I felt little enough!) some irresistible mission to reconcile her to a world to which she was essentially hostile. There is absolute balm in the thought of poor Minny and *rest*—rest and immortal absence!

But viewed in a simple human light, by the eager spirit that insists upon its own—her death is full of overflowing sadness. It comes home to me with irresistible power, the sense of how much I knew her and how much I loved her. As I look back upon the past, from the time I was old enough to feel and perceive, her friendship seems literally to fill it—with proportions magnified doubtless by the mist of tears. I am very glad to have seen so little of her suffering and decline—but nevertheless every word in which you allude to the pleasantness of that last visit has a kind of heart-breaking force. "Dear bright little Minny" as you most happily say: what an impulse one feels to sum up her rich little life in some simple compound of tenderness and awe. Time for you at home will have begun to melt away the hardness of the thought of her being in future a simple memory of the mind—a mere pulsation of the heart:

to me as yet it seems perfectly inadmissible. I wish I were at home to hear and talk about her: I feel immensely curious for all the small facts and details of her last week. Write me any gossip that comes to your head. By the time it reaches me it will be very cheerful reading. Try and remember anything she may have said and done. I have been raking up all my recent memories of her and her rare personality seems to shine out with absolute defiant reality. Immortal peace to her memory! I think of her gladly as unchained from suffering and embalmed forever in all our hearts and lives. Twenty years hence what a pure eloquent vision she will be.

But I revert in spite of myself to the hard truth that she is *dead*—silent—absent forever—she the very heroine of our common scene. If you remember any talk of hers about me— any kind of reference or message—pray let me know of it. I wish very much father were able to write me a little more in detail concerning the funeral and anything he heard there. I feel absolutely *vulgarly* eager for any fact whatever. Dear bright little Minny—God bless you dear Mother, for the words. What a pregnant reference in future years—what a secret from those who never knew her! In her last letter to me she spoke of having had a very good photograph taken, which she would send. It has never come. Can you get one—or if you have only the house copy can you have it repeated or copied? I should very much like to have it—for the day when to think of her will be nothing but pure blessedness. Pray, as far as possible, attend to this. Farewell. I am melted down to such an ocean of love that you may be sure you all come in for your share.

Evening. I have had a long walk this afternoon and feel already strangely familiar with the idea of Minny's death. But I can't help wishing that I had been in closer relation with her during her last hours—and find a solid comfort at all events in thinking of that long never-to-be-answered letter I wrote to her from Florence. If ever my good genius prompted me, it was then. It is no surprise to me to find that I felt for her an affection as deep as the foundations of my being, for I always knew it; but I now become sensible how her image, softened and sweetened by suffering and sitting patient and yet expectant, so far away from the great world with which so many of her old dreams and impulses were associated, has operated in my mind as a gentle incentive to action and enterprise. There have been so many things I have thought of telling her, so many stories by which I had a fancy to make up her lack to her,—as if she were going to linger on as a graceful invalid to listen to my stories! It was only the other day, however, that I dreamed of meeting her somewhere this summer with Mrs. Post. Poor Minny! how much she was not to see! It's hard to believe that she is not seeing greater things now. On the dramatic fitness— as one may call it—of her early death it seems almost idle to dwell. No one who ever knew her can have failed to look at her future as a sadly insoluble problem—and we almost all had imagination enough to say, to murmur at least, that life—poor narrow life—contained no place for her. How all her conduct and character seem to have pointed to this conclusion—how profoundly inconsequential, in her history, continued life would have been! Every happy pleasant hour in all the long course of our friendship seems to return to me, vivid and eloquent with the light of the present. I think of Newport as with its air vocal with her accents, alive with her movements. But I have written quite enough—more than I expected. I couldn't help thinking this afternoon how strange it is for me to be pondering her death in the midst of this vast indifferent England which she fancied she would have liked. Perhaps! There was no answering in the cold bright landscape for the loss of her liking. Let me think that her eyes are resting on greener pastures than even England's. But how much—how long—we have got to live without her! It's no more than a just penalty to pay, though, for the privilege of having been young with her. It will count in old age, when we live more than now, in reflection, to have had such a figure in our youth.

But I must say farewell. Let me beg you once more to send me any possible talk of reminiscences—no matter how commonplace. I only want to make up for not having seen her—I resent their having buried her in New Rochelle.[1] She ought to be among her own people. Good night. My letter doesn't read over-wise, but I have written off my unreason. You promise me soon a letter from Alice—the sooner the better. Willy I trust will also be writing. Good night, dearest Mother,

Your loving son,
H. James

Write me who was at the funeral and I shall write next from here—then possibly from London.

To GRACE NORTON

Cambridge May 20th, 1870

My dear Grace.

Nothing more was needed to make me feel utterly at home—utterly *revenu* and awake from my dream again—than to get your letter of May 2d. Hearty thanks for it! Here I am—here I have been for the last ten days—the last ten years. It's very hot! the window is open before me: opposite thro' the thin trees I see the scarlet walls of the president's *palazzo*. Beyond, the noble grey mass—the lovely outlines, of the library: and

---

1 She was actually buried in the Temple family plot in Albany.

above this the soaring *campanile* of the wooden church on the *piazza*. In the distance I hear the carpenters hammering at the great edifice in process of erection in the college yard—and in sweet accordance the tinkle of the horse-cars. Oh how the May-wind feels like August. But never mind: I am to go into town this p.m. and I shall get a charming breeze in the cars crossing the bridge.—Nay, *do* excuse me: I should be sorry wilfully to make you homesick. I could find in my heart to dwell considerately only on the drawbacks of Cambridge life: but really I know of none: or at least I have only to look at that light elegant campanile—that simple devout Gothic of the library— or indeed at that dear quaint old fence of wood, of stone (which is it most?) before the houses opposite—to melt away in ecstasy and rapture.—My voyage I am happy to say, was as prosperous as if I had received your good wishes at its beginning instead of its close. We made it in nine days and a half, without storms or serious discomforts. I will agree with you in any abuse of the cabins and state-rooms of the Scotia: but the deck is excellent and there I chiefly spent my time. I find all things here prosperous, apparently, and all people decently happy. My own family may be well reported of. My sister is in strength and activity quite an altered person and my brother inspires me with confident hopes. My parents are particularly well. I lately spent an evening in Kirkland Street where of course I found many questions to answer; and boasted hugely of all your favors. Miss Theodora[1] [Sedgewick] is a most delightful young lady: I say it because I don't believe you adequately know it. Arthur[2] [Sedgewick] I have seen several times: we enjoy very much reminding each other of you. The Gurneys[3] too I have seen and

1 Mrs. Norton's youngest sister.
2 Mrs. Norton's brother.
3 The family of Ephraim Whitman Gurney, professor of history at Harvard.

the Howells—all very well. Howells is lecturing very pleasantly on Italian literature. I go to the lecture room in Boylston hall; and sit with my eyes closed, listening to the sweet Italian names and allusions and trying to fancy that the window behind me opens out into Florence. But Florence is within and not without. When I'm hopeful of seeing Florence again not ten years hence —that *is* Florence!—all that you tell me is delightful. I can fancy what a game Florence and May are playing between them. Poor May just here has rather an irresponsible playmate. But when May is a month older she will amuse herself alone.—I congratulate you on Charles and Susan [Norton] having returned from Rome. When I think that in this latter season they have made that journey thro' the very vitals of Italy, I feel almost as if it were a merry world. Indeed when I hear that you really think of summering (not simmering) in Venice, I pronounce it altogether a mad world—using the term in no invidious sense. Thrice happy thought! I could say horrible things—invent the fiercest calumnies, about Siena, to drive you to Venice. If you write to me not from Venice—I shall—I shall almost delay to answer your letter. Siena would be all very well if you had never thought of Venice—but having done this I don't see how you can escape going there. There are things the immortal gods don't forgive. Beware them.—I wish I were able to tell you where I am going to outlast the genial season—or what, now that I have got America again, I am going to do with it. Like it enormously *sans doute:* they say there is nothing like beginning with a little aversion. My only fear is that mine is too old to end in a grand passion. But America is American: that is incontestable, and consistency is a jewel. I wish I could tell you how characteristic everything strikes me as being—everything from the vast white distant sky—to the stiff sparse individual blades of grass.

To GRACE NORTON [*1870*]

22d. a.m. I went yesterday to lunch at Shady Hill. Don't think me very cruel when I tell you how lovely it was—in the very sweetest mood of the year—the fullness of the foliage just all but complete and the freshness of the verdure all undimmed. The grass was all golden with buttercups—the trees all silver with apple blossoms, the sky a glorious storm of light, the air a perfect hurricane of zephyrs. We sat (Miss C. Hooper, Miss Boott &c)[4] on a verandah a long time immensely enjoying the fun. But oh my dear Grace it was ghostly. For me the breeze was heavy with whispering spirits. Down in that glade to the right three women were wading thro' the long grass and a child picking the buttercups. One of them was you, the others Jane and Susan[5]—the child Eliot. Mesdemoiselles Hooper and Boott talked of Boston, I thought of Florence. I wanted to go down to you in the glade and we should play it was the Villa Landor. Susan would enact Miss Landor. But the genius of my beloved country—in the person of Miss Hooper— detained me. I don't know indeed whether I most wanted you to be there or to be myself in Florence. Or rather I do very well know and I am quite ashamed of my fancy of robbing that delightful scene of its simple American beauty. I wished you all there for an hour, enjoying your own.—But my intended note is turning into a very poor letter. One of these days I shall intend a letter. —I ought to tell you by the way, that my having taken a turn for the worse in England, was partly concerned in my return home. I was wise in doing as I did apparently: for I am already vastly better. At all events, economy had begun to make my return necessary. I don't feel very much further from you here than I was in England. I may safely assume—mayn't I?—that you are to be abroad two or three years yet. Largely within that

---

[4] Marion "Clover" Hooper, later Mrs. Henry Adams and Elizabeth Boott.
[5] Jane, sister of C. E. Norton and Susan (Sedgewick), Norton's wife.

time we shall meet again. When I next go to Italy it will be not for months but years. These are harmless visions, but I utter them only to you.—Wherever you go this summer, remember that—*I* care most about hearing the whole story. This is not modest, but I maintain it. Live, look, enjoy, write a little for me. Tell all your companions how fondly I esteem them. I implore your mother to exert her maternal authority in favor of Venice. I perceived no bad smells there: and as for mosquitoes, I imagine that a private house properly furnished with curtains needn't in the least fear them. Howells tells me *they* never suffered. Wherever you go, however, I shall be happy in your contentment and shall believe you blessed with peace and prosperity. Farewell. Love to one and all. Believe me dear Grace yours most faithfully

HENRY JAMES jr.

I don't ask about Sara[6] because I have just written to her and have hopes of an answer if she has time before her return.

To ELIZABETH BOOTT

Cambridge [*April 1871*] *Friday*

My dear Miss Lizzie—

A destiny at once cruel and kind forbids my acceptance of your amiable proposition for Monday evening. I am engaged to meet the Bret Hartes at Mrs. Howells's. An opportunity to encounter these marvellous creatures is, I suppose, not lightly to be thrown aside. On the other hand I shall pine for the marvellous creatures assembled in your *atelier* and *salon*. But such is life!—Such as it is, however, I pray it may last till we meet again.—Primed with your compliment, and your father's, about

---

6 Sara, Norton's eldest daughter.

the P[assionate] P[ilgrim],[1] I shall really quite hold up my head
to the author of the Heathen Chinee. With cordial regards to
your father and many regrets.

Yours most faithfully

H. James jr.

To HIS FATHER

Paris [*Nov. 1872*]

Dear Father:

I received promptly your letter of Oct. 14th: and I had a couple of days before received the last *Atlantic*. For both many
thanks. The photograph from J[ohn] La Farge's drawing, and
Bob Temple's letter were both welcome, too, in their respective
and very different manners. The drawing seems to be a weaker
thing than John ought to be doing, now-a-days (though certainly
very pretty;) and Bob's letter is touching in its amiable demoralization. It's an event worthy of Thackeray that his *spelling*
should have degenerated!—I have not yet heard from Aunt
K[ate] and Alice. I must allow them a few days more. By this time
I suppose, you feel as if they had never been away. The dresses
are unpacked, and the photographs, and the stories told, and
Alice is all ready to take ship again. You must remind her that
she is to write me the most *intime* details of her impressions of
home. My love to Aunt Kate, who will have written me, I
trust, whatever she is able to do. May she, on reaching home,
have found this more than it seemed to be here!—I am fast
becoming a regular Parisian *badaud;* though, indeed, I led a
far madder and merrier life in Cambridge than I seem likely to
do here. The waiters at the *restaurants* are as yet my chief
society. The weather, since my return, has been wet but soft

1 James's tale "A Passionate Pilgrim" had appeared in the March-April issues
of the *Atlantic Monthly*.

and I have had a blissful respite from suffering with the cold. This little room of mine, in the Hotel Rastadt, is a most delightful spot: hardly larger than a state room on the *Algeria,* but with everything needful and all the warmer for its smallness. Today is bright and the sun is pouring in over the opposite house tops in a way that I wish Aunt Kate could see. A gentleman has just come in to try me on a shirt. Imagine Mr. Chaffin calling in Quincy St.[1] for this purpose or entertaining the idea that a shirt could be tried on! Mine is an elegant fit and *très echanchré* in the neck.—I did wrong just now to speak slightingly of my society; for I have struck up a furious intimacy with James Lowell, whom I lived side by side with for so many years in Cambridge without sight or sound of. I called on him the other day, with a message from Charles Norton; he returned my call, the next day and we went out to walk and tramped over half Paris and into some queer places which he had discovered on his own walks. There is a good deal of old Paris left still. Lowell is very pleasant and friendly, and apparently very happy: driving great bargains in old books, some wonderfully handsome and cheap. The cheapness of books here must make Paris a paradise of bibliophilists. A few days later I went over and dined at Lowell's *table d'hôte* in the Rue de Beaune, just off the Quai Voltaire. He lives in a little old genuine French hotel in a snug little apartment, with fabulous cheapness. The dinner at 3 frs.50 was the cheapest entertainment I ever enjoyed, not only on account of the food which was very savoureux, but of the company, which was more succulent still. The scene was indescribable; I only wish Willy could have seen it. It consisted of a political fight between four conservatives (one the Marquis de Grammont, a deputy and

---

[1] The James family residence was at 20 Quincy Street in Cambridge, opposite the Harvard Yard.

legitimist,) and a solitary republican, a Wallachian by birth. All the classic qualities of the French nature were successively unfolded before us and the *manner* of it beat the best comedy. One of the conservatives, a doctor of the complacent sapient epigrammatic sort, was a perfect specimen of a certain type of Frenchman and the way he rolled his eyes and chucked his epigrams into the air with his chin (as if he were balancing a pole on the end of it) was something not to miss. He clamored for a despotism stronger than any France has ever had, absolute suppression of the press, and that all radicals should be *fusillés*. The Marquis de Grammont thought *suppression* of the press a little severe but went in for *lois très répressives* and declared that his party hoped to carry such in the next session of the chamber. He then worked himself into a rage, against the Wallachian, more purple, more frantic, more grotesque, than anything you can imagine. The wildest parody couldn't approach it, and it was wondrous to see the rest of them quietly eating their dinner instead of running for a straight-jacket. I shall know in future what to *s'échauffer* means. The state of mind exhibited by the whole thing was incredibly dark and stupid— stupidity expressed in epigrams. If the discussion was really as typical as it seemed to be, the sooner France shuts up shop the better. I mean to return often to the Hotel de Lorraine, and if the other table d'hôtes in that region are as good, I shall take them all in turn. Mr. John Holmes, by the way, is with the Lowells, with his aroma of Cambridge quite undiluted.—Rowse and C. Wright have gone and the latter, I suppose, will have turned up in Cambridge before this reaches you. I know of no one due in Paris whom I am likely to see, except the Masons and Bob James, whom I mean to receive till every other resource has failed.—For your liberal advice about drawing money, beloved father, many thanks. I shall do very well without ruining you. I mean to act in accordance with what you say about having my cheques sent to you; it is the best plan. Tell Alice and Willy to read the *full correspondence* of Henri Regnault just published. I have just sent a review of it to the *Nation*.[2] You say nothing about the boys, so that I suppose there is nothing new with them. Tell Willy I mean soon to write to him. Love to my incomparable mammy. Address Hotel Rastadt &c. Farewell. Ever your loving son

H. JAMES jr.

To CHARLES ELIOT NORTON

Rome, March 31st [1873]

Dear Charles—

Nothing could have given me more substantial pleasure than your note about Ruskin—the indivious comparison as to Mr. Colvin[1] included. If there is any stimulus in the case it is certainly I who have felt it. I can well understand that it should be a gratification to Ruskin to encounter late in life a cordial assent to a cherished opinion never very popular and to which years have not, I suppose, brought many adherents. Tintoret I have never seen (save by Ruskin) spoken of with the large allowance that he demands.—Your letter has been the great news with me—I don't know that I have any other. I am growing daily fonder of Rome, and Rome at this season is growing daily more loveable. My only complaint is of the climate, which takes a good deal more strength from you than it gives. But Rome with a *snap* in the air would not be Rome, and the languor that one continually feels has something harmonious

2 It appeared, unsigned, in the issue of 2 January 1873.
1 Sidney Colvin, art critic, had just been appointed Slade Professor at Cambridge. John Ruskin, who had the corresponding post at Oxford, had insisted that no one should occupy a chair of art criticism without being able to draw.

and (intellectually) profitable in it. "Society" continues, in spite
of the departure of two or three of its ornaments. Last night at
the Story's[2] I met Matthew Arnold and had a few words with
him. He is not as handsome as his photographs—or as his
poetry. But no one looks handsome in Rome—beside the
Romans.—So you're acquainted with Story's Muse—that brazen
hussy—to put it plainly. I have rarely seen such a case of
prosperous pretention as Story. His cleverness is great, the
world's good nature to him is greater.—I am very sorry your
harsh weather continues, for an English spring is too good a
thing to be spoiled. I wish I could take you out on my balcony
and let you look at the Roman house-tops and loggias and sky
and feel the mild bright air. But this is questionably kind.—
Your note of ten days since came safely and was most welcome.
There were several things in it to reply to which your story of
Ruskin has chased out of my head.—I do, for instance, believe
in criticism, more than that hyperbolical speech of mine would
seem to suggest. What I meant to express was my sense of its
being, latterly, vastly over-done. There is such a flood of pre-
cepts and so few examples—so much preaching, advising, re-
buking and reviling, and so little *doing:* so many gentlemen
sitting down to dispose in half an hour of what a few have
spent months and years in producing. A single positive attempt,
even with great faults, is worth generally most of the comments
and amendments on it. You'll agree to that.—Again, I wished
to repudiate the charge of my patriotism being "serene". It has
come to that pass, you see, that I'm half ashamed of it. I wish
it *were* serene. I don't pretend in the least to understand our
national destinies—or those of any portion of the world. My
philosophy is no match for them, and I regard the march of

2 William Wetmore Story, American sculptor (1819-95), whose biography
James wrote after the turn of the century.

history very much as a man placed astride of a locomotive, without knowledge or help, would regard the progress of that vehicle. To stick on, somehow, and even to enjoy the scenery as we pass, is the sum of my aspirations.—As to Christianity in its old applications being exhausted, civilization, good and bad alike, seems to be certainly leaving it pretty well out of account. But the religious passion has always struck me as the strongest of man's heart, and when one thinks of the scanty fare judged by our usual standards, in which it has always fed, and of the nevertheless powerful current continually setting towards all religious hypotheses, it is hard not to believe that some application of the supernatural idea, should not be an essential part of our life.—I don't know how common the feeling is, but I am conscious of making a great allowance to the questions agitated by religion, in feeling that conclusions and decisions about them are tolerably idle.—But I meant to write you no letter—only to thank you: and this is more than a note and less than what it should be otherwise. Farewell dear Charles. Love to each and all—I sent you a criticism of *Middlemarch* in the *Galaxy*[3] lately. Did it come? If you positively don't at all like *M.* you will probably say that such criticism as that ought to be silenced.

Yours always

H. James jr.

To THE JAMES FAMILY

Story's Hotel, Dover St.
Piccadilly Sunday Nov. 1st [*1875*]

Dear People all—

I take possession of the old world—I inhale it—I appropriate it! I have been in it now these twenty-four hours, having

---

[3] James's review of George Eliot's novel appeared unsigned in the March 1873 issue.

arrived at Liverpool yesterday at noon. It is now two o'clock, and I am sitting, in the livid light of a London November Sunday, before a copious fire, in my own particular sitting-room, at the establishment mentioned above. I took the afternoon train from Liverpool yesterday, and having telegraphed in advance, sat down at 10 p.m. to cold roast beef, bread and cheese and ale in this cosy corner of Britain. I have been walking up Piccadilly this morning, and into Hyde Park, to get my land-legs on; I am duly swathed and smoked and chilled, and feel as if I had been here for ten years.—Of course you got my letter from Sandy Hook, and learned that my voyage began comfortably. I am sorry to say it didn't continue so, and I spent my nights and my days declaring that the sea shouldn't catch me again for at least twenty years. But of course I have already forgotten all that and the watery gulf has closed over my miseries. Our voyage was decently rapid (just 10 days) owing to favouring winds; but the winds were boisterous gales, and after · the second day we tumbled and tossed all the way across. I was as . . . usual, but I kept pretty steadily on deck, and with my rugs and my chair, managed to worry thro'. The steamer is a superb one, but she was uncomfortably crowded and she presumably bounced about more than was needful. I was not conversational and communed but little with my multitudinous passengers. My chief interlocutor was Mrs. Lester Wallack, whose principal merit is that she is the sister of Millais the painter. She offers to take me to his studio if he returns to town before I have—which he won't. We had also Anthony Trollope,[1] who wrote novels in his state room all the morning (he does it literally every morning of his life, no matter where he may be,)

[1] James's essay on Trollope, appeared in the July 1883 issue of the *Century* magazine and was reprinted in *Partial Portraits* (1888).

and played cards with Mrs. Bronson[2] all the evening. He has a gross and repulsive face and manner, but appears *bon enfant* when you talk with him. But he is the dullest Briton of them all. Nothing happened, but I loathed and despised the sea, more than ever. I managed to eat a good deal in one way and another, and found it, when once I got it well under way, the best help to tranquillity. It isn't the eating that hurts one, but the stopping.—I shall remain in this place at most a week. It is the same old big black London, and seems, as always, half delicious, half dismal. I am profoundly comfortable, thanks to Mr. Story, the usual highly respectable retired butler, who gives me a sitting room, a bedroom, attendance, lights and fire, for three guineas a week. Everything is of the best, and it is a very honorable residence. Why didn't Aunt Kate and Alice bring me here in '72? I shall probably start for Paris a week from tomorrow, and hope to find there a line from home. If anything very interesting befalls me here I will write again, but in my unfriended condition this is not probable. I hope the Western journey has been safely and smoothly executed and insist upon hearing full particulars. If A[unt] K[ate] has gone to N.Y. let her see this. Each of you hold Dido an hour against your heart for me. The sight of all the pretty genteel dogs in Hyde Park a while since brought tears to my eyes. I think that if I could have had D. in my berth I would have been quite well. But perhaps *she* would have been sea-sick. I have been haunted since I left home by the recollection of three small unpaid bills, which I pray mother to settle for me.

1. At Dollard's, the cobbler's. About 2 dollars.
2. Schoenhof and Moellers. About $3.00

2 Mrs. Arthur Bronson (Katherine de Kay) who settled in Venice and became a distinguished hostess and intimate of artists and writers, notably of Browning and Henry James.

3d. At Smith's, the tailor's, 7$ for that summer coat: not 7.50, as his bill said, which I left on my bedroom table. Excuse these sordid details. This sitting still to write makes me swim and roll about most damnably. Your all-affectionate

. H. James jr.

To WILLIAM JAMES

Etretat, July 29th [*1876*]

Dear William,

Your long and charming letter of July 5th came to me just before I left Paris—some ten days since. Since then, directly after my arrival here, I wrote a few words to Alice by which you will know where I am "located." Your letter, with its superior criticism of so many things, the Philadelphia Exhibition especially, interested me extremely and quickened my frequent desire to converse with you. What you said of the good effect of the American pictures there gave me great pleasure; and I have no doubt you are right about our artistic spontaneity and sensibility. My chief impression of the Salon was that four-fifths of it were purely mechanical, (and *de plus* vile). I bolted from Paris on the 20th feeling a real need of a change of air. I found it with a vengeance here, where as I write I have just had to shut my window for the cold. I made a mistake in not getting a room with sun, strange, and even loathesome, as it may appear to you! The quality of the air is delicious—the only trouble is indeed that it has too shipboard and mid-ocean a savor. The little place is picturesque, with noble cliffs, a little Casino, and your French bathing going on all day long on the little pebbly beach. But as I am to do it in the *Tribune*,[1] I won't

---

[1] It appeared in the New York *Tribune,* 26 August 1876 titled "A French Watering Place" and was reprinted in *Portraits of Places* (1883).

steal my own thunder. The company is rather low, and I have no one save Edward Boit[2] and his wife (of Boston and Rome) who have taken a most charming old country house for the summer. Before I left Paris, I spent an afternoon with the Bootts, who are in Paradise—though with Ernest Longfellow and lady as fellow-seraphs. They have a delightful old villa, with immense garden and all sorts of picturesque qualities, and their place is (as I found by taking a walk with Boott) much prettier than I supposed—in fact very charming, and with the air of being 500 miles from Paris. Lizzie and Longfellow are working with *acharnement,* and both, I ween, much improving. I have little to tell you of myself. I shall be here till August 15-20, and shall then go and spend the rest of the month with the Childes,[3] near Orléans (an ugly country, I believe), and after that try to devise some frugal scheme for keeping out of Paris till as late as possible in the Autumn. The winter there always begins soon enough. I am much obliged to you for your literary encouragement and advice—glad especially you like my novel.[4] I can't judge it. Your remarks on my French tricks in my letters are doubtless most just, and shall be heeded. But it's an odd thing that such tricks should grow at a time when my last layers of resistance to a long-encroaching weariness and satiety with the French mind and its utterance has fallen from me like a garment. I have done with 'em, forever and I am turning English all over. I desire only to feed on English life and the contact of English minds—I wish greatly I knew some. Easy and smooth-flowing as life is in Paris, I would throw it over tomorrow for an even very small chance to plant myself for a while in England.

2 An American water-colorist.

3 Edward Lee Childe, an American expatriate whom James had met through the Nortons.

4 Serialization of *The American* had begun in the *Atlantic Monthly* during the preceding month.

To WILLIAM JAMES [1876]

If I had but a single good friend in London I would go thither. I have got nothing important out of P[aris] nor am likely to. My life there makes a much more succulent figure in your letters, as my mention of its thin ingredients, comes back to me, than in my own consciousness. A good deal of Boulevard and third rate Americanism: few retributive relations otherwise. I know the Théâtre Français by heart!—Daniel Deronda (Dan'l himself) is indeed a dead, though amiable failure. But the book is a large affair; I shall write an article of some sort about it.[5] All desire is dead within me to produce something on George Sand;[6] though perhaps I shall, all the same, mercenarily and mechanically—though only if I am forced. *Please make a point of mentioning*, by the way, whether a letter of mine, upon her, exclusively, *did* appear lately in the *Tribune*. I don't see the T. regularly and have missed it. They misprint sadly. I never said e.g. in announcing her death, that she was "*fearfully* shy": I used no such vile adverb, but another—I forget which.—I am hoping, from day to day, for another letter from home, as the period has come round. I hope father is getting on smoothly and growing able to enjoy life a little more. I am afraid the extreme heat does not help him and I fear also that your common sufferings from it have been great—though you, in your letter, didn't speak of it. I hope Alice will have invented some plan of going out of town. Is there any one left in Cambridge whom the family sees? I am glad you went to Mattapoissett, which I remember kindly, tho' its meagre nature seems in memory doubly meagre beside the rich picturesqueness of this fine old Normandy. What you say of nature putting Wendell H. and his

---

[5] "Daniel Deronda, A Conversation," by James appeared in the *Atlantic Monthly* of December 1876 and was reprinted in *Partial Portraits* (1888).

[6] George Sand had died recently and James had written a column devoted to her in the New York *Tribune* of 22 July 1876. He was to write three long papers on her in 1897, 1902 and 1914, all reprinted in *Notes on Novelists* (1914).

wife under a lens there is very true. I see no one here; a common and lowish lot; and the American institution of "ringing in" is as regards the French impossible. I hope your own plans for the summer will prosper, and health and happiness &c be your portion. Give much love to father and to the ladies.—Yours always—H. James jr.

To HIS MOTHER

[*3 Bolton Street W*]
March 15th [*1878*]

Dearest Mammy—

Only a word to thank you for your letter of March 2d, acknowledging my explanation about the Scribner cheque last summer. Now it is all right.—I am much pleased with your other news—about William's success in Baltimore of which I was sure in advance; and A[lice's] visit to N. Y. I am sorry W's eyes still demand care, as I suppose that in consequence I shall have no details from him: but I trust A. will write me a keen analysis of her N. Y. observations. I congratulate her female-lunch-cooperative-society which strikes me as a brilliant idea. I would willingly be present in the humble garb of an Irish waiter—or are the waiters female too? I am surprised father has not yet received a copy of my book [*French Poets and Novelists*] which I posted instantly with my own hands: I hope it promptly turned up. A number of people here have spoken to me of it with much appreciation. The story Howells is about to publish is *by no means* the one of which I wrote you last summer that it would be to the *American* "as wine unto water." *That*[1] is still in my hands; but I hope to do something with it this summer. I have offered it again to Lippincott. (*Silence* on this point.)

[1] James had begun writing *The Portrait of a Lady*.

The Europeans is a much slighter and shorter affair—which I have pledged myself to get into a 100 pages of the *Atlantic,* and which will be much squeezed and minimized by this circumstance. Still, I think you will find it pretty and good. The donnée is interesting—and the art will be superior. Howells has quite enough of it in his hands to begin immediately: but I am afraid he wont. (Please say *nothing* about the other story, which is the one that will cover you with fame.) If I could only afford to wait, *that* might come out here also in the *Cornhill* or *Macmillan;* but for this I must wait for what I do next afterward. I have dined out a good deal lately; but with moderate interest and will reserve the record till I next write to A[lice]. Blessings on all from

Your faithful H.

To ALICE JAMES

Tillypronie, Aberdeen. Sept. 15th [*1878*]

Dearest sister.

On this howling stormy Sunday, on a Scotch mountainside, I don't know what I can do better than give you a little old-world news. I have had none of yours in some time; but I venture to interpret that as a good sign and to believe that peace and plenty hover over Quincy St. I shall continue in this happy faith and in the belief that you are gently putting forth your strength again, until the contrary is distinctly proved. Behold me in Scotland and very well pleased to be here. I am staying with the Clarks, of whom you have heard me speak and than whom there could not be a more tenderly hospitable couple. Sir John caresses me like a brother, and her ladyship supervises me like a mother. It is a beautiful part of the country—the so-called Deeside—the mountains of Aberdeenshire—the region of Balmoral and Braemar. This supremely comfortable house—lying deep among the brown and purple moors—has the honor, I believe, of being the highest placed laird's house in Scotland. On such a day as this it is quite in the clouds; but I wish that, in the beautiful weather that we have been having, you might contemplate the glorious view of sweeping hills and gleaming lochs that lies forever before the windows. I have been here for four or five days and I feel that I have done a very good thing in coming to Scotland. Once you get the hang of it, and apprehend the type, it is a most beautiful and admirable little country—fit, for "distinction" &c. to make up a trio with Italy and Greece. There is a little very good company in the house, including my brilliant friend Lady Hamilton Gordon,[1] and every day has brought with it some pretty entertainment. I wish I could relate these episodes in detail but I shall probably do a little of it in mercenary print. On the first day I went to some Highland sports, given by Lord Huntly, and to a sumptuous lunch, in a coquettish marquee, which formed an episode of the same. The next day I spent in roaming over the moors and hills, in company with a remarkably nice young fellow staying in the house, Sidney Holland, grandson of the late Sir Henry; (his father married a daughter of Sir Charles Trevelyan, sister of my friend Mrs. Dugdale). Nothing can be more breezy and glorious than a ramble on these purple hills and a lounge in the sun-warmed heather. The real way to enjoy them is of course supposed to be with an eye to the grouse and partridges but this is, happily, little of a shooting house, though Holland keeps the table—one of the best in England (or rather in Scotland, which is saying more) supplied with game. The next day I took part in a cavalcade across the hills to see a ruined castle; and in the evening, if

[1] Daughter of Herschel, the physicist and astronomer, Lady Hamilton Gordon was a lady-in-waiting to Queen Victoria.

you please, stiff and sore as I was and am still, with my exploits
in the saddle, which had been sufficiently honorable, I went to
a ball fifteen miles distant. The ball was given by a certain old
Mr. Cunliffe Brooks, a great proprietor hereabouts and possessor
of a shooting-lodge with a ball-room; a fact which sufficiently
illustrates the luxury of these Anglo-Scotch arrangements. At
the ball was the famous beauty Mrs. Langtry,[2] who was staying
in the house and who is probably for the moment the most celebrated woman in England. She is in sooth divinely handsome
and it was "extremely odd" to see her dancing a Highland reel
(which she had been practising for three days) with young Lord
Huntley, who is a very handsome fellow and who in his kilt and
tartan, leaping, hooting and romping, opposite to this London
divinity, offered a vivid reminder of ancient Caledonian barbarism and of the roughness which lurks in all British amuse-
ments and only wants a pretext to explode. We came home from
our ball (where I took out two young ladies who had gone with
us for a polka apiece) at 4 a.m. and I found it difficult on that
morning, at breakfast, to comply with that rigid punctuality
which is the custom of the house. But for all that we went on a
twelve-mile drive and picnic through a glorious country and
under a yellow autumnal sun, to the beautiful old baronial
castle of Craigievar—a perfect specimen of Franco-Scottish
architecture. There we sat on the grass, under the trees and
towers and imbibed one [of] those admirable cold lunches which
English butlers, whatever their faults, know how to put up so
neatly in English hampers. Today our fine weather has come to
an end and we are closely involved in a ferocious wet tornado.
But I am glad of the rest and the quiet and I have just bolted
out of the library to escape the "morning service" read by the

2 Mrs. Emily Charlotte Langtry (1852-1929), a famous beauty, known as "the
Jersey Lily."

worthy Nevin, the American Episcopal chaplain in Rome, who is staying here, to which the dumb and decent servants are tramping in. I am fast becoming a good enough Englishman to respect, inveterately, my own habits, and do, wherever I may be, only exactly what I want. This is the secret of prosperity here—provided of course one has a certain number of sociable and conformable habits, and civil inclinations, as a starting point. After that, the more positive your idiosyncrasies, the more positive the convenience. But it is drawing toward lunch and I can't carry my personality quite so far as to be late for that.— I have said enough, dear sister, to make you see that I continue to see the world with perhaps even enviable profit. But don't envy me too much; for the British country-house, has at moments, for a cosmopolitanized American, an insuperable flatness. On the other hand, to do it justice, there is no doubt of its being one [of] the ripest fruits of time—and here in Scotland, where you get the conveniences of Mayfair dove-tailed into the last romanticism of nature—of the highest results of civilization. Such as it is, at any rate, I shall probably have a little more of it. I shall be here a few days more and then go, via Aberdeen and Edinburgh, to spend a few days with my hospitable, though somewhat irregular friend, Mrs. Rogerson.[3] I spent a day at Edinburgh on my way hither (it's a long journey from London) and was immensely taken with its grand air. I shall hardly get back to town and settle down to my winter's work, which probably this year will be copious, before the last of the month. But I shall have had a very pretty holiday and have got all kinds of valuable impressions. Scotland is decidedly a thing to see and which it would have been idiocy to have foregone. Did I tell

[3] Mrs. Rogerson, a London hostess described by James as "a clever, liberal woman, who invites me to dinner every four or five days."

you I was now London correspondent of the *Nation?*[4] I parted with the good Gurneys just before leaving town; they will tell you an immense deal about me. Farewell, dearest child and sister. I wish I could blow you a little of the salubrity of bonnie Scotland. The lunch bell is striking up and I hurry off with comprehensive blessings. Ever your faithfullest

H.J. Jr.

To ROBERTSON JAMES

723 15th Street
Washington
Jan. 27th. [*1882*]

My dear Bob.

Your note has just arrived and I am filled with grief and horror at the news of poor Mother's illness. Give her my tender love and assure her of my liveliest sympathy. I cannot bear to think that she suffers, and would come on to see her if I believed it would help her through. But if Aunt Kate has come, and you are there, she has care enough, (with what father and Alice can also give) and I should only be in the way. I earnestly hope moreover that she has seen the worst and I depend upon your writing to me again immediately to let me know how she prospers.—You don't tell me when she was taken ill—nor whether she had been ailing; but I hope that if her attack was sudden her recovery will be equally so. I was very glad to hear from you apart from this—as we have corresponded so little and particularly pleased that you are able to tell me that you are better in health and spirits and are you painting in Cambridge? That is a resource that I advise you to cultivate, the more things one can do the better.

---

4 In this capacity James wrote several articles on British politics as well as his usual literary and artistic chronicles.

To MRS. FRANCIS MATHEWS [*1882*]

I am amused at the impression my Washington life makes upon you for, seen from my own near standpoint, it is not at all fairy-like. I have learned no State secrets, nor obtained the inside view of anything, neither have I acquired any valuable familiarities. The number of persons here at present asking for consulates is I suppose about 5000. I dined last night with Mr. De Biedt, Swedish secretary of Legation, and went afterwards to a ball at the British Legation; however, I remained but half an hour.

Do keep me informed about Mother and tell her that I embrace her as firmly as she can endure. I trust father and Alice are equal to the occasion and am happy at the advent of Aunt Kate. I am delighted those poor $250 have given you any obligation but don't see how they can so long as they repose in the bank. An equal sum is at your disposal as often as you need it. Ever yours affectionate   Henry James.

To MRS. FRANCIS MATHEWS

Boston, Feb. 13th [*1882*]

My dear Mary.[1]

I have been intending to write to you ever since I came back to America, more than three months ago—I wished to give you news both of myself and my people, over here—whom I always consider a little as yours also. Today I have more reason than ever for sending you a friendly missive—but, I grieve to say, it is a very sad one. You will feel much sympathy for us when I tell you that my dear mother, for whom you were named, died a fortnight ago. It seems a great deal longer—her death has made

[1] Mrs. Mathews was the former Mary Wilkinson, daughter of Dr. J. J. Garth Wilkinson, Swedenborgian friend of the elder Henry James. She had been named Mary after the novelist's mother.

the days move slowly! I am very happy to say that her death was tranquil and painless—she passed away from one moment to another as my father and sister were sitting with her in the twilight. She had had a rather sharp (but not at all alarming) attack of bronchial asthma, from which she was apparently happily convalescent—and in the midst of her cheerful sense of recovery she suddenly died. I was not at my father's house at the time—but in Washington, and I reached home but twenty-six hours after all was over. I didn't see my dear mother living— but I saw her with a tranquil, beautiful appearance of life. My three brothers had all arrived—it was the first time in fifteen years that we had been together—and we carried her to her rest on one of those splendid days of winter that are frequent here— when the snow is high and deep, but the sky as blue as the south, and the air brilliant and still. You will know for yourself that our loss is great. She was the perfection of a mother—the sweetest, gentlest, most beneficent human being I have ever known. I am extremely happy that I had come to America this year, after so long an absence—all my last recollections of her are inexpressibly tender. I thank heaven, however, that it is given to us to feel this particular pang but once. My father is infirm, but very tranquil; he has a way of his own of taking the sorrows of life—a way so perfect that one almost envies him his troubles. Alice, I am happy to say, after many years of ill health has been better for the last few months than for a long time; she is able to look after my father and take care of his house—and as she is a person of great ability it is an extreme good fortune that she is now able to exert herself. You were always interested in Wilky—whom I lately saw for the first time in ten years. He is not particularly successful, as success is measured in this country; but he is always rotund and good-natured and delightful. Please tell your father and mother all this—I know they will think of us affectionately. My mother's death has changed my present plans. I was to have returned to England in May—but I have put off my departure till somewhat later, in order to be a while longer near my father. When I do go you shall soon see me; and as I expect to spend the remainder of my life in England I don't grudge my native land a few additional months. I greatly hope that you are all well, and I send you the very best wishes. Commend me kindly to your valiant husband, and to your father and mother and believe me ever faithfully yours

Henry James Jr.

II

HOUSE OF LIFE, PALACE OF ART

FROM the time that he dispatched his first book review (with a formal two-sentence covering letter) to late middle life, Henry James conducted his own business affairs. The literary market was a much simpler place in those days than it is today: no tangled questions of stage or movie rights, no radio, no television, no paper-bound reprints, no book digests. On the contrary, an absence of adequate copyright protection that resulted in frequent "piracies," much more limited markets, and literary buying and selling by simple gentlemen's agreements. James did not suffer unduly from publishing pirates, although *Daisy Miller*, after its appearance in England, was very promptly republished in America in two journals without benefit of royalties. The novelist learned quickly through such experiences how to protect his rights and how to bargain effectively alike with magazine editors and book publishers.

The letters given in this section show his methods of negotiation, the manner in which he posed his terms and fought for his reputation. As his publications increased—and there was a time when he almost glutted his own market by excess of production—he found it more difficult to serialize his work in the magazines. For a brief interval he used the services of the pioneer London literary agent, A. P. Watt. Then, at the turn of the century, he turned his business affairs over to James B. Pinker, through whose office there passed virtually all the great literature of the late Victorian era. Pinker relieved James of much of the burdensome problem of administering what was now a substantial literary capital—for James had been producing shelf upon shelf of volumes for more than three decades.

Most of the business letters addressed to Pinker have been preserved in the Yale University Library and these reveal how closely James kept abreast of his affairs. There are probably few agents who have been prodded as regularly and supplied with such abundant material for the marketplace. James kept up a flow of fiction into Pinker's office and expected in return a substantial flow of money. Pinker was successful in obtaining adequate and sometimes substantial advances on most of James' late productions, but the royalty returns were—given James's years and reputation—smaller than those of the best-selling writers. This was a source of intermittent anxiety to James and his long illness of 1910 was partially the result of worry that took its cue from the failure of the long-prepared New York Edition of his novels and tales to earn him substantial returns.

In this section will be found not only examples of James's correspondence with editors and publishers, but his concern over questions of copyright; the manner in which he planned his books; his exacting demand to see proof at each stage of production; his method of choosing names for characters; and his attitude towards illustration. Included also is an unique letter to a reviewer of his books. He shuttled with ease in the letters relating to his profession from the palace of art to the house of life—that life which he confronted with a shrewd and practical sense of the realities to be faced and conquered.

To THE NORTH AMERICAN REVIEW

13 Ashburton Place
[*Boston*] *30 July* [*1864*]

Gentlemen.
I take the liberty of enclosing a brief review of [Nassau W.] Senior's *Essays on Fiction* published in London a few months ago. Hoping that you may deem it worthy of a place among your Literary Notices, I remain, yours respectfully HENRY JAMES Jr.

To F. B. CHURCH

Cambridge, Oct. 23d [*1867?*]

My dear sir:—
I recd. your note and the inclosed cheque—for which many thanks.—I am sorry the story is not a little shorter but I am very glad that you are to print all at once. As for adding a paragraph I should strongly object to it. It doesn't seem to me necessary. Silence on the subject will prove to the reader, I think, that the marriage *did* come off.[1] I have little fear that the reader will miss a positive statement to that effect and the story closes in a more dramatic manner, to my apprehension, just as I have left it. Yours most truly

H. James Jr.

P.S. Let me reiterate my request that I may see a proof. This I should particularly like to do.

H. J. Jr.

1 The allusion here appears to be to "The Story of a Masterpiece" published in the *Galaxy* January-February 1868. From the first James seems to have had difficulty convincing editors that fiction should imitate life and not provide tidy endings. In this instance, however, James yielded, for the story has a final explanatory paragraph announcing that the marriage did take place. Church, to whom the letter is addressed, was one of the owners and editors of the *Galaxy*.

To WILLIAM DEAN HOWELLS

Florence March 10th. [*1874*]

Dear Howells—

This is grim business, and yet I must be brief. Your dear friend Dr. Holland[1] has just proposed to me to write a novel for *Scribner,* beginning in November next. To write a novel I incline and have been long inclining: but I feel as if there were a definite understanding between us that if I do so, the *Atlantic* should have the offer of it. I have therefore sent through my father a refusal to Dr. H. to be retained or forwarded according to your response. Will the *Atlantic* have my novel, when written?[2] Dr. H's offer is a comfortable one—the novel accepted at rate (that is if terms agree,) and to begin, as I say, in November and last till the November following. He asks me to name terms, and I should name $1200. If the *Atlantic* desires a story for the year and will give as much I of course embrace in preference the *Atlantic.* Sentimentally I should prefer the *A.*; but as things stand with me, I have no right to let it be anything but a pure money question. Will you, when you have weighed the matter, send me a line through my father or better, perhaps, communicate with him *viva voce*—This is not a love-letter and I won't gossip. I expect to be in Europe and, I hope, in Italy, till midsummer. I sent you lately, at three or four weeks interval, the two parts of a tale.[3] You have them, I hope? Farewell, with all tender wishes to your person and household. Yours ever

H. James jr.

---

[1] Josiah Gilbert Holland (1819-81) first editor of *Scribner's Monthly,* from 1871 to 1881.

[2] Howells came to terms with James, and *Roderick Hudson,* his first major novel, was published in the *Atlantic* from January to December 1875.

[3] Presumably "Eugene Pickering," which appeared in the October-November 1874 issues of the *Atlantic Monthly.*

To WILLIAM DEAN HOWELLS

Paris, Rue de Luxembourg 29
Feb. 3rd. [*1876*]

Dear Howells—

Ambiguous tho' it sounds, I was sorry to get your letter of the 16th ult. Shortly after coming to Paris, finding it a matter of prime necessity to get a novel on the stocks immediately, I wrote to F. P. Church, offering him one for the *Galaxy,* to begin in March, and I was just sending off my first instalment of MS. when your letter arrived. (The thing has been delayed to April.) It did not even occur to me to write to you about it, as I took for granted that the *Atlantic* would begin nothing till June or *July,* and it was the money question solely that had to determine me. If I had received your letter some weeks before I think my extreme preference to have the thing appear in the *Atlantic* might have induced me to wait till the time you mention. But even of this I am not sure, as by beginning in April my story, making nine long numbers, may terminate and appear in a volume by next Christmas. This, with the prompter monthly income (I have demanded $150 a number,) is a momentous consideration. The story is *The American*—the one I spoke to you about (but which, by the way, runs a little differently from your memory of it.) It was the only subject mature enough in my mind to use immediately. It has in fact perhaps been used somewhat prematurely; and I hope you find enough faults in it to console you for not having it in the *Atlantic*. There are two things to add. One is that the insufferable *nonchalance,* neglect and ill-manners of the Churches have left me very much in the dark as to whether my conditions are acceptable to them: and I have written them that if they are not satisfied they are immediately to forward my parcel to you. The other is that I would, at any rate, rather give a novel to the Atlantic next year, (beginning, that is, in January) than this.[1] So far as one party can make a bargain, I hereby covenant to do so. I expect to have the last half of the summer and the autumn to work on such a tale; for I shall have obviously to settle down and produce my yearly romance. I am sorry, on many accounts, that the thing for the present, stands as it does, but I couldn't wait. I hope you will find something that will serve your turn.

—Why didn't you tell me the name of the author of the very charming notice of R[oderick] H[udson] in the last *Atlantic,* which I saw today at Galignani's? I don't recognize you, and I don't suspect Mrs. Wister. Was it Lathrop? If so please assure him of my gratitude. I am doing as I would be done by and not reading your story in pieces.[2] Will you mail me the volume when it appears? I should like to notice it.

—Yes, I see a good deal of Tourgueneff and am excellent friends with him. He has been very kind to me and has inspired me with an extreme regard. He is everything that one could desire—robust, sympathetic, modest, simple, profound, intelligent, naif—in fine angelic. He has also made me acquainted with G. Flaubert, to whom I have likewise taken a great fancy, and at whose house I have seen the little *coterie* of the young realists in fiction. They are all charming talkers—though as editor of the austere *Atlantic* it would startle you to hear some of their projected subjects. The other day Edmond de Goncourt (the best of them) said he had been lately working very well on his novel—he had got upon an episode that greatly interested him, and into which he was going very far. *Flaubert:* "What is it?" *E. de G.* "A whore-house *de province.*"

I oughtn't to give you any news—you yourself were so brief.

[1] *The American* appeared in the *Atlantic* from June through December 1876 and January through May 1877.

[2] Apparently an allusion to *Private Theatricals* by Howells which ran in the *Atlantic* from November 1875 through May 1876.

To WHITELAW REID [*1876*]

Indeed I have no news to give: I lead a quiet life, and find Paris more like Cambridge than you probably enviously suppose. I like it—(Paris)—much, and find it an excellent place to work.— I am glad my *Tribune* letters amuse you.—They are most impudently light-weighted, but that was part of the bargain. I find as I grow older, that the only serious work I can do is in story-spinning.—Farewell. With a friendly memory of your wife and children

Yours very truly
H. James jr.

To WHITELAW REID

Chateau de Varennes [près Montargis]
Aug. 30th [*1876*]

Dear Mr. Reid

I have just received your letter of August 10th. I quite appreciate what you say about the character of my letters, and about their not being the right sort of thing for a newspaper. I have been half expecting to hear from you to that effect. I myself had wondered whether you could make room for them during the present and coming time at home,[1] and I can easily imagine that the general reader should feel indisposed to give the time requisite for reading them. They would, as you say, be more in place in a magazine. But I am afraid I can't assent to your proposal that I should try and write otherwise. I know the sort of letter you mean—it is doubtless the proper sort of thing for the *Tribune* to have. But I can't produce it—I don't know how and I couldn't learn how. It would cost me really more trouble than to write as I have been doing (which comes tolerably easy to me) and it would be poor economy for me to try and become "newsy" and gossipy. I am too finical a writer and I should be

---

1 An allusion to the impending presidential elections.

constantly becoming more "literary" than is desirable. To resist this tendency would be rowing up stream and would take much time and pains. If my letters have been "too good" I am honestly afraid that they are the poorest I can do, especially for the money! I had better, therefore, suspend them, altogether. I have enjoyed writing them, however, and if the *Tribune* has not been the better for them I hope it has not been too much the worse. I shall doubtless have sooner or later a discreet successor. Believe me, with the best wishes,

Yours very truly
Henry James Jr.

To WILLIAM DEAN HOWELLS

3 Bolton St. W.
March 30th. [*1877*]

Dear Howells—I am supposed to be busily scribbling for lucre this morning; but I must write you three lines of acknowledgment of your welcome long letter. Its most interesting portion was naturally your stricture on the close of my tale, which I accept with saintly meekness. These are matters which one feels about as one may, or as one can. I quite understand that as an editor you should go in for "cheerful endings"; but I am sorry that as a private reader you are not struck with the inevitability of the *American* dénouement. I fancied that most folks would feel that Mme. de Cintré *couldn't,* when the finish came, marry Mr. N[ewman]; and what the few persons who have spoken to me of the tale have expressed to me (e.g. Mrs. Kemble t'other day) was the fear that I should really put the marriage through. *Voyons;* it would have been impossible: they would have been an impossible couple, with an impossible problem before them. For instance—to speak very materially—where would they have lived? It was all very well for Newman to talk of giving her the whole world to choose from: but Asia and Africa being counted out, what would Europe and America have offered? Mme. de C. couldn't have lived in New York; depend upon it; and Newman, after his marriage (or rather *she,* after it) couldn't have dwelt in France. There would have been nothing left but a farm out West. No, the interest of the subject was, for me, (without my being at all a pessimist) its exemplification of one of those insuperable difficulties which present themselves in people's lives and from which the only issue is by forfeiture—by losing something. It was cruelly hard for poor N. to lose, certainly: but *que diable allait-il faire dans cette galère?* We are each the product of circumstances and there are tall stone walls which fatally divide us. I have written my story from Newman's side of the wall, and I understand so well how Mme. de Cintré couldn't really scramble over from *her* side! If I had represented her as doing so I should have made a prettier ending, certainly; but I should have felt as if I were throwing a rather vulgar sop to readers who don't really know the world and who don't measure the merit of a novel by its correspondence to the same. Such readers assuredly have a right to their entertainment, but I don't believe it is in me to give them, in a satisfactory way, what they require.—I don't think that "tragedies" have the presumption against them as much as you appear to; and I see no logical reason why they shouldn't be as *long* as comedies. In the drama they are usually allowed to be longer—*non è vero?*— But whether the *Atlantic* ought to print unlimited tragedy is another question—which you are doubtless quite right in regarding as you do. Of course you couldn't have, for the present, another evaporated marriage from me! I suspect it is the tragedies in life that arrest my attention more than the other things and say more to my imagination; but, on the other hand, if I fix my eyes on a sun-spot I think I am able to see the prismatic

[69]

colors in it. You shall have the brightest possible sun-spot for the four-number tale of 1878.¹ It shall fairly put your readers eyes out. The idea of doing what you propose much pleases me; and I agree to squeeze my buxom muse, as you happily call her, into a 100 of your pages. I will lace her so tight that she shall have the neatest little figure in the world. It shall be a very joyous little romance. I am afraid I can't tell you at this moment what it will be; for my dusky fancy contains nothing joyous enough: but I will invoke the jocund muse and come up to time. I shall probably develop an idea that I have, about a genial, charming youth of a Bohemianish father, who comes back from foreign parts into the midst of a mouldering and ascetic old Puritan family of his kindred ([word illegible] imaginary locality in New England 1830,) and by his gayety and sweet audacity smooths out their rugosities, heals their dyspepsia and dissipates their troubles. *All* the women fall in love with him (and he with them —his amatory powers are boundless;) but even for a happy ending he can't marry them all. But he marries the prettiest, and from a romantic quality of Christian charity, produces a picturesque imbroglio (for the sake of the picturesque I shall play havoc with the New England background of 1830!) under cover of which the other maidens pair off with the swains who have hitherto been starved out: after which the beneficent cousin departs for Bohemia (with his bride, oh yes!) in a vaporous rosy cloud, to scatter new benefactions over man—and especially, womankind!—(Pray don't mention this stuff to any one. It would be meant, roughly speaking, as the picture of the conversion of a dusty, dreary domestic circle to epicureanism. But I may be able to make nothing of it. The merit would be in the amount of *color* I should be able to infuse into it.) But I shall

¹ The story James had in mind became *The Europeans* serialized in the *Atlantic* from July through October 1878.

give you it, or its equivalent, by November next.—It was quite
by accident I didn't mention the name of your admiress. Nay
there are two of them! The one I spoke of, I think, is Lady
Clark—a handsome charming woman, of a certain age, the wife
of a retired and invalid diplomatist who lives chiefly on her
estate in Scotland. She takes in the *Atlantic* and seems to affect
you much. The other is Mrs. Coltman, a modest, blushing and
pleasing woman, who also has the *Atlantic,* and who can best be
identified by saying that she is the sister of the widow of A. H.
Clough, the poet—Lowell's friend. She is to take me some day
soon down to Eton to show me an inside-view of the school,
where her rosy little British boys are. Both of these ladies
descanted to me on the *Atlantic,* and your productions and said
nary a word to me of my own masterpieces: whereby I consider
my present action magnanimous! Apropos: the young girl in
your comedy[2] is extremely charming; quite adorable, in fact;
and extremely real. You make them wonderfully well.—What
more shall I say?—Yes, I find London much to my taste—entertaining, interesting, inspiring, even. But I am not, as you seem
to imply, in the least in the thick of it. If I were to tell you
whom I see; it would make a tolerably various list: but the
people only pass before me panoramically, and I have no relations with them. I dined yesterday in company with Browning,
at Smalley's[3]—where were also Huxley and his wife and the
editor and editress of the *Daily News:*[4] among the cleverest
people I have met here. Smalley has a charming house and wife,
and is a very creditable American representative; more so than
the minister who, I am told, has never returned a dinner since
he has been here. Browning is a great chatterer but no *Sordello*

2 Apparently an allusion to Howells' *Out of the Question* which appeared
in the *Atlantic* from February to April 1877.
3 G. W. Smalley, European correspondent of the *Tribune.*
4 Mr. and Mrs. F. H. Hill.

at all.—We are lost in admiration of Mr. Hayes; may his shadow never grow less. Blessing on your home. Yours always truly

H. James jr.

To W. E. HENLEY

3 Bolton Street
Aug. 24th. [*1878*]

My dear Mr. Henley

Your note ought to have had a prompt answer but it came to me in the country, where I had taken a religious vow not to put pen to paper, for a few days, and I kept it till my return to town, which took place only last evening.—I like the idea of "helping" any one, in any degree, to read Turgenieff: but I am afraid the assistance I can now render you will not seem valuable. I am sorry to say I have *none* of Turgenieff's works near me at present—I possess the whole collection, but it is no nearer than America. Many of them I read in one of the German translations, the best of which is the best of any. *Helene* has been (unless I am grossly mistaken) translated into English under the title of *On the Eve;* whether by Ralston[1] or not I forget. *Pères et Enfants* has been also translated into—American. (Ralston translated the *Nichu* as *Lisa* and it is better than the French version.) Do you know the *Nouvelles Moscovites?*—the *Étranges Histoires?*—the *Reliques Vivantes* (the last a small masterpiece?) *Smoke* has been done into English. It is poor comfort to tell you of these things, without sending them to you. But I am destitute. (The *Mémoires d'un Seigneur Russe* and the *Récits d'un Chasseur* are one and the same thing; having but the respective names of two different French translations. The first published by Hachette cheaply, at a franc a volume—there are two—is easily obtain-

[1] W. R. S. Ralston, Turgenev's English friend and translator.

able. The other—which is better—is scarce and out of print.) I am glad you are interested in Turgenieff and envy you the high pleasure of making acquaintance with him. Do you ever read at the British Museum? You would find there, in back volumes of the *Revue des Deux Mondes* 10 and 15 years ago—2 or 3 *superb* things of T's: notably the *Journal d'un Homme de Trop* (reprinted with *Dimitri Roudine*) and *Faust* (a masterpiece) never reprinted.—I am extremely sorry you are disconnected with *London,* but hope you are in for something as good or better. Also that you are well. I am on the point of bringing out a small fiction which I will send you.—Very truly yours

H. James jr.

To MRS. F. H. HILL

3 Bolton Street,
March 21st [*1879*]

My dear Mrs. Hill¹—

I must thank you without delay for the little notice of *Daisy*

1 This letter, generously furnished by Mr. Robert H. Taylor, is unique among the thousands extant: it is the only one found so far written to a reviewer of one of Henry James's works. James, however, had met Mrs. Hill, wife of the editor of the *Daily News* in London drawing-rooms and seems to have felt acutely that he could not allow her strictures to go unanswered. His usual rule was to ignore reviews and reviewers and there exist letters to various publishers instructing them not to send him any cuttings about himself from the press. This letter was written at a moment when James was being sharply criticized in the United States for having committed an "outrage" upon American girlhood in his portrait of Daisy Miller, and he now found himself under English fire for his social satire of certain English types. On Jan. 18th, 1879 he had written to his mother about "An International Episode": "It is an entirely new sensation for them (the people here) to be (at all delicately) *ironized* and satirized, from the American point of view, and they don't at all relish it. Their conception of the normal in such a relation is that the satire should be all on their side against the Americans; and I suspect that if we were to push this a little further we would find that they are extremely sensitive. But I like them too much and feel too kindly to them to go into the satire-business or even the light-ironical in any case in which it would wound them—even if in such a case I should see my way to it very clearly."

Miller and the "Three Meetings,"² in this morning's D[aily]
N[ews], in which you say so many kind things so gracefully. You
possess in great perfection that amiable art. But, shall I confess
it? (you will perhaps guess it,) my eagerness to thank you for
your civilities to two of my tales, is slightly increased by my im-
patience to deprecate your strictures with regard to the third.
I am distressed by the evident disfavour with which you view
the "International Episode;"³ and meditating on the matter as
humbly as I can, I really think you have been unjust to it. No,
my dear Mrs. Hill, *bien non,* my two Englishmen are not represented as "Arries;" it was perhaps the fond weakness of a creator,
but I even took to myself some credit for the portrait of Lord
Lambeth, who was intended to be the image of a loveable, sympathetic, excellent-natured young personage, full of good feelings and of all possible delicacies of conduct. That he says "I
say" rather too many times is very probable (I thought so, quite,
myself, in reading over the thing as a book:) but that strikes me
as a rather venial flaw. I differ from you in thinking that he
would, in fact, have been likely to say it with considerable fre-
quency. I used the words because I remembered that when I
was fresh to England and first began to "go out," I was struck
with the way in which they flourished among the younger generation, especially when the younger generation was of the idle
and opulent and pleasure-loving type. Depend upon it, it is not
only "Arry" who says "I say." There are gentlemen and gentle-

2 The volume reviewed was *Daisy Miller and Other Stories,* issued in two volumes by Macmillan on Feb. 15, 1879. James makes an interesting slip of the pen
here in speaking of "Three Meetings" although the title of his story was "Four
Meetings," which suggests that perhaps his title was inspired by one of Turgenev's tales which did bear the title "Three Meetings."

3 "An International Episode" had originally appeared in the *Cornhill Magazine*
of December 1878 and January 1879. It tells of the adventures of two Englishmen, one a peer, in New York and in Newport and then of the experiences of
two American women in England. The peer falls in love with an American girl
who, however, in the end refuses to marry him.

men—those who are constantly particular about what they say, and those who go in greatly for amusement and who say anything, almost, that comes into their heads. It has always seemed to me that in this latter racketing, pleasure-loving "golden-youth" section of English society, the very atmosphere was impregnated with slang. A year ago I went for six months to the St. James's Club, where (to my small contentment personally,) the golden youth of every description used largely to congregate, and during this period, being the rapacious and shameless observer that you know, I really made studies in London colloquialisms. I certainly heard more "I says" than I had ever done before; and I suppose that 19 out of 20 of the young men in the place had been to a public school. However, this detail is not of much importance; what I meant to indicate is the (I think) incontestable fact that certain people in English society talk in a very offhand, informal, irregular manner, and use a great many roughnesses and crudities. It didn't seem to me that one was bound to handle their idiosyncrasies of speech so very tenderly as to weigh one idiom very long against another. In a word the Lord Lambeths of the English world are, I think, distinctly liable, in the turn of their phrases, just as they are in the gratification of their tastes—or of some of them—to strike quiet conservative people like your humble servant as vulgar. I meant to do no more than just rapidly indicate this liability— I meant it to be by no means the last impression that he would leave. It doesn't in the least seem to have been so, with most people, and if it didn't sound fatuous I should say that I had been congratulated by several people whom I supposed to be of an observing turn upon the verisimilitude of his conversation.— If it didn't seem fatuous, too, or unmannerly, to inflict upon you so very bulky a bundle of exposition as this letter has grown into, I should go on to say that I don't think you have been liberal to the poor little women-folk of my narrative. (That liberal, by the way, is but a conciliatory substitute for some more rigid epithet—say *fair,* or *just.*) I want at any rate to remonstrate with you for your apparent assumption that in the two English ladies, I meant to make a resumé of my view of English manners. My dear Mrs. Hill—the idea is fantastic! The two ladies are a picture of a special case, and they are certainly not an over-charged one. They were very determined their manners should not be nicer; it would have quite defeated the point they wished to make, which was that it didn't at all suit them that a little unknown American girl should marry their coveted kinsman. Such a consummation certainly does not suit English duchesses and countesses in general—it would be quite legitimate to draw from the story an induction as to my conviction on that point. The story was among other things an attempt at a sketch of this state of mind, and, given what I wished to represent, I thought the touches by which the attitude of the duchess and her daughter is set forth, were rather light and discreet than otherwise. A man in my position, and writing the sort of things I do, feels the need of protesting against this extension of his idea in which in many cases, many readers are certain to indulge. One may make figures and figures without intending generalizations—generalizations of which I have a horror. I make a couple of English ladies doing a disagreeable thing— *cela c'est vu:* excuse me!—and forthwith I find myself responsible for a representation of English manners! Nothing is my *last word* about anything—I am interminably super-subtle and analytic—and with the blessing of heaven, I shall live to make all sorts of representations of all sorts of things. It will take a much cleverer person than myself to discover my last impression —among all these things—of anything. And then, in such a matter, the bother of being an American! Trollope, Thackeray,

Dickens, even [sic] with their big authoritative talents, were free to draw all sorts of unflattering English pictures, by the thousand. But if I make a single one, I am forthwith in danger of being confronted with a criminal conclusion—and sinister rumours reach me as to what I think of English society. I think more things than I can undertake to tell in 40 pages of the Cornhill. Perhaps some day I shall take more pages, and attempt to tell some of these things; in that case, I hope, there will be a little, of every sort, for every one! Meanwhile I shall draw plenty of pictures of disagreeable Americans, as I have done already, and the friendly Briton will see no harm in that!—it will seem to him a part of the natural fitness!—Since I am in for it—with this hideously egotistic document—I do just want to add that I am sorry you didn't find a little word of appreciation for the two other women's figures in the *I. E.,* which I really think a success. (You will smile at the artless crudity of my vanity!) The thing was the study—a very sincere, careful, intendedly minute one—of the state of mind of a couple of American women pressed upon by English circumstances—and I had a faith that the picture would seem life-like and comprehensible. In the case of the heroine I had a fancy it would even seem charming. In that of the elder sister, no, I hadn't such a faith: she is too garrulous, and, on the whole, too silly;—it is for a silly woman that she is offered. But I should have said it was obvious that her portrait is purely objective—she is not in the least intended to throw light upon the objects she criticizes, (English life and manners &c;) she is intended to throw light on the American mind alone, and its way of taking things. When I attempt to deal with English manners, I shall approach them through a very different portal than that of Mrs. Westgate's intelligence. I was at particular pains to mark the limitations of this organ—by some of the speeches I have put into her mouth—such as the grotesque story about the Duke who cuts the Butterworths.[4] In a word she is, throughout, an ironical creation!—Forgive this inordinate and abominable scrawl—I certainly didn't mean to reward you for your friendly zeal in reading so many of my volumes by despatching you another in the innocent guise of a note. But your own frankness has made me expansive—and there goes with this only a grain of protest to a hundredweight of gratitude. Believe me, dear Mrs. Hill, very faithfully yours

H. James jr.

To T. B. ALDRICH

Paris, Feb. 13th [1884]
Hotel de Hollande

My dear Aldrich.

It is all right about poor H. Aidé.[1] My application to you was purely perfunctory and I sacrificed you without scruple to a social tie! You will already have received my note asking you to please send back his MS. to *Queen Anne's (Garden) Mansion, St. Jame's Park, London, S.W.* and this is the end of that.

Yes—I think I should like to do you a serial to begin in 1865 [sic].[2] Only I don't think I should be able to begin it in January. It would suit me better to open, as the theatrical papers say, in July. I gather, from the way you express yourself, that this would not be inconsistent with your plan. I have in my head,

---

[4] Mrs. Westgate's story in "An International Episode" concerns the Duke of Green-Erin who enjoys the hospitality of the Butterworths in New York but ignores them when they come to London. When he does encounter them by accident at Ascot he pays Mr. Butterworth £10 he owes him with the suggestion that the American had sought him out to recover this sum.

[1] Hamilton Aidé, a London dilettante and familiar figure in the drawing-rooms of high Victorian society.

[2] This and the subsequent slips of the pen in this letter, in which James writes 1865 instead of 1885, are discussed in *Henry James: The Untried Years* by Leon Edel, (New York 1953), in the chapter titled "Heroine of the Scene."

and have had for a year or two a very good *sujet de roman* of which I should make use. What I desire is that you should give me twelve monthly instalments of 25 pages each: that my novel should in other words run exactly a year. Please let me hear from you in regard to this matter of beginning in July 1865, and as to when in this case you should desire the first batch of copy. I think too that for a work beginning upwards of a year and a half from now there would probably be something to be said about terms: pregnant word! between this and that the *Century* is to publish, de moi, 1/a story in three parts. 2/a story in two parts. 3/a story in six parts, and three or four short tales, from my turning hand are to appear (this is a profound secret)— have been, in a word, secured, *à prix d'or* in—je vous en donne en mille—the New York Sunday *Sun!!*[3] This last fact, I repeat, is really as yet *a complete and sacred secret.* Please bury it in oblivion and burn my letter. I mention it, with the preceding items, simply to denote that by July 1865 I expect to be in the enjoyment of a popularity which will require me to ask $500 a number for the successive instalments of *The Princess Casamassima* (which will probably be the name of my novel, though on this I am not yet fixed.) I should like also to say that it will probably be a good thing for all of us that I should send you between this and the end of the year three or four short critical articles which I have in my head and which crave to be written. Besides relieving my mind of thoughts that ferment in it, they will do to complete a volume of essays which I desire to put forth by the end of the year and which will probably represent the last of this sort of work which I shall do for a long time to come.—This latter is a reason which says more of course to me than to you; but I leave it in its naiveté: one learns to be so naif

3 "Pandora" appeared in the *Sun* June 1 and 8, 1884 and "Georgina's Reasons" July 20, 27 and August 3.

in Paris.—I have been here (for that and other advantages,) for the last fortnight and shall remain to the end of the month. Paris is charming; bright, mild and a little dull, and "naturalism" is in possession *sur toute la ligne*. I spent last evening at Alph. Daudet's, and was much impressed with the intense seriousness of that little group—himself, Zola, Goncourt, &c. About Daudet's intensity of effort there is something tragical, and his wasted, worn extraordinarily beautiful and refined little face expresses it in a way which almost brings tears to my eyes. The torment of style, the high standard of it, the effort to say something perfectly in a language in which everything has been said, and re-said,—so that there are certain things, certain cases, which can never again be attempted—all this seems to me to be wearing them all out, so that they have the look of galley-slaves tied to a ball and chain, rather than of happy producers. Daudet tells me that the act of production, and execution, for him, is nothing but effort and suffering—the only joy, (and that he admits is great) is that of conception, of planning and arranging. This all proves, what one always feels that (in their narrow circle) terrible are the subtleties they attempt. Daudet spoke of his envy and admiration of the "serenity of production" of Turgenieff—working in a field and a language where the white snow had as yet so few foot-prints. In French, he said, it is all one trampled slosh—one has to look, forever, to see where one can put down his step. And he wished to know how it was in English. What do you think I ought to have told him?—Your account of your work gives me yearnings even in the Rue de la Paix. But you will probably see me here (that is in London,) before I see you in your savoury halls. I am very sorry to hear of Howells's visitation. Give him my love, and tell him that I am always theoretically and platonically, writing him letters. Some day before long he shall have a direct sign from me. I thank

To E. L. GODKIN [*1885*]

Mrs. Aldrich very kindly for her attention to the vol. of *Portraits* and am very faithfully yours

Henry James

To E. L. GODKIN

3 Bolton St. Piccadilly
March 3rd 1885

My dear Godkin

Your delightful letter, in answer to my last, gives me more pleasure than I can say. I was morally sure that you had known nothing about the Review[1] in the *Nation,* and that it had found its way in by accident, but it soothes extremely, a certain wounded feeling which had taken possession of me to have your definite confirmation of this. I thank you moreover, most kindly, for the generous and affectionate way in which it is given. I have a tenderness for my poor Father's memory which is in direct proportion to the smallness of the recognition his work was destined to obtain here below and which (in spite of my own personal inability to enter into that work save here and there, or accept most of the premises on which it rests) fill me with a kind of pious melancholy in presence of the fact that so ardent an activity of thought, such a living original expression of spirit may have passed into darkness and silence forever, the waves of time closing straight over it, without one or two signs being made on its behalf, to say, however little it might command general assent, how remarkable and rare it had been. I had a hope that one of such signs might come from the *Nation,* though I was well aware at the same time that it would be next to impos-

[1] The *Nation* had carried an unfavorable review of *The Literary Remains of the late Henry James* (various posthumous papers of the elder James) edited by William James.

[81]

sible, and had been in other cases, to obtain any proper hand
for the work. The volume with my brother's introduction,
seemed to me to have a real literary importance, however into
which even a person outside of my father's religious ideas (as I
am) might enter and in short your critic (or Garrison's rather)
inflicted on me a kind of *deception* which I mention only to
explain my note, not to add to your regrets. *N'en parlons plus!*
  —You say nothing about any chance of your crossing the seas
this year, but I hope there is one, in spite of your silence. You
will find England in a very interesting though a very lugubrious
condition. Difficulties seem to be closing round her, and even at
this moment the newsboys under my window are calling out the
declaration of war with "Roosher" and the recall of the ambassador: which however is anticipating a little. The ministry is
still in office, but hanging only by a hair, Gladstone is ill and
bewildered, the mess in the Soudan unspeakable, London full
of wailing widows and weeping mothers, the hostility of Bis-
marck extreme, the danger of complications with Russia imminent, the Irish in the house of commons more disagreeable than
ever, the dynamiters more active, the income tax threatening
to rise to its maximum, the general muddle, in short, of the
densest and darkest. I must confess that the ministry has none
of my respect; anything more shiftless and uncourageous than
their conduct as to foreign affairs it is impossible to conceive.
The war in the Soudan makes every one simply sick, those who
think it necessary as well as those who don't. Gladstone hates
foreign relations and has tried to shirk them all, and is paying
his penalty in the bitter censure of his own party as well as the
execration of the other. It is a pitiful end of a great career. The
people that abuse him most are the good old liberals.—I am
expecting in a day or two to hear of poor Lowell being superseded—an event which will wring tears from my eyes. I don't
know, or imagine, what will become of him; I don't see his

future. The death of his wife would not in the least interfere with his remaining here if he were left. She had been much out of his life, lately, through her ill-health, and lived in her own manner. Moreover, as she had again been absolutely insane for a month before her death, this event only removes an anxiety.— My sister is at Bournemouth, wretchedly ill, I am sorry to say— not at all the better for a winter in England. I expect to join her about May 1st and to remain near her for the rest of the summer. London becomes impossible at that period for a literary person wishing to work and yet knowing 5000 people, and I already perceive the uncomfortable increase of the pace. I have had nine notes to write this morning and have done no work as yet! If you come out I shall of course come up to town to see you and Mrs. Godkin, to whom I send the friendliest remembrances. I saw Mahlon Sands yesterday[2]—at F. de Rothschild's— and he told me he was going home for a month; so he will take you a late—but exaggerated—impression of me. I wonder if you are at Washington today and what is Mrs. Adam's last. Farewell, my dear Godkin, with every friendly assurance and affectionate remembrance for both of you. Ever faithfully yours

Henry James

To T. B. ALDRICH
London, April 29th. [*1886*]

My dear Aldrich.

I am obliged to throw myself on your mercy—your magnanimity—with regard to the remainder of my *July* Princess, which goes to you to-day, and the still remainder (of August &c) which is to follow. That is, I *must* ask you to give me another month (the 13th—September,) to finish the everlasting tale. Of course for that extra instalment I ask for no payment, as I con-

2 Brother of Mrs. Godkin.

tracted with the publishers to do the things up in 12 numbers.
I can't—I am too damnably voluminous. I must make a Book
Fourth (instead of having only Three, as I intended;) to consist
of the August this added and September part. These will end
the story in flurry;—I hope this won't bother or oppress you too
much. I must *begin* Book Four with Part Eleven—so that, to
divide properly, I have made this July number of a good deal
less than the usual length. I hope you won't mind this—and
don't see why you should—as I am throwing you in a number
gratis,[1] in which all deficiencies of copy will be made up. There
have been several numbers that have fallen a little short of 25
pages. It relieves me immensely to have decided to ask you this
favour—for I have been feeling terribly squeezed, and I pray
you take it not too editorially, but humanely, imaginatively and
with allowances for him whose calculations, provisions and ad-
justments are woefully apt to be erratic, but who is nevertheless
yours with some little pride as well as much contrition   Henry
James

To EDMUND GOSSE

London, October 26th [*1886*]
My dear Gosse.

I was afraid you wouldn't be able to dine with me—but I sent
a word on the chance.

I am infinitely distressed that you should continue to be over-
turned by this whole beastly business[1]—and yet I understand it,

---

[1] The *Atlantic* nevertheless paid James for the extra instalment.
[1] James's counsel contained in this letter was offered to the troubled Gosse
who had been fiercely attacked by a former friend, John Churton Collins (1848-
1908). Collins charged Gosse with slipshod scholarship in his book *From
Shakespeare to Pope*. Some of the criticisms were justified, but they were
venomously made and Gosse took them "hard." Hence this letter.

for iteration will drive any man frantic. It is a matter of sensibility, and sensibility is much. All the same, sensibility apart, I really don't see what you have to consider except your attitude —which I take to be simply that of continued and confirmed interest in your work, and ambition and purpose in regard to the literary life. Don't despair of that or of yourself—and the rest will be of course disagreeable, but still simple and superficial, like having been pushed without warning into a dirty pond, in which one splashes a moment and loses breath. The moment may seem long—especially if one is pushed again—but one scrambles out, as soon as one recovers one's surprise, without having left any vital part whatever behind. I repeat that the whole mass of the public *d'élite* feel the greatest sympathy for you as having been made to an almost unprecedented degree the subject of a peculiarly atrocious and vulgar form of modern torture—the assault of the newspaper—which all civilized and decent people are equally interested in resisting the blackguardism of. As for the *stupid* public, one must simply mind that at one time as little as at another. It is always there and is always a perfectly neglectable quantity, in regard to any question of letters or of art. Above all, however, what I wanted to say to you most especially is that I really don't see the smallest necessity for your *knowing* a word more about this odious matter, nor for your reading the newspapers. I can't too earnestly recommend you not to look at them—for an instant; I urge this upon you as one who has himself been tried. Under what earthly necessity are you, for instance, to know what idiotic rubbish on the subject may be shovelled out in America? Long ago I determined simply never to glance at such stuff and both as a man and an artist *je m'en porte à merveille.* Avert your eyes—and your nose —and the rest will take care of itself. I shall come in and see you, if you have time, on Thursday evening (night)—being engaged tonight and tomorrow. Take my advice, and your nerves will bloom again like roses in June.

Ever, my dear Gosse, yours most faithfully

Henry James.

To THE AMERICAN COPYRIGHT LEAGUE

London, November 15th, 1887

Dear Sirs:

There have been few accidents in my life that I regret more deeply than that of my being separated by so wide a distance from the privilege of taking part in your meetings of the 28th and 29th of this month.[1] I enter with such cordial sympathy into the aims and efforts of the American Copyright League, and entertain such earnest hopes for its success, that it would besides the great personal pleasure, have been an extreme satisfaction to me to feel that I might, in my small measure, testify directly to the excellent cause and help, in however insignificant a degree, to establish the reform we all so eagerly wait for, and remove the wrong we all so deeply deplore. Where justice is so closely in question, and the profession of letters so intimately concerned, I am almost ashamed to be away. I am to some extent consoled, however, by this reflection, that the very fact of my being in London and not in New York, only serves to fortify the conviction which I share with you, and of which I wish I could give you the benefit in some better eloquence—some communication more immediately operative.

For it is through my observation of the case here, while you are observing it at home, that it is impressed upon me that Americans enjoy in another country a courtesy and an advan-

[1] This letter was addressed to the Executive Committee of the American Copyright League on the occasion of Authors' Readings in Chickering Hall.

tage which, among ourselves, we have so long and so ungenerously denied to the stranger, even when the stranger has given us some of the most precious enjoyment we know—has delighted and fortified and enriched us. I have all the material benefit of publishing my productions in England. I have only to put them forth shortly before their appearance in the United States to secure an effective copyright. The circumstance that the profit in question would be much more important if my writings were more so, does not alter my sense of its being sadly out of keeping with the genius of our people to withhold reciprocity in a matter in which my own case is simply a small illustration. It is out of keeping with the genius of our people to have to take lessons in liberality—in fair dealing—from other lands, and to keep its citizens, in relation to those more hospitable countries, in a false, indefensible, intolerable position. To feel this strongly, indeed,—to know our unenviable eminence in this respect,—I do not mean to imply that the American must cross the Atlantic; for your organized existence is in itself a proof of our active conscience, of the manner in which all informed, all intelligent feeling seeks expression. But I speak as one who happens to have had for a good while this particular light, and this particular humiliation, of seeing the right thing done and not being able to feel that it is *we* who do it—being condemned to feel, on the contrary, that it is we who have refused to do it,—erratically, perversely, and so incongruously that it would be grotesque if it were not lamentable.

This consciousness is in general so unfamiliar and so odious to our liberal national spirit, that I should not venture to allude to it even at a family party like the present occasion, if it did not seem that of the two forms of indiscretion the greater would be to blink the fact of an anomaly so gross. What, indeed, could be a grosser one than that on a point of public policy so closely

connected with our national honor, the American should have
to give up his case? What could be in greater contradiction with
the way he feels in general about his country than that he should
have to admit that, in this especial and conspicuous instance,—
covering so vast a ground,—her practice is lamentably at fault,
her sagacity densely clouded, her behavior unenlightened and
uncivilized? That her sense of honesty has really failed her is an
admission he will not make, for he *knows*, in all his instincts,
that it has only to feel the monitory touch through other preoccupations, to place itself immediately at the service of a better
wisdom. The attention of the American people has only to be
effectually called to the cause you advocate, to exert a considerable retrospective resentment upon those who have endeavored
to perpetuate their mistake, and to introduce those who have
suffered by it to the enjoyment of a full equality. To see vividly
that we cannot hold up the American head about the world,
when the subject of copyright is broached, is to number the days
of a system which carries such detestable incidents in its bosom.

You all know how the truth shines on this subject, but one is
tempted to lengthen a letter which helps one to reach across the
Atlantic. Having been witness of the fact that whatever other
discomforts they may suffer, the English people have not been
disastrously affected by allowing copyrights to be within reach
of that branch of the Anglo-Saxon stock which uses, on the
whole, the same ideals,—having satisfied myself of that, I must
give the assurance of my belief that our own adoption of the
straight course would be equally free from calamity. Let it not
be said—for then we may as well quit the field altogether—
that we cannot *afford* the straight course. If the English can
afford it in the manner in which I have touched—in regard to
the American when the American lives among them—they can
afford it also when the American does not; and I absolutely

decline to believe (let no one attempt to persuade you) that we are not a whit less equipped for the strain—if strain there would in any degree be. I know of no honorable thing that we cannot afford to do, least of all a thing that concerns our being as clever as other people. We are so clever that there is only one more thing we want, to be in complete possession of our birthright, and that is the rupture of the last loose knot that ties us to a dead tradition. Our denial of copyright to the stranger has been, it is said, in the interest of universal reading. But our universal reading has done us little good if it has not taught us that it is better to be strong than to be coddled—and coddled in the least invigorating of all ways, at other people's expense. We know not how strong we are until we try, and we cannot try till we are in the erect attitude. Then it will be found, I think that we do not want easier terms than our fellows.

Seeing English people ready to pay for their American books, and enjoying them the more from feeling that, having paid, they have a right to criticise (substantial privilege and delightful freedom!), I perceive no shadow of ground why we should plead incapacity; for our power to pay is certainly as great as our power to understand, and our power to understand is certainly as great as theirs. It is precisely because we *are* a universally reading public that it is of the greatest importance there should be no impediment to our freedom. There is a fatal impediment so long as there is this odious awkwardness in our confessing how we came by our pleasure. The real impediment is not in the burden of paying for the English books we think good enough to read, but not good enough to thank the authors for; . . . the real impediment is that this irresponsibility of ours is tainted with a vice which passes into our intelligence itself. The taint pervades our whole attitude, and it prevents us from being free—it prevents us from being frank—it prevents us from being validly and comfortably founded in our intellectual culture as we are in other matters. It condemns us to be tongue-tied; for, if you may not look a gift horse in the mouth, in what queer relation do you stand to a book which is not only a gift, but a gift whether the giver has willed or no? So long as we withhold copyright from the stranger whom we make a stranger only by our passing strange process of domesticating him—so long as we go in for bargains of which the profit are all for ourselves, and the burden all for the other party, so long must we relinquish the precious prerogative of free appreciation and of criticism. . . .

The bright American mind does not want exceptional terms, or humiliating bargains, or baby-treatment, or pilfered pleasures of any kind, and it has a total disbelief in any privileges of which the source is not pure. It owes too much to books—which are the blessings of life—not to open its heart to the whole body of our English utterance, not to feel that we have all inherited together the magnificent library of our race, not to detest the idea of refusing the tax which will keep up the institution. The institution is essentially ours, and its honor and health, its competition with other institutions of the same order, depend on its not being mutilated—chopped into two. Let us not introduce small differences into great harmonies. Let us work for each other and with each other, and not condemn any of those who work for us to work without us. I am with you in sympathy, in spirit, and am completely of your opinion that we will read better, and write better, and think better, and *feel* better, as we say, when the air is clearer, and that the air will be clearer only when justice is done.

Believe me, dear sir, yours very faithfully,

Henry James.

To EDMUND GOSSE and
WALTER BESANT
Private   *34 De Vere Gardens W.*
                                             July 12th. [*1888*]
Dear Gosse
Dear Walter Besant

I feel that I shall perhaps excite on your part a mixture of surprise and resentment—but in answer to your note just received I *must* again most respectfully and regretfully plead complete inability. I really *can't* be present at the dinner of the 25th. I am afraid no exhibition of reasons can make my refusal less ungracious—especially when the first I put forth is necessarily my fixed rule of never assisting at a public dinner. I dislike them so much (and the better I love any cause the more I dislike its connection with them) that I ask myself by what means I can best do something to discourage them. The only means open to me I inevitably take. Moreover let me candidly and confidentially say that I now even less understand the why and the wherefore and the general *raison d'être* of the banquet in question. What is one doing?—what is one in for? I ask myself—not you. Why, at this particular hour, *should* a dinner be given by the English authors to the American? I see no reason apart from the extravagantly hospitable impulse of the former body: and that impulse seems to me to be exercised at a moment to the awkwardness of which they are blinded by their generosity. I thank you both for giving me a chance to repent but verily I can't. Please believe in the validity of the reasons that govern my apparent perversity and leave me to the unglorious enjoyment of it. Most faithfully yours

                                             Henry James

To JOSEPH PENNELL

London
Jan. 6 [*1888*]

Dear Mr. Pennell,

I am much obliged to you for your inquiry—for your interest in my article; though rather appalled that the *Century*, to whom I made it over just a year ago, is now only putting it into hand.[1] I am afraid that at this rate it will be a long business.—As for the illustrations I have really nothing to suggest save that you follow your own fancy. If you too are fond of London let that fondness be your guide and you will fall in sufficiently with my text. The article from being so general is difficult to illustrate—and the thing, I should say, ought to be freely and fancifully done; *not* with neat, definite, photographic "views". Into that, however, you are not in danger of falling. Street vistas, characteristic corners (that of Hyde Park, say) something in the City, or on the way to it (say that church at the end of the Strand, where the road forks) &c. I should put in a plea for some view of (or in) the Green Park—with the dim and ugly pinnacles of Buckingham Palace. I lived close to it for nine years and was always crossing it. But do your own London, and it will be sufficiently mine.

Very truly yours
Henry James

To THE DEERFIELD SUMMER SCHOOL

[*Summer 1889*]

I am afraid I can do little more than thank you for your courteous invitation to be present at the sittings of your de-

---

[1] The article, "London," appeared in the December 1888 issue of the *Century* with Pennell's illustrations.

lightfully sounding school of romance,[1] which ought to inherit happiness and honour from such a name. I am so very far away from you that I am afraid I can't participate very intelligently in your discussions, but I can only give them the furtherance of a dimly discriminating sympathy. I am not sure that I apprehend very well your apparent premise, 'the materialism of our present tendencies,' and I suspect that this would require some clearing up before I should be able (if even then) to contribute any suggestive or helpful word. To tell the truth, I can't help thinking that we already talk too much about the novel, about and around it, in proportion to the quantity of it having any importance that we produce. What I should say to the nymphs and swains who propose to converse about it under the great trees at Deerfield is: "Oh, do something from your point of view; an ounce of example is worth a ton of generalities; do something with the great art and the great form; do something with life. Any point of view is interesting that is a direct impression of life. You each have an impression coloured by your individual conditions; make that into a picture, a picture framed by your own personal wisdom, your glimpse of the American world. The field is vast for freedom, for study, for observation, for satire, for truth." I don't think I really do know what you mean by 'materializing tendencies' any more than I should by 'spiritualizing' or "etherealizing'. There are no tendencies worth anything but to see the actual or the imaginative, which is just as visible, and to paint it. I have only two little words for the matter remotely approaching to rule or doctrine; one is life and the other freedom. Tell the ladies and gentlemen, the ingenious inquirers, to consider life

1 During the summer of 1889 James was invited to attend the Summer School at Deerfield, Massachusetts for a discussion of the art of the novel. He sent, instead, the following letter, which was read during the proceedings and later published in the New York *Tribune* (4 August 1889).

directly and closely, and not to be put off with mean and puerile falsities, and be conscientious about it. It is infinitely large, various and comprehensive. Every sort of mind will find what it looks for in it, whereby the novel becomes truly multifarious and illustrative. That is what I mean by liberty; give it its head and let it range. If it is in a bad way, and the English novel is, I think, nothing but absolute freedom can refresh it and restore its self-respect. Excuse these raw brevities and please convey to your companions, my dear sir, the cordial good wishes of yours and theirs,

Henry James.

To SIR FREDERICK MACMILLAN

London, March 28th. 1890.

My dear Macmillan.

I thank you for your note and the offer of £70.0.0.[1] Don't, however, think my pretensions monstrous if I say that, in spite of what you tell me of the poor success of my recent books, I still do desire to get a larger sum, and have determined to take what steps I can in this direction. These steps I know will carry me away from you, but it comes over me that that is after all better, even with a due and grateful recognition of the readiness you express to go on with me, unprofitable as I am. I say it is "better" because I had far rather that in those circumstances you should *not* go on with me. I would rather not be published at all than be published and not pay—other people at least. The latter alternative makes me uncomfortable and the former makes me, of the two, feel least like a failure; the failure that,

1 James had offered the book publication of *The Tragic Muse* after its serialization in the *Atlantic Monthly* to the house of Macmillan. Apparently James's terms were ultimately met, or a compromise was reached, for Macmillan did publish the novel.

at this time of day, it is too humiliating to consent to be without trying, at least, as they say in America, to "know more about it." Unless I can put the matter on a more remunerative footing all round I shall give up my English "market"—heaven save the market! and confine myself to my American. But I must experiment a bit first—and to experiment is of course to say farewell to you. Farewell then, my dear Macmillan, with great regret—but with the sustaining cheer of all the links in the chain that remain still unbroken.

Yours ever
Henry James

P.S. I am not unaware or oblivious that I am actually in your debt to the extent of whatever fraction of £200 on account (which you paid me July 9th 1888,) is represented by the third of the books then covenanted for here and in the U.S.—the *Aspern Papers* and *A London Life* being the two others. I will engage that this last member of the batch (about five short tales) shall appear in the autumn—if that will suit you.—H.J.

To HORACE E. SCUDDER

Paris—March 4th 1891

Dear Mr. Scudder.

Your letter demands a frank answer. My "deathly silence" has been the result of the fact that when after last writing to you I read over *The Pupil* in the light of your remarks about it, I quite failed to see that you had treated me fairly: I could *not* see that it was a performance that the *Atlantic* ought to have declined—nor banish from my mind the reflection that the responsibility, in any case, as regards the readers of the magazine, the public, should, when it's a question of an old and honourable reputation, be left with the author himself. The editor, under such circumstances, may fairly leave it to him— and I should not have shrunk from any account the readers might have held me to. These impressions were distinctly chilling as regards the production of further work. I had in my hands a litle story which I had meant to send to you—but there was nothing in it to assure me that it would seem to you to have a different quality from its predecessor, and I couldn't bring myself to despatch it. The pen fell out of my hand and I took refuge in other work, which has proved fruitful and [in] which I am now immersed. I fear I shall remain so—certainly all this month—which I am spending in this place. But on my return to London on April 1st I will do my best to get back to some tales. I feel uncertain as to how I shall do them—and as if the spell, for today, were rather broken. But you shall have a couple of specimens and I will do my best to keep them really short. Please destroy the copy of *The Pupil* you have—if you still have it—in your hands. I sent the story to *Longman,* to which I had long promised a tale, and it presently appears.[1] The other little thing comes out in the new illustrated weekly, a London periodical *Black and White.*[2] Yours very truly

Henry James

To CLEMENT SHORTER

London, February 24th, 1896.

Dear Mr. Shorter,

I should be very glad to write you a story energetically designed to meet your requirement of a "love-story"—and to let you have it at the time and of the dimension that you mention—

[1] In the issue of March-April 1891.
[2] "Brooksmith" in *Black and White* 2 May 1891.

but the sum you name is less than that which I am in the habit of receiving: it is, in fact, rating the instalments, individually, at my usual fee, a great deal less. I should however like to capture the public of the *Illustrated News,* and should be glad to surrender you the English serial rights of the work in question for £300, if you see your way to meeting me on that figure. The particular story I conceive Mrs. Clifford to have spoken to you of is—must be—a plan I narrated to her more than a year ago[1] and have carried for longer than that in my head: an idea that would, as I remember telling her, lend itself about equally well to a play "of incident"—or to a novel—of the same. Two girls are indeed in the forefront of it. If you accept my amendment to your terms I should be able presently to fall to work on it. Believe me yours very truly,

Henry James

To CLEMENT SHORTER

London, February 26th, 1896.

Dear Mr. Shorter,

Thanks for your note of yesterday.

Three hundred Pounds then for the English serial rights of a story in 65,000 words, to be printed in the *Illustrated London News* in Thirteen instalments of 5,000 during July, August and September next. I shall endeavour to be thrilling, and my material is such that I think I shall succeed. I shall be able to get at this business very soon, and shall then be in a position to give you notice of the sort of date at which I can send you the first half at least of my copy. Of this I will advise you at the earliest possible moment, and I hope to finish the whole before

---

1 The novel was *The Other House* serialized by Shorter July 4 through September 26, 1896.

you begin to publish. You shall then (when I give you this date) know my title.

I am much obliged for the invitation to the Omar Khayyam dinner, which it gives me great pleasure to accept for March 27th.—Believe me yours very truly,

Henry James

To CLEMENT SHORTER

Rye, Sussex. May 6th, 1896.

Dear Mr. Shorter,

As (for any purpose of illustration) it may be a convenience to you to have even such a piece of my little serial as I am able to send you today, I despatch you apart from this in a registered cover, typed, the copy for the first instalment. I confess I am afraid your artist—although I regard my story as essentially and absolutely dramatic—won't find in my situations a great deal of suggestion for variegated or panoramic pictures. But I *like* so little to be illustrated (I resent it so, amiably speaking, on behalf of good prose and *real* writing) that I won't hypocritically pretend to pity him too much. For the title I won't claim finality if you don't care for it. I like it myself—it closely fits and seems (to me, at least, who know what it means) suggestive and convenient. But I *may* find a better—or, on the other hand, may have to decline on a proper name, i.e. "Anthony Bream." I have lost several days in moving down here from town—on purpose to peg away uninterrupted, taking a little house, settling myself, etc. But if you will have patience with me a little—about the middle of the month, a very few days will right me, and I shall be able to send you another batch. They will follow each other steadily and fast, and I think I can promise you that the whole thing shall practically be in your hands by the time the beginning appears. Of course I shall like to see proof—and will deal with it very promptly. Kindly let me have *duplicates.*—

Believe me yours most truly,

Henry James

To ANTON CAPADOSE

London, *13 Oct. 1896.*

My dear Sir,

You may be very sure that if I had ever had the pleasure of meeting a person of your striking name I wouldn't have used the name, especially for the purpose of the tale you allude to.

It was exactly because I had no personal or private association with it that I felt free to do so. But I am afraid that (in answer to your amiable inquiry) it is late in the day for me to tell you how I came by it.

The Liar was written (originally published in the *Century Magazine*[1]) 10 years ago—and I simply don't remember.

Fiction-mongers collect proper names, surnames, &c.—make notes and lists of any odd or unusual, as handsome or ugly ones they see or hear—in newspapers (columns of births, deaths, marriages, &c.) or in directories and signs of shops or elsewhere; fishing out of these memoranda in time of need the one that strikes them as good for a particular case.

"Capadose" must be in one of my old note-books. I have a dim recollection of having found it originally in the first columns of *The Times,* where I find almost all the names I store up for my puppets. It was picturesque and rare and so I took possession of it. I wish—if you care at all—that I had applied it to a more exemplary individual! But my romancing Colonel was a charming man, in spite of his little weakness.

[1] In the May-June 1888 issues.

To JAMES B. PINKER [*1903*]

I congratulate you on bearing a name that is at once particularly individualizing and not ungraceful (as so many rare names are).

I am, my dear Sir,

Yours very truly

Henry James.

To WILLIAM BLACKWOOD

London

October 28th, 1897

Dear Mr. Blackwood.

It gives me great pleasure to hear from you that you accept my proposal in regard to the volume on Mr. [William Wetmore] Story;[1]—£250 "down" as before mentioned (as fee for the Work) and £100 in case of its selling 7000—and again any, or every further 2000 sold. This to cover *all rights*. I shall not, as I was [able to make] clear to the Waldo S[torys] get at the business (be at all *able* to) immediately: but I shall attack it at my very first leisure and then with much concentration, and so, in fine, my very best for it. I shall live—with it—among many old friends and old ghosts. Believe me yours very truly

Henry James

To JAMES B. PINKER

Rye, Aug. 13th. 1903

Dear Mr. Pinker.

I just get your note about Methuen's request for expedition. I have indeed done everything in my power, but the Harpers

---

[1] Although contracted for at this time, *William Wetmore Story and His Friends* was not written by James until he had completed his last three big novels, *The Ambassadors*, *The Wings of the Dove* and *The Golden Bowl*. It was published by Blackwood in 1903.

have been of a mortal slowness in sending me proof of the last third of the Book—which I received but three or four days ago, and returned to Albermarle Street immediately, after due correction, to be sent as fast as possible back to New York. It is this remaining third that has not yet been supplied to Methuen, and, as the proof in question will have left for New York only yesterday, I am afraid there will be at least twenty days delay in its returning hither again with the numerous corrections embodied. The thing therefor is for the New York people immediately to be cabled to that they send a full set of proof of this portion (*exactly the same chapters and pages they last sent to me through Albemarle Street*) again, without delay, straight to you, to be handed over to Methuen—I mean without waiting for the corrections; though I shall thus quite tiresomely have to make them all again in Methuen's proof. This botheration would have been obviated if the New York people had shown the least heed for my reiterated request for duplicates of proof, of the serial form, from the first.[1] This request was made them from the first, both by letter and by personal supplication in Albemarle Street, but entirely without result. I went to see McIlvaine about it myself, and he interviewed me on the subject in the attesting presence of Mr. Sidney Brooks, declaring that my request should have effect—but all to no purpose. I am writing to Albemarle Street today to ask them, urgently, to cable, but shall be greatly obliged to you if, without prejudice

1 The fact that James did not receive all the proof of the American edition of *The Ambassadors* resulted in a publishing error which exists in all American copies of the novel. Chapters 28 and 29 are reversed. The error was first detected by an American student, Robert E. Young, in 1950, almost fifty years after publication. Moreover, it was perpetuated in the New York Edition of James's works. Thus the English edition, published by Methuen, which James saw through the press, acquires a certain rarity as the only accurate edition of *The Ambassadors*. The novelist, in his anger at Harper for their failure to follow his directions, seems to have never examined the finished book, and to have been unaware of the violence done to his text by the publisher.

to this, you will kindly prod them in the same sense as hard as ever you can. They require all that can be administered of that. And will you also render me a small service which will help?— send, namely, over to Bedford Street and procure for me the *North American Review*[2] which is due to be issued by Heine-mann on the 15th, and have it immediately despatched to me here? It requires a small interpolation that I shall be able to make, but when I then post it off to Methuen the latter will have received, for setting up the Book, eight out of the twelve numbers of the Serial. Up to now he has sent me proof of a quantity represented but by three—so there is still a margin for his going forward. Let me add, moreover, that I shall be able to help him materially by sending him a duplicate Type-Copy of the M.S., which I fortunately have clung to, and have not sent him hitherto because the printed text of the Serial contains inevitable little amendments and alterations. (Besides this I am afraid I lack duplicate of some passages omitted in the serial form and subsequently supplied to Harpers for insertion in the Book.) However, these things will help to sustain Methuen in patience till the still wanting proof arrives from New York. I am myself writing to him today in this full sense. Pardon my long-windedness. Yours very truly

Henry James

To ELIZABETH JORDAN

Paris, May 3rd 1907

Dear Miss Jordan.

I have, to my shame, two or three unanswered communica-tions from you, and I can only let the fact of my being in Paris

---

[2] *The Ambassadors* was serialized in the *Review* from January through December 1903.

still (these nine weeks, with a couple more to come,) plead for me; since that represents an agitated and abnormal life, with a terrible, even though profitable and inevitable leakage of precious hours—that of the writing table in particular. One of your letters replied to my proposal about a few short American "impressionist" papers—to the effect that the *Bazar* would find use for three if they should take the form of being specifically addressed to women. This I well understand to be your necessity—though I am not sure I had it as distinctly present to me when I made you my proposal. I am not sure either, that I shall be quite *able* to give them that complexion in an adequate degree—though again, with a swing of the pendulum I remember that I mostly feel myself able to do anything I sufficiently try. (I had to sufficiently try to do the Married Son, for instance.) At any rate I *will* try, and if the things don't seem to me to come in a shape exactly to correspond with your need I won't send them to you. In fine I will do this only if they come out specifically right—I shall ask you to kindly leave the question open till I break with the agitated life and get back to the peace of home; which will be by the middle of June (I go down very briefly to Rome and Venice meanwhile.) And then you sent me Mrs. Phelps Ward's contribution to the *Whole Family*[1]—which I began to read the other day, but which immediately affected me as subjected to so pitiless an ordeal in the searching artistic light and amid the intellectual and literary associations of Paris that I tenderly forebore, and laid it away to await resuscitation in a medium in which I shall be able to surround my perusal of it with more precautions. Lastly there comes your note asking me to consult, on the question of my favourite fairy-tale the

1 Elizabeth Jordan, editor of Harper's *Bazar,* had induced a group of authors to write a composite novel. This was serialized in the magazine and published as a book titled *The Whole Family* (N. Y. 1908). James contributed the chapter "The Married Son."

dreadfully dim and confused and obscure memories of my ante-diluvian childhood.[2] I'm not very sure I *had* a favourite fairy-tale—so beguiling and absorbing to me were *all* such flowers of nursery legend (I mean when I was very infantine indeed) for I seem to make out that I got through them, through Perrault and Mme D'Aunoy, through the Brothers Grimm and H. C. Andersen, very early indeed and began to prefer "stories of Real Life"—amid which I ranked promiscuously Robinson Crusoe, Nicholas Nickleby, The Parents' Assistant, *The Initials* —a novel "of manners" new and much esteemed at that time— and several of the productions of Captain Marryat.) However I *had* thrilled by the nursery fire, over a fat little Boys'—or perhaps Children's Own Book which contained all the "regular" fairy-tales, dear to that generation—an enormous number, amid which I recall "Hop o'my Thumb," *Le Petit Poucet,* as my small romance of yearning predilection. I seem to remember that story in some other particularly thrilling and haunting form, with a picture of the old woodcutter and his wife sitting at night in the glow of the fire and the depths of the wood and plotting for the mislaying of their brood; a very dreadful and romantic image of a strange far-off world in which the enchanting hero-ism of the small boy, smaller than one's self, who had in that crisis gained immortality, gave one's fond fancy the most attach-ing of possible companions. There was no boy one had ever heard of one would have given so much to know—and one focussed him as a tiny brown mite much more vividly and saliently, in the picture, at the great moment, than any of the terrible big people by whom he was surrounded. It is the vague memory of this sense of him as some small precious object, like

[2] James's account of his favorite fairy tale was reproduced from this letter in *Favorite Fairy Tales,* The Childhood Choice of Representative Men and Women (N. Y. 1907).

a lost gem, or a rare and beautiful insect on which one might inadvertently tread, or might find under the sofa or behind the window-curtain, that leads me to think of Hop-o'-my-Thumb as my earliest and sweetest and most repeated cupful at the fount of fiction.

Yes, the photograph Evelyn Smalley, poor dear invincible heroine must have given you, will have reached my house *after* I left home and be lying actually on my table, in all safety, with other matter of the packet or extensive kind that is never forwarded to me. But I shall find it as soon as I return, and will carefully and zealously write upon it to you with every precaution.

Yours most truly
Henry James.

To ELIZABETH LEE

London, February 10th. 1913.

Dear Miss Lee,

Alas, my knowledge of poor unpleasant little Ouida was a very limited thing indeed. I met her two or three times in Florence and went once to see her—before she had fallen on her later most evil days, though there even then hung about her an air as of very precarious resources and very tarnished lustre. I had later on, here, two or three letters from her—short, very sprawling notes (which I didn't keep: they were so abusive of two or three very harmless persons); and a small painted panel, a view of a Lucca street—this an *offrande* but of a childishly primitive "art": really a child of seven or eight might have done it. Frankly she was not sympathetic—and I scarce envy you the task of undertaking a book about her. But she was *curious*, in a common little way: she suggested somehow having come out of such a very "low-down" or even base little past, of unfathomable things, and yet being withal of a most uppish, or dauntless, little spirit of arrogance and independence. The best and most sincere thing about her I seemed to make out, was—or had been—her original genuine perception of the beauty, the distinction and quality of Italy: this almost inspired her—yet was mixed with such vulgarities and falsities too. She must have gone—and for many years—through absolute horror of growing poverty and final want—though for long too she was arrogant about her debts and obligations. The only way to treat her would be really, and quite frankly, I think, as a little terrible and finally pathetic *grotesque;* but even as such she *means* nothing—is too without form and void! However, she is doubtless a challenge to the bookmaking art—if you can but get *documents,* of sorts.[1] Old Florentines (of the cosmopolite colony) could tell you things—and I could tell you two or three—yet unimportant or irreproducible. But the trouble is we are all gone or going—dead or dying! I *have* the little painted panel (in the country) I think—but that would be the most irreproducible of all! Believe me yours very truly,

Henry James.

To AUGUSTE MONOD

September 7th, 1913

Dear Auguste Monod,

I have too long owed you an acknowledgment to your most kind letter of a date so distant that I am ashamed to remind you of it. But I live in arrears—they are a necessity and a penalty of my condition and there are good friends who have more to forgive me even than you.

I take it as a great benevolence that you let me know of your

---

[1] Elizabeth Lee's *Ouida, A Memoir* was published in London in 1914.

appreciation of my jumble of childish memories, which I rejoice that you found interesting. The book was a fond experiment, determined by personal considerations it would take me some time to explain; but I found the experiment succeed, from my own point of view, as soon as all sorts of dimnesses of far past began to *like* to wake up again at pressure of the spring. They kept waking and waking and I grew more and more touched and amazed by their doing so, and thus my rather fatuous emotions became *un gros volume*. And monstrous to say, I am doing another, complementary to it and relating to the next ten years —it was in fact for the sake of this latter part of the case more particularly that I began to maunder at all. You understand the value I attach to your attention to what I do—yet I confess that it is a relief to me this time to have so utterly defied translation.[1] The new volume will complete that defiance and express for me how much I feel that in a literary work of the least complexity the very form and texture are the substance itself and that the flesh is indetachable from the bones! Translation is an effort— though a most flattering one!—to *tear* the hapless flesh, and in fact to get rid of so much of it that the living thing bleeds and faints away! forgive the violence of my figure. I believe truly that I feel myself to have lost less blood at your hands than (in those past little adventures) I could have done at any other's. But without having in the least sought the effect, it does interest me, it does even partly exhilarate me to recognise that the small Boy, while yet so tame and intrinsically safe a little animal, is locked fast in the golden cage of the *intraduisible!* It's all the more genial of you to look at him so patiently through that gilt wire of the bars. You will say I make much of the gilding, so good night before I appear to make more! I

---

1 Monod had been translating some of James's stories into French. The novelist here is discussing his memoirs, *A Small Boy and Others*, 1913.

thank you again and wish you peace and ease and am most truly yours

Henry James

To MRS. G. W. PROTHERO

Rye.

Sept. 14th, 1913.

This, please, for the delightful young man from Texas,[1] who shews such excellent dispositions. I only want to meet him half way, and I hope very much he won't think I don't when I tell him that the following indications as to five of my productions (splendid number—I glory in the tribute of his appetite!) are all on the basis of the Scribner's (or Macmillan's) collective and revised and prefaced edition of my things, and that if he is not minded somehow to obtain access to *that* form of them, ignoring any others, he forfeits half, or much more than half, my confidence. So I thus amicably beseech him—! I suggest to give him as alternatives these two slightly different lists:

1. Roderick Hudson.
2. The Portrait of a Lady.
3. The Princess Casamassima.
4. The Wings of the Dove.
5. The Golden Bowl.

———

1. The American.
2. The Tragic Muse.
3. The Wings of the Dove.
4. The Ambassadors.
5. The Golden Bowl.

[1] The young man from Texas was Stark Young, who had appealed to Mrs. Prothero for guidance in reading James. Mrs. Prothero in turn conveyed the appeal to the author himself and received this reply.

The second list is, as it were, the more "advanced." And when it comes to the shorter Tales the question is more difficult (for characteristic selection) and demands separate treatment. Come to me about that, dear young man from Texas, later on—you shall have your little tarts when you have eaten your beef and potatoes. Meanwhile receive this from your admirable friend Mrs. Prothero.

Henry James

III

THE SCENIC ART

FROM 1890 to 1895 Henry James devoted himself to the writing
of plays. He gave as his main reason the need to earn more
money than his books were yielding. There is no doubt that he
was impressed by the substantial royalties derived by play-
wrights from a successful box-office. Dependent as he still was
then upon his literary earnings, he had also experienced some
anxiety over the continued limited sale of his books and his
increasing difficulties in placing his longer works in the magazines. It seemed to him that an immediate solution was to confine himself to the writing of short stories—*à la Maupassant*, he
wrote in his notebooks—and to devote the time he would have
normally given his longer fictions to "pot-boiling" for the
theatre. His was a calculated siege of the theatre. He promised
himself that he would persist even if at first he encountered
defeat.

The immediate impulse to commence serious writing for the
stage had been given by Edward Compton, an actor-manager
whose company played a repertoire of classical comedies in the
provinces throughout the British Isles. Compton asked for a
dramatization of *The American*, seeing in Christopher Newman
a role with which he might try to establish himself in London.

The play was produced first at Southport and gave James high hopes. In London, however, it had a modest run of seventy performances without bringing the novelist the returns he had anticipated.

He wrote a series of four comedies, later published as *Theatricals* and one of these was accepted by the American producer Augustin Daly who, however, lost interest in it as James's angry letter here given shows. In the meantime he sold another play *Guy Domville* to George Alexander the actor-manager of the St. James's Theatre. Alexander wanted a costume play "tailored" to enable him to give his devoted audiences a great deal of himself. James tried to meet these specifications and on January 5, 1895 the play had its first night. Well-acted, handsomely mounted, artistically costumed, its first act charmed a distinguished audience that included three young drama critics, Bernard Shaw, Arnold Bennett and H. G. Wells. The play fell apart in the second act and the third did not repair the damage. Alexander, aware of the restlessness of a segment of the audience, nevertheless brought James on-stage at the end, and while a large measure of applause greeted him he was jeered, hissed and booed by the gallery. The novelist renounced further attempts at conquering the theatre and returned to his author's study to write fiction.

The letters which follow sketch these episodes and show how "hard" James took the theatre. His feeling after *Guy Domville* was that he had tried to make "a silk purse out of a sow's ear." Nevertheless his interest in the stage was profound and continued to manifest itself—under less trying conditions than those to which he exposed himself from 1890 to 1895. He wrote a one-act play, for Ellen Terry—but she did not do it. He remained one of the group in London that fought the battle for Ibsen. He tilted amicably with Bernard Shaw, who would have had him drastically revise one of his plays; and he experienced, in a play he did for Gertrude Elliott (Lady Forbes-Robertson), the chagrin of an author whose audience applauds the wrong speeches. An inveterate playgoer, he himself applauded the advent of Repertory; and as he had done in the days of the copyright controversy, he joined the battle, this time against censorship of plays.

The first letter in this section is the earliest of the novelist's extant—written when James was eleven from Paris to his playmate Eddy Van Winkle, a neighbor of the Jameses in 14th Street. It testifies to the boyhood interest in theatricals which flowered in middle life into his "dramatic years."

To MASTER E[DGAR] VAN WINKLE
14 st. N. York

[*Paris 1854*]

Dear Eddy, As I heard you were going to try to turn the club into a Theatre. And as I was asked w'ether I wanted to belong here is my answer. I would like very much to belong. Yours truly   H. James.

To WILLIAM ARCHER

London
Dec. 27th. 1890

Dear Sir, I am much obliged to you for your interest in an obscure and tremulous venture. It *is* true that a play of mine[1] is to be produced at a mysterious place called Southport, which I have never seen, a week from tonight, and it is further true that the production is one to which I myself, and every one con-

---

1 A dramatization of his novel *The American*.

cerned, have, and has, contributed as seriously as the particular conditions would allow. The performance is not a "scratch" one, to establish copyright, but a carefully prepared one to which I have lent a zealous hand and in which the performers, wholly deficient in celebrity, but inflamed, I think, with something of the same zeal, will do their individual best. I won't deny that I should be glad to know that the piece was seen by a serious critic, and by yourself in particular, but I shrink from *every* responsibility in the way of recommending such a critic to attempt so heroic a feat. The place is far, the season inclement, the interpretation *extremely* limited, different enough, as you may suppose, from what I should count on for representation in London. The circumstances *may* be definitely uncomfortable. I have carefully followed rehearsals, but the whole thing is a leap in the dark, and my hope is greater than my confidence. On the other hand it is apparently to be months before the play comes to town—as I accepted at the outset the essence of the proposal made me (and of which the general attempt was the direct result:) the proviso, namely, that the piece should be produced (and only *occasionally!*) in the provinces for upwards of a year before being brought out in London. England, Scotland and Ireland will behold it before the starved metropolis. But it will come—I believe—before long, considerably nearer town than Southport, and probably in more seductive weather. At any rate I have hopes that I may be represented otherwise in London before the drama in question is revealed here; for if I have made up my mind to make a resolute theatrical attempt, I am far from considering that one makes it with a single play. I mean to go at it again and again—and shall do so none the worse for knowing that you may give some heed to the undiscourageable flounderings of yours very truly   Henry James

Telegram to ALICE JAMES

Southport Jan. 4, 1891

Unqualified triumphant magnificent success universal congratulations great ovation for author great future for play Comptons radiant and his acting admirable writing Henry

To ALICE JAMES *and* K. P. LORING

Southport, Jan. 4th. 1891.

My dear children,[1]

I wired you an half hour ago a most veracious and historical account of yesterday's beautiful evening. It was really *beautiful* —the splendid success of the whole thing, reflected as large as the surface presented by a Southport audience (and the audience was very big indeed) could permit. The attention, the interest, the outbursts of applause and appreciation hushed quickly for fear of losing (especially with the very bad acoustic properties of the house) what was to follow, the final plaudits, and recalls (I mean after each act) and the big universal outbreak at the end for 'author, *author*, AUTHOR!! in duly *delayed* response to which, with the whole company grinning delight and sympathy (behind the curtain) I was led before by Compton to receive the 1st 'ovation,' but I trust not the last, of my life—all this would have cured you (both) right up if you could only have witnessed it. The great feature of the evening was the surprising way Compton 'came out,' beyond anything he had done, or shown, at rehearsal,—acting really exceedingly well and putting more force, ability and above all art and charm and *character* into his part than I had at all ventured to expect of him.

1 This letter was written to James's sister, by now a confirmed invalid, and her friend and companion Katherine P. Loring. In all that he wrote to her, and in his talks with her, (which Alice recorded in her journal), it is clear that both substance and tone were designed to enliven the sick-room.

He will improve it greatly, ripen and *tone* it, as he plays it more, and end, I am sure, by making it a *celebrated* modern creation. He *may* even become right enough in it to do it in America—though as to that one must see. The Comptons, of course are intensely happy, and their supper with me here, with Balestier[2] for a 4th, was wildly joyous, as you may infer when I tell you it lasted from 11 to 1.45 a.m. Mrs. Compton was 'cured right up' by our success—she acted, in her own Mrs. Comptonish way, *very* neatly and gracefully, for a lady who had been ill in bed for a week. She was exceedingly well-dressed—all Liberty, but very good Liberty. Every one, in fact, worked his and her hardest and did his and her best; and though some of them, notably Valentin, who made himself very handsome, were much impaired by extreme nervousness, there was no real flaw on the extreme smoothness of the performance, which 'went' as if it were a 50th. On the other hand, of course, I felt freshly the importance of a change of Mme. de B[ellegarde] and Mrs. Bread, of Lord Deepmere and perhaps, or probably even of Valentin and the Marquis for the London production. As for Newman, Compton simply *adores* the part and will, I feel sure, make it universally beloved. Well, he *may* like it, for though I say it who shouldn't, I was freshly struck, in my little 'cubby' beside the curtain in the right wing (where I stuck all the evening, save to dash out and embrace every one in the entractes) I was more than ever impressed, I say, with its being *magnificent*—all the keyboard, the potential fortune of an actor. The wondrous Balestier dashed out between the 3rd and 4th acts and cabled to the *New York Times* 50 vivid words which will already have been laid on every breakfast table (as it were) in

2 Wolcott Balestier (1861-91), an enterprising young American writer and publisher. He had become a close friend of James's and assisted him in the business negotiations arising from his theatricals.

that city. I strongly suspect they will bring in prompt applications for the 'American rights.' I will tell you a droll anecdote of William Archer's behaviour and attitude.[3] I go part of the way to Cheltenham tonight, sleep at Birmingham and spend tomorrow at C. Expect to see you Tuesday evening. If Katherine could send me a word—telegraphic—about how you are—to 4 Promenade Terrace C.—I should be glad. I am writing to William but you might send him on this letter just as it stands. Ever yours

Henry James.

P.S. *Sunday noon.* Compton has just come in to tell me that he has already seen a number of people present last night who were *unanimous* about the success of the piece, the great hit he has made it and ergo—the large fortune that opens to it. His own high spirits indeed tell everything.

To GEORGE W. SMALLEY

London, Oct. 19th. 1891.

My dear Smalley. I can't help thanking you for your note—for very soothing and welcome letter I should rather say. I am delighted that your evening at the O[pera] C[omique][1] didn't prove such a bad quarter of an hour as some of the portents might justly have led you to fear. I have no illusions whatever about the play or its prospects (which latter however now define

3 The anecdote was recorded by Alice James in her journal. Apparently Archer offered James gratuitous advice on how to improve his play immediately after the curtain calls, when the novelist was too elated to appreciate the unsolicited counsel.

1 *The American* ran for seventy performances at the Opera Comique Theatre from late September to mid-November, 1891. The full story of this production and of James's other play-writing activities is told in *The Complete Plays of Henry James* (ed. Edel) London and New York 1949. James's dramatic criticism was collected by Allan Wade in *The Scenic Art.*

themselves rather more rosily,) and I regard it simply as a
beginning—accomplished in conditions that somewhat injuri-
ously imposed themselves and will never present themselves
again. If I hadn't done this particular thing—with all its drawbacks—I should never have begun at all—which, as I now feel—
would have been much of a pity. Compton proposed to me this
particular thing (for the sake of the character of C[hristopher]
N[ewman] which it would give him to do;) and *didn't* propose
to me—more, perhaps, was the pity!—a play in general—on a
subject residing in my own bosom. I agreed for the sake of the
character of Newman, and of the chance to take a definite first
step—to say nothing of that of the advantage of having been the
approached and not the approacher. But I shall never again
move in the straight-jacket of a novel originally conceived from
a point wholly non-scenic, containing a damnable element (the
machinery by which the denouement is brought about) which I
had long ago outlived, and forcing one into the corner of at
once keeping to it, to get the benefit of its associations, and yet
violating it, at every step, to make it an organism—the drama—
utterly distinct from the story-form. I loathed, of course, the
"'secret," and tout-ce-qui-s'en suit, but recognized that my only
chance was in having, in a business-like way, the courage of it—
in putting it frankly and clearly through, on a romantic basis,
and making it as interesting as I could—not sprawling it but
condensing it and letting it give my play the romantic and not
the comedy-of-manners stamp—which last any critic who had
taken an intelligent glance at the book would have seen it
couldn't for a moment pretend to have. Then, alas, in my inexperience and good nature—my sympathy with a new young
manager's expenses and timidities—I consented to Compton's
doing what he should never have been so short-sighted as [to]
wish to do—retain the four or five members of his provincial

company (people of small salaries,) who had "created" their parts in the country. It's a folly we have paid for—and the end is not yet! The play would obviously have done much better from the first if—with all its intrinsic infirmities—it had been produced at the Garrick or the Haymarket. Excuse my inflicting all this on you—and *don't*, at your peril answer! I am moved to this épanchement by seeming to gather from your note that you have discerned all I want, after all, to *leave* as a residuary impression in an intelligent spectator's (if there *be* such a creature!) mind—the circumstance that I shall write—though so late in the day—far better plays than *The American*, do, in a word, a very different sort of thing.—This episode has done what I am quite content with its having done—simply put me in the saddle. Now (if stone walls don't circumvent me) I intend to *ride*—to ride as far as I can: I feel as if your note had been a stirrup-cup and am, my dear Smalley, yours always   Henry James.

To AUGUSTIN DALY

Brighton,
September 1st, 1892.

My dear Mr. Daly,

I am much obliged to you for reading my play[1]—as to which I think I may say that I haven't any illusions—any that prevent my understanding that you shouldn't be 'satisfied' with it. I am far from satisfied myself, but as the thing cost me, originally, a good deal of labour and ingenuity, I was unable to resist the desire to subject it to some sort of supreme probation. If it had a fault of which I was very conscious, I thought it perhaps had other qualities which would make it a pity that I shouldn't

---

[1] The play was then tentatively known as *Mrs. Jasper*. Later it was renamed *Disengaged*.

[119]

give it a chance—since a chance so happily presented itself. To tell the truth, now that I have given it this chance my conscience is more at rest, and I feel as if my responsibility to it were over. Its fault is probably fundamental and consists in the slenderness of the main motive—which I have tried to prop up with details that don't really support it; so that—as I freely recognize —there is a lack of action vainly dissimulated by a superabundance (especially in the last act) of movement. This movement cost me such pains—and I may add such pleasure!—to elaborate that I have probably exaggerated its dramatic effect—exaggerated it to myself, I mean. The thing has been my first attempt at a *comedy,* pure and simple, and as first attempts are, in general, mainly useful as lessons, I am willing to let it go for that. At any rate I am far from regarding it as my necessary last word. You will wonder perhaps that as I defend Mrs. Jasper so feebly I could still care to talk with you about her. But this will give me pleasure, all the same, and I shall avail myself of your leave to do so. I am spending a few days at this place, but I shall be in London tomorrow, Friday, and if I hear nothing from you, here to the contrary, will call on you at (say) three o'clock. I can't forego any opportunity of seeing a manager! Believe me,

Yours very truly,

Henry James.

To GEORGE ALEXANDER

Ramsgate. [*Summer 1893*]

Dear Mr. Alexander: I have considered the terms that you offer me in your note of Monday—with the result of being moved to say that they *don't* strike me as all I could desire. It seems to me that in the arrangement you propose you would become very easily and quickly possessor, owner—for your personal use—of the play[1] for the rest of the ten years. I can't help

---

[1] *Guy Domville.*

considering the enjoyment of the half share with you in the profit arising from the use of the piece by others as too indefinite and undetermined a compensation for this. I am perfectly willing to make an arrangement with you by which you shall have control of the play *everywhere* for ten years. But I don't like my share in your performances stopping at £2000. Does not this limit very unduly my profit if the play is successful? If it isn't, my profit will stop of itself; but if it is, I think my gains ought to run further—from *your* performance, I mean, which will be *the* performance. Also is £5.0.0 a night as much as I ought to receive? If this is your definite conviction—and I have no other source of information on the subject—I should probably be willing to let it stand so; but in this case I should like the enjoyment of the £5.0.0 to run a good deal longer. I should be very glad if you would let me have an alternative proposal. Is there none you can make me that should be more attractive to me than this, based on a royalty? I spoke to you myself of a fixed sum, but I am not wedded to it. At any rate I should be obliged to you if you can put the case to me more dazzlingly another way.

I came back here yesterday and am already launched very promisingly in my second act. I think I shall be able to send it to you in a really very moderate space of time—a quite near date. It *goes* so. Yours very truly, Henry James.

To AUGUSTIN DALY

34 De Vere Gardens W.
Dec. 7, 1893

Dear Mr. Daly,

My play may *not* contain the elements of success, and at my stage of relationship to the theatre I am much too nervous a subject not to accept as *determining*, in regard to my own action

—any sound of alarm, or of essential scepticism, however abrupt, on the part of a manager. That makes my nervousness operative and simplifies the case. I should none the less have been very glad to be informed at an earlier moment (of the year it has been in your hands) of your discovery that the piece is fundamentally unsuited to your purpose—an earlier moment, I mean, than the eve of what I had been looking forward to as a serious preparation. Your few words of Saturday so definitely express, in spite of their brevity, or perhaps indeed by reason of the same, the sudden collapse of your own interest in it, that I withdraw it from your theatre without delay and beg you to send me back the ms. For myself—I cannot for a moment profess that the scene I witnessed on your stage yesterday[1] threw any light on the character of the play that might not have been thrown by *any* repetition on re-reading of the lines. The only slightly fresh or somewhat intenser impression I derived from it was that of the quick brevity of the three acts and their closeness and crispness of texture. I could recognize it in no degree as a test constituted by even an approach to the tentative or experimental *representation* of a delicate and highly finished piece, each of whose steps and stages was to have been essentially dependent on expression. I was, in other words, unable to see in it, any measure or any intimation of what *acting* could do for my intentions. Nor can I meet you on the ground—which if I mistake not there was a moment when you invited me to do— of taking account of the actor's "conception" (and last of all of its finality) either of the parts or of the total—in a piece that I am surprised the author was deprived of the indispensable preliminary of communicating to them or giving them a hint about, and as to which not one of them had had the interest or

---

[1] *Mrs. Jasper,* designed for Ada Rehan, had had its first and only reading by the cast the day before this letter was written.

curiosity to approach him for a suggestion; or in illustration of the said conception and even while uninterruptedly reading from the book, to seek to exhibit an acquaintance with the text.

Truly yours,

Henry James.

To WILLIAM HEINEMANN

London, [November 1894]

My dear Heinemann,

I feel as if I couldn't thank you enough for introducing me to Ibsen's prodigious little performance![1] I return it to you, by the same post conscientiously after two breathless perusals,— which leave me with a yearning as impatient, an appetite as hungry, for the rest, as poor Rita's yearning and appetite are for the missing caresses of her Alfred. Do satisfy me better or more promptly than he satisfied her. The thing is immensely characteristic and immensely—immense. I quite agree with you that it takes hold as nothing else of his has as yet done—it appeals with an immoderate intensity and goes straight as a dose of castor oil! I hope to heaven the thing will reach the London stage: there ought to be no difficulty, if Rita, when she offers herself, can be restricted to a chair, instead of lying on her back on the sofa. Let her *sit,* and the objection vanishes—I mean let her eschew the sofa. Of course I don't know what the rest brings forth—but this act and a half are a pure—or an impure—perfection. If he really carries on the whole play simply with these four people—and at the same high pitch (it's the *pitch* that's so magnificent!) it will be a feat more extraordinary than any he's achieved—it will beat *Ghosts.* Admirable, gallant old man! The success of this would be high! I greatly enjoyed our "lovely

1 Heinemann, who was to publish several of James's works, had sent the novelist the English translation of *Little Eyolf.*

luxurious" (as Rita would say), *fin de soirée*, on Monday. Tree is[2] as dewily infantine as Eyolf!

Yours truly,

Henry James

P.S. *Do* remember that I'm on the sofa, with my hair down—and pink lamp shades!

To HENRIETTA REUBELL

34, De Vere Gardens W.

Jan. 10, 1895

Dearest Miss Etta,

I rejoice in the warm glow of your friendship and of your indignation. I encountered on Saturday evening[1] the most horrible hours of my life—*but* the demonstration didn't come from the audience in any real sense of the term—infinite numbers of whom have deluged me—even when complete strangers—with letters and visits to tell me they had been delighted with the play. An ill-disposed, vicious, brutish *gallery*[2] was in the house, and bent, for particular and backstairs[3] reasons, on mischief. They made it effectually, and the newspapers in general, have by their vulgar stupidity and density increased the damage of the mob. I send you, however, Clement Scott in the *Telegraph,* and will send you W. Archer (in the *World*) next week: these are the only two critics who in the least count. Of course however the play has *du plomb dans l'aile,* and it remains to be seen what will become of it. I am prepared for the worst, and had no

---

[2] Herbert Beerbohm Tree, (1853-1917), the London actor-manager.

[1] The first night of *Guy Domville* was on Saturday, January 5.

[2] Henry James inserted a footnote at this point in his letter which reads: "The *row* was all the gallery, though much of the stupidity was elsewhere too."

[3] An allusion to a report that the gallery's hostility was in reality directed against the actor manager, George Alexander, for having slighted an actress.

real illusions at any time. You can take my word for it that the piece is extremely charming and skilful *je ne suis pas une bête,* either to write a silly play, or not to know it if I had. But when I stood in the presence of that yelling crew (gallery pure and simple—out-vociferating the applause thanks to leathern lungs,) I felt with bottomless dismay how the atmosphere of any London theatre is in mortal danger of becoming a complete nonconductor of any fine intention or of any really civilized artistic attempt—and I saw in one sickened moment (it wasn't pleasant) the *effondrement* of my labour and my hope. *Are* they really effondrés? It is too soon to say: but this week will show. The *seconde,* on Monday went admirably to a full and enthusiastic house. But that was an inevitable manifestation, on the part of the public, of shame and remorse for the brutishness of an element on Saturday, and may mean nothing in relation to a "run." So I am prepared, as I say, for the worst, and am, thank God, absolutely philosophic. The only thing they understand, or want here, is *one kind* of play—the play of the same kind as the unutterable kind they already know. With anything a little more delicate they are like a set of savages with a gold watch. Yet God knows I had *tried* to be simple, straightforward and British, and to dot my i's as big as with targets. The subject doubtless is too far away—an episode in the history of an old English Catholic family in the last century—treated as I thought, at least, very ingeniously and humanly. But the theatre is verily a black abyss—and one feels stained with vulgarity rien que d'y avoir passé. Thank heaven there is another art. I embrace you, dear Etta Reubell, for your prompt participation in my little *ennui,* and am yours more than ever

Henry James

To ELLEN TERRY

34, De Vere Gardens W.

Aug. 31st. '95

My Dear Ellen Terry.

Your farewell note was very genial and graceful, and I thank you most kindly for your cheque for £100—to which, and its species, I make not the smallest pretension to be indifferent or superior for I shouldn't be able to keep it up.[1] "Teach" you, dear source of instruction?—yes, every scrap that your genius leaves a margin for. I fear that will be a narrow edge. Let this lucid and punctual acknowledgment, at any rate, fly after you in your flight. It's so hot and still and stagnant here that I feel the Atlantic will have no steeper an incline than the mere slope of the footlights. May you therefore sail grandly on—and may the same serenity float you through the whole business. It will seem a long year—but art *is* long, ah me! At all events, if the Americans are not to have the Gem, do excruciate them with a suspicion of what they lose. Save for that, be only a blessing and blest and come back fluent in the idiom of Mrs. G[racedew][2] and above all believe me yours, dear Ellen Terry, very devotedly

Henry James

To ELIZABETH ROBINS

London, Dec. 18, 1896

Dear Miss Robins.

I am coming to the Avenue to-night and hoping to see you once or twice in the entr'actes and even, if you can, to drive home with you—or, rather, to *drive* you home; and this is a word of warning to make my application at the Stage door more

---

1 The advance for the one-act play *Summersoft,* later *The High Bid.*
2 Name of the heroine in the play.

convenient to you. It is above all an overflow of my exaltation over the 1st 2 Acts of 'John-Gabriel' which I have just read in the French of the *Revue de Paris*: an exaltation prepared and confirmed by Mrs. Green's[1] telling me last night of your blessed possession of the play and preparedness to produce it. It is magnificent and Ella Rendheim *for* you from top to toe and floor to ceiling. She is a part to do *everything* with, a wondrous chance. DO *ask Mrs. Crowe[2] to do Mrs. Borkman.* It seems to me she's for *her*, too. Ah, who will 'do' J.—Gabriel? He's immense. What an old boy is our Northern Henry!—he is too delightful—an old darling! The possible *when* &c., &c. are thrilling things you must tell me. I shall be, to-night, probably, in the 1st or 2nd row of stalls. I have let you alone with a severity worthy of a better cause—if there *were* a better than saving you any *extra* human strife and personal fatigue. But *do* try to see me to-night as much as possible—as Mrs. G. tells me of your immediate flight to Redcar. There are a 100 things I wish to ask and to say—above all: Go it, Ella! I go to-morrow afternoon to see Tessa Gosse do Mr. Puff in the 'Critic,' and in the evening to see Irving do—what he *does* do, alas, in 'Richard'! A bientôt:

Ever yours
Henry James

P.S. Tessa in Mr. Puff, is of course inspired by Sarah in 'Lorenzaccio!'

---

1 Alice Stopford Green, wife of the historian, John Richard Green.
2 Kate Josephine Bateman (Mrs. Crowe) (1842-1917) an American actress who had played in the London production of *The American*.

To GERTRUDE ELLIOTT

Rye, October 22d. 1908.

Dear Mrs. Forbes-Robertson. It has been very interesting to me to hear from you and of your intention and prospects even though these appear to include no very early production of *The High Bid.* I greatly regret to learn that its apparent effect on returns during its few country performances in the spring was a *downward* influence—this I take in for the first time, and the view is of course not exhilarating. I can only hope that an experience on a larger scale and in the longer piece, as it were, will point another way. I have no fixed, no hard and fast view whatever, as you seem to suppose, of the difference between the attitude of London and provincial audiences *on the whole* in respect to any work of mine, but quite incline to believe that these attitudes are—on the whole, as I say, pretty even as regards *all* productions. I only conceive that the London conditions are *generally* better and that the trial there gives a longer and fairer test. In the long run (of returns) no doubt the cases are equal—as to favor or disfavor.—When you come to the question of the Second Act and its effect and its possibilities and impossibilities I *don't,* I confess altogether follow—and perhaps I don't understand you. I only get the sense that you are asking of the little play, with its exceedingly simple and limited origin, that one-act essence of it, stamped on its every square-inch of surface, a range of appeal and effect, a *bearing* that it didn't and couldn't pretend to have, and that can no more be inserted into it after the fact than seeds, say, can be inserted into a (seedless) California orange (I have just eaten one for lunch!) after the tight-skinned golden ball has been exposed on the fruit-stall. I think you mix things and—pardon the expression!—earnestly and eloquently "muddle" them in your plea for "bed-rock!"[1] My small comedy treats its subject—and its subject is Mrs. Gracedew's appeal and adventure—on Mrs. Gracedew's grounds and in Mrs. Gracedew's spirit, and any deflection from these and that logic and that consistency would send the whole action off into a whirlwind of incoherence. Remember that my little piece was conceived quite primarily for *American* production (it was largely on that delusive ground that it took birth in response to Miss Terry's appeal—and she immediately started for America waving it over her head.) That character intensely abides in it, and *can* only intensely do so, and stared out of it from the outset, and had so to be reckoned with.

If however you ask me whether then I can't entertain the idea of taking the second act, and especially its central part, in hand again on the possibility of making it go better, my reply is, on the contrary, that it will interest me greatly to see what I *can* do, as soon as I can get a free mind. It is always interesting to measure and reconsider things in the light of their apparent effect (or non-effect) on audiences—if they [are] not things of the *essence*. I claim for myself infinite ingenuity in the whole dramatic and theatric mystery and craft, and I am quite ready to say that I will give the thing the benefit of my most earnest attention in the light of those resources—and in the measure of the possible. I can imagine, I think, already a more amusing *breaking-up*—of the centre of Act II—amusing in the sense of more generally attaching and thrilling and dramatic. But the very *stuff* of the thing can only remain of course—and there it is. Leave me, however, to shut myself up with it. I will see what

1 Miss Elliott had complained that audiences were not responding to her big speech pleading for preservation of old traditions and old English "show" houses but were applauding loudly her husband's brief rejoinder (in his role as a radical young politician) that there were thousands in England who had no houses to show at all.

I can do. Only I must wait till I have some very urgent present work off my mind, and as I gather that you expect to run your present play *through* your season at Terry's this leaves a margin. But will you please meanwhile send me the text of the alteration of the beginning of the first act of the H[igh] B[id]—the Cora and Young Man bit—which are not *with* the three bound acts (of the whole) you sent me some time since? I am appalled at what has "come out" of the play as I see the scale of the streaked excisions in these three volumes.—I've had no copy of my own since long ago. It will at least give attraction to the idea of putting something in!—I am very glad to infer that you have a country refuge, and hope it is doing you both great good, but as it may be only for Sundays—or week-ends—I address this to the Theatre. Believe me yours very truly

Henry James

To G. BERNARD SHAW

Rye, 20th Jan: 1909

My dear Bernard Shaw,

Your delightful letter is a great event for me,[1] but I must first of all ask your indulgence for my inevitable resort, to-day, to this means of acknowledging it. I have been rather sharply unwell and obliged to stay my hand, for some days, from the pen. I am, thank goodness, better, but still not penworthy—and in fact feel as if I should never be so again in presence of the beautiful and hopeless example your inscribed page sets me. Still another form of your infinite variety, this exquisite applica-

---

[1] Shaw had read James's one act pay *The Saloon* at the Stage Society and was asked by the executive committee to write the letter of rejection. This he did by suggesting to James that he rewrite the play and have the hero kill the ghost instead of being killed by it. Victory, he argued, could be given as artistically to the one or the other.

tion of your ink to your paper! It is indeed humiliating. But I bear up, or try to—and the more that I *can* dictate, at least when I absolutely must.

I think it is very good of you to have taken such explanatory trouble, and written me in such a copious and charming way, about the ill-starred *Saloon*. It raises so many questions, and you strike out into such illimitable ether over the so distinctly and inevitably circumscribed phenomenon itself—of the little piece as it stands—that I fear I can meet you at very few points; but I will say what I can. You strike me as carrying all your eggs, of conviction, appreciation, discussion etc., as who should say, in one basket, where you put your hand on them all with great ease and convenience; while I have mine scattered all over the place—many of them still under the hens!—and have therefore to rush about and pick one up here and another there. You take the little play "socialistically", it first strikes me, all too hard: I use that word because you do so yourself, and apparently in a sense that brings my production, such as it is, up against a lion in its path with which it had never dreamed of reckoning. Yes, there literally stands ferocious at the mouth of your beautiful cavern the very last formidable beast with any sop to whom I had prepared myself. And this though I thought I had so counted the lions and so provided the sops!

But let me, before I say more, just tell you a little how *The Saloon* comes to exist at all—since you say yourself "WHY have you done this thing?" I may not seem so to satisfy so big a Why, but it will say at least a little How (I came to do it;) and that will be perhaps partly the same thing.

My simple tale is then that Forbes Robertson and his wife a year ago approached me for the production of a little old one-act comedy written a dozen years or so previous, and that in the event was to see the light but under the more or less dissimulated form of a small published "story". I took hold of this then, and it proved susceptible of being played in three acts (with the shortest intervals)—and was in fact so produced in the country, in a few places, to all appearances "successfully"; but has not otherwise yet affronted publicity. I mention it, however, for the fact, that when it was about to be put into rehearsal it seemed absolutely to require something a little better than a cheap curtain raiser to be played in front of it; with any resources for which preliminary the F.R.'s seemed, however, singularly un-provided. The matter seemed to be important, and though I was extremely pressed with other work I asked myself whether I, even I, mightn't by a lively prompt effort put together such a minor item for the bill as would serve to help people to wait for the major. But I had distractingly little time or freedom of mind, and a happy and unidiotic motive for a one-act piece isn't easy to come by (as you will know better than I) offhand. Therefore said I to myself there might easily turn up among all the short tales I had published (the list being long) some-thing or other naturally and obligingly convertible to my pur-pose. That would economise immensely my small labour—and in fine I pounced on just such a treatable idea in a thing of many years before, an obscure pot-boiler, "Owen Wingrave" by name—and very much what you have seen by nature. It was treatable, I thought, and moreover I was in possession of it; also it would be very difficult and take great ingenuity and expertness—which gave the case a reason the more. To be brief then I with consummate art lifted the scattered and expensive Owen Wingrave into the compact and economic little Saloon— very adroitly (yes!) but, as the case had to be, breathlessly too; and all to the upshot of finding that, in the first place, my friends above-mentioned could make neither head nor tail of it; and in the second place that my three-act play, on further exploitation, was going to last too long to allow anything else of importance. So I put The Saloon back into a drawer; but so, likewise, I shortly afterwards fished it out again and showed it to Granville-Barker, who was kind about it and apparently curious of it, and in consequence of whose attention a member of the S[tage] S[ociety] saw it. That is the only witchcraft I have used!—by which I mean that that was the head and front of my undertaking to "preach" anything to anyone—in the guise of the little Act—on any subject whatever. So much for the modest origin of the thing—which, since you have read the piece, I can't help wanting to put on record.

But, if you press me, I quite allow that this all shifts my guilt only a little further back and that your question applies just as much, in the first place, to the short story perpetrated years ago, and in the re-perpetration more recently, in another specious form and in the greater (the very great alas) "maturity of my powers." And it doesn't really matter at all, since I am ready serenely to answer you. I do such things because I happen to be a man of imagination and taste, extremely interested in life, and because the imagination, thus, from the moment direction and motive play upon it from all sides, absolutely enjoys and insists on and incurably leads a life of its own, for which just this vivacity itself is its warrant. You surely haven't done all your own so interesting work without learning what it is for the imagination to *play* with an idea—an idea about life —under a happy obsession, for all it is worth. Half the beautiful things that the benefactors of the human species have produced would surely be wiped out if you don't allow this adventurous and speculative imagination its rights. You simplify too much, by the same token, when you limit the field of interest to what you call the scientific—your employment of which term in such a connection even greatly, I confess, confounds and bewilders

me. In the one sense in which The Saloon *could* be scientific—
that is by being done with all the knowledge and intelligence
relevant to its motive, I really think it quite supremely so. That
is the only sense in which a work of art can be scientific—though
in that sense, I admit, it may be so to the point of becoming an
everlasting blessing to man. And if you waylay me here, as I
infer you would be disposed to, on the ground that we "don't
want works of art," ah then, my dear Bernard Shaw, I think I
take such issue with you that—if we didn't both *like* to talk—
there would be scarce use in our talking at all. I think, frankly,
even, that we scarce want anything else at all. They are capable
of saying more things to man about himself than any other
"works" whatever are capable of doing—and its only by thus
saying as much to him as possible, by saying, as nearly as we can,
all there is, and in as many ways and on as many sides, and with
a vividness of presentation that "art", and art alone, is an adequate mistress of, that we enable him to pick and choose and
compare and know, enable him to arrive at any sort of synthesis
that isn't, through all its superficialities and vacancies, a base
and illusive humbug. On which statement I must rest my sense
that all *direct* "encouragement"—the thing you enjoin on me—
encouragement of the short-cut and say "artless" order, is really
more likely than not to be shallow and misleading, and to make
him turn on you with a vengeance for offering him some scheme
that takes account but of a tenth of his attributes. In fact I view
with suspicion the "encouraging" *representational* work, altogether, and think even the question not [an] *a priori* one at all;
that is save under this peril of too superficial a view of what it is
we have to be encouraged or discouraged *about*. The artist helps
us to know this,—if he have a due intelligence—better than
anyone going, because he undertakes to represent the world to
us; so that, certainly, if *a posteriori,* we can on the whole feel

encouraged, so much the better for us all round. But I can imagine no scanter source of exhilaration than to find the brute undertake that presentation without the most consummate "art" he can muster!

But I am really too long-winded—especially for a man who for the last few days (though with a brightening prospect) has been breathing with difficulty. It comes from my enjoying so the chance to talk with you—so much too rare; but that I hope we may be able before too long again to renew. I am comparatively little in London, but I have my moments there. Therefore I look forward—! And I assure you I have been touched and charmed by the generous abundance of your letter.

Believe me yours most truly,

Henry James

To JOHN GALSWORTHY

I answer your appeal on the censor question[1] to the best of my small ability. I *do* consider that the situation made by the Englishman of letters ambitious of writing for the stage has less dignity—thanks to the Censor's arbitrary rights upon his work—than that of any other man of letters in Europe, and that this fact may well be, or rather *must* be, deterrent to men of any intellectual independence and self-respect. I think this circumstance represents accordingly an impoverishment of our theatre; and it tends to deprive it of intellectual life, of the *importance* to which a free choice of subjects and illustration directly ministers, and to confine it to the trivial and the puerile.

1 This letter was read on August 12, 1909 by John Galsworthy into his evidence before the Joint Select Committee of the House of Lords and the House of Commons investigating the censorship of plays by the Lord Chamberlain.

To JOHN GALSWORTHY

It is difficult to express the depth of dismay and disgust with which an author of books in this country finds it impressed upon him, in passing into the province of the theatre with the view of labouring there, that he has to reckon anxiously with an obscure and irresponsible Mr. So-and-So, who may by law preemptorily demand of him that he shall make his work square, at vital points, with Mr. So-and-So's personal and, intellectually and critically speaking, wholly unauthoritative preferences, prejudices and ignorances, and that the less original, the less important and the less interesting it is, and the more vulgar and superficial and futile, the more it is likely to square. He thus encounters an arrogation of critical authority and the critical veto, with the power to enforce its decisions that is without a parallel in any other civilized country and which has in this one the effect of relegating the theatre to the position of a mean minor art, and of condemning it to ignoble dependencies, poverties and pusillanimities. We rub our eyes, we writers, accustomed to freedom in all other walks, to think that this cause has still to be argued in England.

IV

"ADMIRABLE FRIEND . . . ILLUSTRIOUS CONFRÈRE"

(i)

AT one time or another Henry James came to know, during his half century of writing, the celebrated men of letters on both sides of the water. In America he had known most of the Boston Brahmins; he counted the older, as well as the younger, generation of writers among his friends. In London there were few distinguished men of letters who did not sooner or later cross his path—not to speak of many lesser scribblers whom James treated with a professional cameraderie that made them seem his peers. In France he knew most of the members of Flaubert's circle; and he became an intimate later of Alphonse Daudet and of Paul Bourget. When in Italy, he occasionally moved in Italian literary circles, as his essays on D'Annunzio and Matilde Serao suggest.

Unfortunately his correspondence with his fellow craftsmen is not as abundant as his social correspondence, perhaps because his contemporaries were readily accessible in club or drawing room or salon. He was a friend of George Meredith whom he visited at Box Hill, but there seems to have been little correspondence between them. He saw Browning so often that he probably had no occasion to write to him: indeed they were neighbors for a while in Kensington. On the other hand a substantial correspondence with Robert Louis Stevenson has survived, as well as letters to H. G. Wells, to Conrad, to Henley, to Daudet and others. But these give only a partial view of the extent of James's literary fraternizing.

The group of letters published here has been selected largely to show the tone in which James wrote to his fellow-craftsmen: in some cases it was a little stiff and formal; in others however it was easy and loquacious. He was inevitably at his easiest with some of his fellow-Americans as well as the younger men who sought him out and called him "Master." But he was equally lively and readily explanatory when interrogated by minor Victorian writers: whether he was explaining the character of Daisy Miller to Lynn Linton, a busy writer in her day, or effusively greeting his younger confrères, a vein of professional pride runs through his banter, his talk about their common craft, his discourse on art. He clung to all the codes and conventions of his guild.

To ELIZA LYNN LINTON

[*ca. August 1880*]

My dear Mrs. Linton,—I will answer you as concisely as possible—and with great pleasure—premising that I feel very guilty at having excited such ire in celestial minds, and painfully responsible at the present moment.

Poor little Daisy Miller was, as I understand her, above all things *innocent*. It was not to make a scandal, or because she took pleasure in scandal, that she 'went on' with Giovanelli. She never took the measure really of the scandal she produced, and had no means of doing so: she was too ignorant, too irre-

flective, too little versed in the proportions of things. She intended infinitely less with G. than she appeared to intend—and
he himself was quite at sea as to how far she was going. She was
a flirt, a perfectly superficial and unmalicious one, and she was
very fond, as she announced at the outset, of 'gentlemen's
society.' In Giovanelli she got a gentleman—who, to her un-
cultivated perception, was a very brilliant one—all to herself,
and she enjoyed his society in the largest possible measure.
When she found that this measure was thought too large by
other people—especially by Winterbourne—she was wounded;
she became conscious that she was accused of something of
which her very comprehension was vague. This consciousness
she endeavoured to throw off; she tried not to think of what
people meant, and easily succeeded in doing so; but to my perception she never really tried to take her revenge upon public
opinion—to outrage it and irritate it. In this sense I fear I
must declare that she was not *defiant,* in the sense you mean.
If I recollect rightly, the word 'defiant' is used in the text—
but it is not intended in that large sense; it is descriptive of the
state of her poor little heart, which felt that a fuss was being
made about her and didn't wish to hear anything more about it.
She only wished to be left alone—being herself quite unaggres-
sive. The keynote of her *character* is her innocence—that of her
conduct is, of course, that she has a little sentiment about
Winterbourne, that she believes to be quite unreciprocated—
conscious as she was only of his protesting attitude. But, even
here, I did not mean to suggest that she was playing off Giovanelli against Winterbourne—for she was too innocent even for
that. She didn't try to provoke and stimulate W. by flirting
overtly with G.—she never believed that Winterbourne was
provokable. She would have liked him to think well of her—
but had an idea from the first that he cared only for higher

game, so she smothered this feeling to the best of her ability (though at the end a glimpse of it is given), and tried to help herself to do so by a good deal of lively movement with Giovanelli. The whole idea of the story is the little tragedy of a light, thin, natural, unsuspecting creature being sacrificed as it were to a social rumpus that went on quite over her head and to which she stood in no measurable relation. To deepen the effect, I have made it go over her mother's head as well. She never had a thought of scandalising anybody—the most she ever had was a regret for Winterbourne.

This is the only witchcraft I have used—and I must leave you to extract what satisfaction you can from it. Again I must say that I feel 'real badly,' as D. M. would have said, at having supplied the occasion for a breach of cordiality. May the breach be healed herewith! . . . Believe in the very good will of yours faithfully,

H. James

To GEORGE DU MAURIER

London, March 18th. [*1884*]

My dear du Maurier.

I just receive your honorific note. I shall be delighted to come up on Sunday at about 11.30 and let you do anything you please with my head, except punch it.[1] The amiability of your designs upon it causes me a flutter of mingled pride and modesty; I hang the head which you propose to exalt.—I have been meditating a pilgrimage to your hill-top any one of these next days—but Sunday makes its definite.—Of the time that has elapsed since I saw you last I have passed a month in Paris:

---

[1] Du Maurier had invited James to pose for a sketch of his head which he intended to incorporate into a group picture.

I will tell you of that. I thank you again for your kind offer to make me if not beautiful, at least visible, forever and am always yours

Henry James

To JAMES RUSSELL LOWELL

Bournemouth, May 29th [*1885*]

My dear Lowell,

My hope of coming up to town again has been defeated, and it comes over me that your departure is terribly near. Therefore I write you a line of hearty and affectionate farewell[1]—mitigated by the sense that after all it is only for a few months that we are to lose you. I trust, serenely, to your own conviction of this fact, but for extra safety just remark that if you don't return to London next winter I shall hurl myself across the ocean at you like a lasso. As I look back upon the years of your mission my heart swells and almost breaks again (as it did when I heard you were superseded) at the thought that anything so perfect should be gratuitously destroyed. But there is a part of your function which can go on again, indefinitely, whenever you take it up—and that, I repeat, I hope you will do soon rather than late. I think with the tenderest pleasure of the many fire-side talks I have had with you, from the first—and with a pleasure dimmed with sadness of so many of our more recent ones. You are tied to London now by innumerable cords and fibres, and I should be glad to think that you ever felt me, ever so lightly, pulling at one of them. It is a great disappointment to me not to see you again, but I am kept here fast and shall not be in town

---

[1] Lowell was leaving London after having held the position of American Minister since 1880.

till the end of June. I give you my blessing and every good wish for a happy voyage. I wish I could receive you over there—and assist at your arrival and impressions—little as I want you to go back. Don't forget that you have produced a relation between England and the U. S. which is really a gain to civilization and that you must come back to look after your work. You can't look after it there: that is the function of an Englishman—and if *you* do it there they will call you one. The only way you can be a good American is to return to our dear old stupid, satisfactory London, and to yours ever affectionately and faithfully,

Henry James

To ROBERT LOUIS STEVENSON

London, Oct. 30th. 1891

My dear Louis.

My silences are hideous, but somehow I feel as if you were inaccessible to sound. Moreover it appears that my last letter, despatched many months ago, I admit, never reached you. But Colvin tells me that a post leaves tomorrow for San Francisco, and the effect of diminished remoteness from you is increased . by the fact that I dined last night with Henry Adams, who told me of his visits to you months and months ago. He re-created you, and your wife, for me a little, as living persons, and fanned thereby the flame of my desire not to be forgotten of you and not to appear to forget you. (He lately arrived—in Paris—via New Zealand and Marseilles and has just come to London to learn that he can't go to China, as he had planned, through the closure, newly enacted, and inexorable, of all but its outermost parts. He now talks of Central Asia, but can't find anyone to go with him—least of all, alas, me. He is about to ship [John] La Farge home—now in Brittany with his French relations, (and whom I have not seen.) I feel as if I ought to make my letter a smoking porridge of news; but it's a bewilderment where to begin. Nothing, however, seems more foremost than that [Sidney] Colvin is really in a state of substantially recovered health. I dined with him a few days since at the Athenaeum and he gave me a better impression than he had done for years. He has passed through black darkness—and much prolonged; but I think he sees daylight and hears the birds sing. That little black demon of a Kipling will have perhaps leaped upon your silver strand by the time this reaches you—he publicly left England to embrace you many weeks ago—carrying literary genius out of the country with him in his pocket. As you will quarrel with him at an early day, for yourself, it is therefore not needful I should say more of him than that nature languishes since his departure and art grunts and turns in her sleep. I am told you and Lloyd are waking them both up in the *Wrecker*, but I have had the fortitude not to begin the Wrecker yet. I can't read you in snippets and between the vulgar covers of magazines; but I am only biding my time and smacking my lips. I am a baser cockney even than you left me, inasmuch as now I don't even go to Bournemouth. I have made, in a whole year, but two absences from London—one of six weeks, last spring, in Paris, and another of the same duration, in the summer, in Ireland, which has a shabby foreign charm that touches me. Yet I'm afraid I have little to show for such an adhesion to my chair—unless it be holes in the seat of my trousers. I have written and am still to write a goodish many short tales—but you are not to be troubled with them till they prop each other up in a Volume. I mean never to write another novel; I mean I have solemnly dedicated myself to a masterly brevity. I have come back to it, as to an early love. *"La première politesse de l'écrivain"* says lately the exquisite Anatole France, *"n'est-ce point d'être bref? La nouvelle suffit à tous. On peut y renfermer*

*beaucoup de sens en peu de mots. Une nouvelle bien faite est
le régal des connoisseurs et le contentement des difficiles. C'est
l'élixir et la quintessence. C'est l'onguent précieux."* I quote
him because *il dit si bien.* But you can ask Kipling. Excuse me
for seeming to imply that one who has distilled the ointment as
you have needs to ask anyone. I am too sceptical even to mention that I sent you ages ago the *Tragic Muse*—so presumable is
it that she never reached you. I lately produced here a play—a
dramatization of my old novel *The American* (the thing was
played last spring in various places in the country,) with circumstances of public humiliation which make it mainly count
as an heroic beginning. The papers slated it without mercy,
and it was—by several of its interpreters—wretchedly ill-played;
also it betrays doubtless the inexperience of its author and suffers damnably from the straight-jacket of the unscenic book.
But if I hadn't done, on solicitation, this particular thing I
shouldn't have begun ever at all; and if I hadn't begun I
shouldn't have the set purpose to show, henceforth, what flower
of perfection I presume to think I can pick from the dusty
brambles—ah meagre vegetation!—of the dramatic form. The
play is in its fifth week—and will probably traverse a goodish
many others; but it has been a time (the first, God knows!) when
I have been on the whole glad you are not in England. Adams
has made me see you a little—both, and I look to John LaFarge
to do so a little more. (He comes in a few days.) Colvin has
read me your letters when he discreetly could, and my life has
been a burden from fearing to unfold the *Times* every morning
to a perusal of Samoan convulsions. But apparently you survive, little good as I get of it. We are all under water here—it
has rained hard for five months—and the British land is a waste
of waters, as in the first pages of geologies. I am consumed with
catarrh and rheumatism and lumbago—and when Adams talked
to me last night of the tropics I could have howled with baffled

desire. My poor sister—slowly and serenely dying—is too ill for me to leave England at present: she has a house in London now: I don't know whom to tell you about more that you would care to hear of. Edmund Gosse has written a novel—as yet unpublished—which I wot little of. Hall Caine has put forth *A Scapegoat* to the enrichment, I believe, of all concerned—but I am not concerned. I will send you the work as soon as it is reduced in bulk. The Frenchmen are passing away—Maupassant dying of locomotor paralysis, the fruit of fabulous habits, I am told. *Je n'en sais rien;* but I shall miss him. Bourget is married and will do good things yet—I send you by this post his (to me very exquisite, as perception and as expression—that is as literature,) *Sensations d'Italie.* I saw Daudet last winter, more or less in Paris, who is also *atteint de la moelle épiniere* and writing about it in the shape of a novel called *La Douleur,* which will console him by its sale. I greet your wife, my dear Louis, most affectionately,—I speak to you too, dear Mrs. Louis, in every word I write. I desire to express the very friendliest remembrance of your heroic mother—who accounts for her son, and still more wonderfully for her daughter-in-law and grand young stepson. My love to the gallant Lloyd. Vouchsafe me a page of prose and believe in the joy that a statement that you bloom with a tropic luxuriance, will, if made with your hand, convey to your flaccid old friend

Henry James

To EDMUND GOSSE

London [Dec. 13th, 1894.]

My dear Gosse,

I return with much appreciation the vivid pages on Pater.[1] They fill up substantially the void of one's ignorance of his

---

[1] Gosse's study of Walter Pater was included in his volume *Critical Kit-kats* published in 1896.

personal history, and they are of a manner graceful and lumi-
nous; though I should perhaps have relished a little more insistence on—a little more of an inside view of—the nature of his
mind itself. Much as they tell, however, how curiously negative
and faintly-grey he, after all telling, remains! I think he has had
—will have had—the most exquisite literary fortune: i.e. to
have taken it out all, wholly, exclusively, with the pen (the
style, the genius,) and absolutely not at all with the person. He
is the mask without the face, and there isn't in his total super-
ficies a tiny point of vantage for the newspaper to flap his wings
on. You have been lively about him—but about whom *wouldn't*
you be lively? I think you'd be lively about *me!*—Well, faint,
pale, embarrassed, exquisite Pater! He reminds me, in the dis-
turbed midnight of our actual literature, of one of those lucent
matchboxes which you place, on going to bed, near the candle,
to show you, in the darkness, where you can strike a light: he
shines in the uneasy gloom—vaguely, and has a phosphorescence,
not a flame. But I quite agree with you that he is not of the
little day—but of the longer time.

Will you kindly ask Tessa if I may *still* come, on Saturday?
My visit to the country has been put off by a death—and if
there is a little corner for me I'll appear. If there isn't—so late—
no matter. I daresay I ought to write to Miss Wetton. Or will
Tessa amiably inquire?

Yours always,
Henry James

To EDMUND GOSSE

De Vere Gardens
Monday [April 8] 1895

My dear Gosse:

Yes, I will come with pleasure to-morrow, Tuesday. Yes, too, it has been, it is, hideously, atrociously dramatic[1] and really interesting—so far as one can say that of a thing of which the interest is qualified by such a sickening horribility. It is the squalid gratuitousness of it all—of the mere exposure—that blurs the spectacle. But the *fall*—from nearly 20 years of a really unique kind of "brilliant" conspicuity (wit, "art," conversation —"one of our 2 or 3 dramatists, etc.") to that sordid prison cell and this gulf of obscenity over which the ghoulish public hangs and gloats—it is beyond any utterance of irony or any pang of compassion! He was never in the smallest of degree interesting to me—but this hideous human history has made him so—in a manner. À demain—Yours ever,

HJ

To ALPHONSE DAUDET

34, De Vere Gardens. W.
ce 12 fevrier
Londres [1895]

Cher ami et confrère,

Je n'ai pas voulu, avant de l'avoir longuement savouré, vous remercier de votre nouveau livre, que vous m'envoyiez l'autre jour si amicalement. Je suis très touché et tout réchauffé (au temps où nous sommes,) de ce signe de votre bon souvenir. J'ai lu *Petite Paroisse* comme je vous lis toujours—dans un doux receuillement traversé de frissons pénétrants. Il n'y a pas de

1 The Oscar Wilde case.

[147]

manière de faire qui me contente aussi pleinement que la vôtre; je l'avais constaté de nouveau, justment ces jours-là, en relisant—chacun pour la troisieme fois—*Sapho* et *l'Immortel.* Ça m'est une véritable joie de vous voir trouver au sortir (il y parait bien,) de vos sombres années, ce beau et riche roman, où la vie se joue si largement et librement, où l'observation et la poésie s'etreignent et se confondment. J'avais soif du timbre si spécial de votre voix de couleur—de votre monde et vous, tel que vous nous la donnez—et m'en voilà tout refraichi. Je tiens à croire que c'est une reprise entière de vos moyens, de vos grandes aises—à croire, c'est à dire, que vous allez bien de mieux en mieux. J'y mettrai plus de foi encore en vous voyant, au mois de mai ou de juin, débarquer sur cette côte hospitalière—qui ne l'aura jamais été pour personne (pas même pour Vallès ou pour Rochefort!) plus que—et de moins entendus!—que moi-même. J'en ai traversé une considérable l'autre jour pour vous —en président à la conférence que ce digne et terne M. Hugue-met a consacré à University Collège, à quelques uns de vos romans. La salle était comble, on y était entassé et debout; je constatais un appétit, une curiosité du sujet qui m'a fait bien regretter que le pauvre conferencier se doutât si peu de ce qu'il y avait à en tirer. J'étais tout tenté de lui arracher la parole— mais j'ai du me borner, en proposant un vote de remerciement, à le qualifier d'intéressant et d'entrâinant et à annoncer à l'audi-toire que je vous ferai connaître le plaisir que nous avions eu à passer une heure avec vous—ce qui m'a valu de longs applaudis-sements. Je viens d'en passer encore une en vous infligeant ces trop nombreuses pages de reconnaisance, de bon espoir et de mauvais français. Trouvez y, mon cher Daudet, pour tous les votres comme pour vous même l'affectueuse pensée de

Henry James

To SIR LESLIE STEPHEN

London, May 6th, 1895

My dear Stephen,

I feel unable to approach such a sorrow[1] as yours—and yet I can't forbear to hold out my hand to you. I think of you with inexpressible participation, and only take refuge from this sharp pain of sympathy in trying to call up the image of all the perfect happiness that you drew and that you gave. I pray for you that there are moments when the sense of that rushes over you like a possession that you still hold. There is no happiness in this horrible world but the happiness we have *had*—the very present is ever in the jaws of fate. *I* think, in the presence of the loss of so beautiful and noble and generous a friend, of the admirable picture of her perfect union with you, and that for her, at any rate, with all its fatigues and sacrifices, life didn't pass without the deep and clear felicity—the best it can give. She leaves no image but that of the high enjoyment of affections and devotions—the beauty and the good she wrought and the tenderness that came back to her. Unquenchable seems to me such a presence. But why do I presume to say these things to you, my dear Stephen? Only because I want you to hear in them the sound of the voice and feel the pressure of the hand of your affectionate old friend,

Henry James

To H. G. WELLS

Rye. Dec. 9th, 1898

My dear H. G. Wells,

Your so liberal and graceful letter is to my head like coals of fire—so repeatedly for all these weeks have I had feebly to

[1] The death of Mrs. Stephen, the former Julia (Jackson) Duckworth, mother of Virginia Woolf.

suffer frustrations in the matter of trundling over the marsh to ask for your news and wish for your continued amendment. The shortening days and the deepening mud have been at the bottom of this affair. I never get out of the house till 3 o'clock, when night is quickly at one's heels. I would have taken a regular day—I mean started in the a.m.—but have been so ridden, myself, by the black care of an unfinished and *running* (galloping, leaping, and bounding,) serial that parting with a day has been like parting with a pound of flesh.[1] I am still a neck ahead, however, and *this* week will see me through; I accordingly hope very much to be able to turn up one of the ensuing days. I will sound a horn, so that you yourself be not absent on the chase. Then I will express more articulately my appreciation of your various signs of critical interest, as well as assure you of my sympathy in your own martyrdom. What will you have? It's all a grind and a bloody battle—as well as a considerable lark, and the difficulty itself is the refuge from the vulgarity. Bless your heart, I think I could easily say worse of the T[turn] of the S[crew], the young woman, the spooks, the style, the everything, than the worst any one else could manage. One knows the most damning things about one's self. Of course I had, about my young woman, to take a very sharp line. The grotesque business I had to make her picture and the childish psychology I had to make her trace and present, were, for me at least, a very difficult job, in which absolute lucidity and logic, a singleness of effect, were imperative. Therefore I had to rule out subjective complications of her own—play of tone etc.; and keep her impersonal save for the most obvious and indispensable little note of neatness, firmness and courage—without which she wouldn't

[1] *The Awkward Age,* serialization of which had begun on October 1, 1898 in *Harper's Weekly.*

have had her data.[2] But the thing is essentially a pot-boiler and a *jeu d'esprit.*

With the little play,[3] the absolute creature of its conditions, I had simply to make up a deficit and take a small *revanche.* For three mortal years had the actress for whom it was written (utterly to try to *fit*) persistently failed to produce it, and I couldn't wholly waste my labour. The B[ritish] P[ublic] won't read a play with the mere names of the speakers—so I simply paraphrased these and added such indications as might be the equivalent of decent acting—a history and an evolution that seem to me moreover explicatively and sufficiently smeared all over the thing. The moral is of course Don't write one-act plays. But I didn't mean thus to sprawl. I envy your hand your needle-pointed fingers. As you don't say that you're *not* better I prepare myself to be greatly struck with the same, and with kind regards to your wife,

Believe me yours ever,

Henry James

P.S. What's this about something in some newspaper?—I read least of all—from long and deep experience—what my friends

2 Many critics have cited this passage as refutation of the thesis that the ghosts in *The Turn of the Screw* were imagined by the governess. James actually is explaining to Wells how he kept the governess "impersonal"—so that she is not even named. In his later preface to the ghostly tale he may have been alluding to Wells's inquiries when he wrote: "I recall . . . a reproach made me by a reader capable evidently, for the time, of some attention, that I hadn't sufficiently 'characterised' my young woman engaged in her labyrinth; hadn't endowed her with signs and marks, features and humors, hadn't in a word invited her to deal with her own mystery as well as with that of Peter Quint, Miss Jessel and the hapless children." To which James added: "We have surely as much of her own nature as we can swallow in watching it reflect her anxieties and inductions."

3 James had included in the volume *The Two Magics* (1898) as a companion piece to *The Turn of the Screw* a story titled *Covering End,* based on the one-act play he had written for Ellen Terry in 1895.

write about me, and haven't read the things you mention. I suppose it's because they know I don't that they dare!

To MRS. W. K. CLIFFORD

Rye.
Wednesday night.
[*Oct. 3, 1901.*]

Dearest Lucy C.

I have waited to welcome you, to thank you for your dear and brilliant Vienna letter, because you stayed my hand (therein) from writing—for want of an address; and because I've believed that not till now (if even now) would you be disengaged from the tangled skein of your adventures. And even at this hour (of loud-ticking midnight stillness,) I don't pretend to do more than greet you affectionately on the threshold of home; promise you a better equivalent (for your so interesting, so envy-squeezing, so vivid record of adventure) at some very near date; and, above all, renew my jubilation at your having made so good and brave a thing of it all—especially as *full* and unstinted a one as you desired. Never mind the money, I handsomely say—you will get it all back and much more—in the refreshment and renewal and general intellectual ventilation your six weeks will have been to you. I'm sure the effect will go far—I want details so much that I wish I were to see you soon—but, alas, I don't quite see when. I'm just emerging from a domestic cyclone that has, in one way and another, cost me so much time, that, pressed as I am with a woefully backward book,[1] I can only for the present hug my writing-table with convulsive knees. The figure doesn't fit—but the postponement of all joy, alas, does. My two old man-and-wife servants (who had been with me sixteen years) were, a few days ago, shot into

---

1 Probably *The Ambassadors.*

space (thank heaven at last!) by a whirlwind of but 48 hours duration; and though the absolute rupture came and went in that time, the horrid accompaniments and upheaved neighbourhoods have represented a woeful interruption. But it's over, and I have plunged again (and am living, blissfully, for the present, with a house-maid and a charwoman, and immensely enjoying my simplified state and my relief from what I see now was a long nightmare).

I read your play in the *Nineteenth Century*, as you invited me, but I can't *write* of it now beyond saying that I was greatly struck by the care and finish you had given it. If I must tell you categorically, however, I don't think it a scenic subject *at all;* I think it bears all the mark of a subject selected for a tale and done as a play as an after-thought. I don't see, that is, what the scenic form does, or *can* do, for it, that the narrative couldn't do better—or what it, in turn, does for the scenic form. The inwardness is a kind of inwardness that doesn't become an outwardness—effectively—theatrically; and the part played in the whole by the painting of the portrait seems to me the kind of thing for which the play is a non-conductor. And here I am *douching* you on your doorstep with cold water. We must *talk*, we must colloquise and compare and *renew* the first moment we can, and I am all the while and ever your affectionate old friend,

Henry James

To FORD MADOX HUEFFER [FORD]

Reform Club,
Pall Mall, S. W.
April 14th, 1904

My dear Hueffer,

Lord bless you, it is all right about your book, [*The Soul of London*] of which I am delighted to hear. Go on with it to felicity and fortune and let it take my hearty benediction with it. Mine is a thing of the far, though not of the contingent future. I agreed nearly a year ago to do for the *Macmillans* (no Heinemann-Pawling) two (wide-printed illustrated) vols. to be called *London Town*,[1] to be illustrated by J. Pennell, and to be of the general type of Marion Crawford's *Ave Roma*, etc. But the essence of my understanding is free margin of *time*, and I haven't *touched* the work yet.

I go to America five months hence (scarce that) and stay there some eight, and while there shall not be able to think of the subject—to do anything but get away and away from it. This means that I can't even begin to "think of" my book for at least a year hence, and when I do begin to think I must collect a great many impressions (by reading) before I can begin to write. So there it is. My work is relegated to a dim futurity. Go on with yours never dreaming of my job. Bring yours out and find all comfort, pride and profit in it; the sooner the better; then I shall be able to crib from you freely—yet shall [be] demurely acknowledging.

All greetings and good wishes.

Yours ever,
Henry James

To W. E. NORRIS

Boston.
[*Dec. 15, 1904.*]

My dear Norris,

There is nothing to which I find my situation in this great country less favourable than to this order of communication; yet I greatly wish, 1st, to thank you for your beautiful letter of as long ago as Sept. 12th (from Malvern), and 2nd, not to fail

---

1 The book was never written.

of having some decent word of greeting on your table for Christmas morning.[1] The conditions of time and space, at this distance, are such as to make nice calculations difficult, and I shall probably be frustrated of the felicity of dropping on you by exactly the right post. But I send you my affectionate blessing and I aspire, at the most, to lurk modestly in the Heap. You were in exile (very elegant exile, I rather judge) when you last wrote, but you will now, I take it, be breathing again bland Torquay (*bland,* not blond)—a process having, to my fancy, a certain analogy and consonance with that of quaffing bland Tokay. This is neither Tokay nor Torquay—this slightly arduous process, or adventure, of mine, though very nearly as expensive, on the whole, as both of those luxuries combined. I am just now amusing myself with bringing the expense up to the point of ruin by having come back to Boston, after an escape (temporary, to New York,) to conclude a terrible episode with the Dentist—which is turning out an abyss of torture and tedium. I am promised (and shall probably enjoy) prodigious results from it—but the experience, the whole business, has been so fundamental and complicated that anguish and dismay *only* attend it while it goes on—embellished at the most by an opportunity to admire the miracles of American expertness. These are truly a revelation and my tormentor a great artist, but he will have made a cruelly deep dark hole in my time (very precious for me here) and in my pocket—the latter of such a nature that I fear no patching of all my pockets to come will ever stop the leak. But meanwhile it has all made me feel quite domesticated, consciously assimilated to the system; I am losing the precious sense that everything is strange (which I began by

[1] James annually wrote a letter to W. E. Norris destined for his breakfast table on Christmas morning. In 1904, however, since he was in the United States, James could not be sure that his letter would reach Norris in time; he therefore took the precaution of writing it a fortnight earlier.

hugging close,) and it is only when I know I am quite whiningly homesick *en dessous,* for L. H. and Pall Mall, that I remember I am but a creature of the surface. The surface, however, has its points; New York is appalling, fantastically charmless and elaborately dire; but Boston has quality and convenience, and now that one sees American life in the longer piece one profits by many of its ingenuities. The winter, as yet, is radiant and bell-like (in its frosty clearness;) the diffusion of warmth, indoors, is a signal comfort, extraordinarily comfortable in the travelling, by day—I don't go in for nights; and a marvel the perfect organisation of the universal telephone (with interviews and contacts that begin in two minutes and settle all things in them;) a marvel, I call it, for a person who hates notewriting as I do—but an exquisite curse when it isn't an exquisite blessing. I expect to be free to return to N. Y., the formidable in a few days—where I shall inevitably have to stay another month; after which I hope for sweeter things—Washington, which is amusing, and the South, and eventually California—with, probably, Mexico. But many things are indefinite—only I shall probably stay till the end of June. I suppose I am much interested—for the time passes inordinately fast. Also the country is *unlike* any other—to one's sensation of it; those of Europe, from State to State, seem to me less different from each other than they are all different from this—or rather this from them. But forgive a fatigued and obscure scrawl. I am really *done* and demoralized with my interminable surgical (for it comes to that) ordeal. Yet I wish you heartily all peace and plenty and am yours, my dear Norris, very constantly,

Henry James

To JOSEPH CONRAD

Rye, November 1st, 1906

My dear Conrad,

I have taught you that I am lumbering and long, but I haven't, I think, yet taught you that I am base, and it is not on the occasion of your beautiful sea green volume[1] of the other day that I shall consent to begin. I read you as I listen to rare music—with deepest depths of surrender, and out of those depths I emerge slowly and reluctantly again to acknowledge that I return to life. To taste you as I do taste you is *really* thus to wander far away and to decently thank you is a postal transaction (quite another affair), for which I have to come *back,* and accept with a long sad sigh the community of our afflicted existence. My silence is thus—after your beautiful direct speech to me too—but that I['ve] been away with you, intimately and delightfully and my only objection to writing to you in gratitude is that I am not reading you, but quite the contrary, when I do it. But I *have* you now, and the charm of this process of appropriation has been to me, with your adorable book for its subject, of the very greatest. And I am touched in the same degree by the grace of your inscription, all so beautifully said and so generously felt. *J'en suis tout confus,* my dear Conrad, and can only thank you and thank you again. But the book itself is a wonder to me really—for it's so bringing home the prodigy of your past experiences: bringing it home to me more personally and directly, I mean, the immense treasure and the inexhaustible adventures. No one has *known*—for intellectual use—the things you know, and you have, as the artist of the whole matter, an authority that no one has approached. I find you in it all, writing wonderfully, whatever you may say of your difficult medium and your *plume rebelle.* You knock about in

---

[1] Apparently *The Mirror of the Sea.*

the wide waters of expression like the raciest and boldest of privateers,—you have made the whole place your own *en même temps que les droits les plus acquis vous y avez les plus rares bonheurs.* Nothing you have done has more in it. The root of the matter of saying you stir me, in fine, to amazement and you touch me to tears, and I thank the powers who so mysteriously let you loose with such sensibilities, into such an undiscovered country—*for* sensibility. That is all for tonight. I want to see you again. Is Winchelsea a closed book?

Are the Ford Madoxes still away? (What a world *they* must then have been let loose into!) I am looking for some sign of them, and with it perhaps some more contempory news of you. I hope the smaller boy is catching up, and your wife reasserting herself and your 'condition' favourable? Ah, one's conditions! But we must *make* them, and you have on every showing, *de quoi!* I pat you, my dear Conrad, very affectionately and complacently on the back and am yours very constantly

Henry James.

P.S. *Milles amitiés* to the fireside and the crib.

To ROBERT HERRICK

Rye, August 7th. 1907

Dear Robert Herrick,

It has been charming to hear from you, but I am always miles and miles behind all proper forms of correspondence. When I have done a day's stint of work—that is of 'literary composition' —with any intensity, any power to write further in any manner, dreadfully abandons me. I am depleted and exanimate, and letters come off as they can—the larger proportion of them never coming off at all. But I must thank you for the gentle gift of *The Common Lot* too (which I want to read and shall read:

it rests on my table only till I shall have got into the traces again for dragging my cart along in its customary ruts. I have been since my return from the U.S. much derailed—but things are running more smoothly). I rejoice heartily that your Breton conditions prove so charming to you and may you [relish?] the romantic experience. Why do you speak of 'sparing' me the expression of your 'unregenerate enthusiasm' for them? I shouldn't have supposed that at this time of day j'en étais encore at having to prove *my* haunting preoccupation with the things of France. You didn't even come—you told me—to my fanatical Balzac lecture!—All thanks, at any rate, for your so curious and urgent remarks on the matter of my revisions,[1] in respect to some of the old stuff I spoke of to you in connection with the plan of an édition définitive. I am greatly touched by your having felt and thought strongly enough on the matter to take the trouble to remonstrate at the idea of my re-touching. The re-touching with any insistance will *in fact* bear but on one book (*The American* —on *R. Hudson* and the *P. of a Lady* very much less) but in essence I shouldn't have planned the edition at all unless I had felt close revision—wherever seeming called for—to be an indispensable part of it. I do every justice to your contention, but don't think me reckless or purblind if I say that I hold myself really right and you really wrong. The *raison d'être* (the edition's) is in its being selective as well as collective, and by the mere fact of leaving out certain things (I have tried to read over *Washington Square* and I *can't,* and I fear it must go!) I exercise a control, a discrimination, I treat certain portions of my work as unhappy accidents. (Many portions of many—of all—men's work are). From that it is but a step further—but it is 1 o'clock

1 For the selective New York Edition of his novels and tales Henry James revised many of his early works. The edition was issued in 24 volumes between 1907 and 1909.

a.m. and I've written seven letters, and I won't attempt to finish that sentence or expand my meaning. Forgive my blatant confidence in my own lucid literary sense! If I had planned not to re-touch—that is revise closely—I would have reprinted *all* my stuff and that idea is horrific. You also will be ravished! Trust me and I shall be justified. But good night and pardon my untidy scrawl and my belated incoherence. Recall me kindly to your wife and believe me,

Yours always,

Henry James

To W. D. HOWELLS

London, February 19th, 1912

My dear Howells,

It is made known to me that they are soon to feast in New York the newest and freshest of the splendid birthdays to which you keep treating us, and that your many friends will meet round you to rejoice in it and reaffirm their allegiance.[1] I shall not be there, to my sorrow, and though this is inevitable I yet want to be missed, peculiarly and monstrously missed; so that these words shall be a public apology for my absence: read by you, if you like and can stand it, but better still read *to* you and in fact straight *at* you, by whoever will be so kind and so loud and so distinct. For I doubt, you see, whether any of your toasters and acclaimers have anything like my ground and title for being with you at such an hour. There can scarce be one, I think, to-day, who has known you from so far back, who has kept so close to you for so long, and who has such fine old reasons—so old, yet so well preserved—to feel your virtue and sound your praise. My debt to you began well-nigh half a cen-

---

[1] The letter was written to be read at a dinner in New York in celebration of Howells's 75th birthday. It was published in the *North American Review,* April 1912.

tury ago, in the most personal way possible, and then kept growing with your own admirable growth—but always rooted in the
early intimate benefit. This benefit was that you held out your
open editorial hand to me at the time I began to write—and I
allude especially to the summer of 1866—with a frankness and
sweetness of hospitality that was really the making of me, the
making of the confidence that required help and sympathy and
that I should otherwise, I think, have strayed and stumbled
about a long time without acquiring. You showed me the way
and opened me the door; you wrote to me, and confessed yourself struck with me—I have never forgotten the beautiful thrill
of *that*. You published me at once—and paid me, above all,
with a dazzling promptitude; magnificently, I felt, and so that
nothing since has ever quite come up to it. More than this even,
you cheered me on with a sympathy that was in itself an inspiration. I mean that you talked to me and listened to me—ever so
patiently and genially and suggestively conversed and consorted
with me. This won me to you irresistibly and made you the most
interesting person I knew—lost as I was in the charming sense
that my best friend was an editor, and an almost insatiable editor, and that such a delicious being as that was a kind of property of my own. Yet how didn't that interest still quicken and
spread when I became aware that—with such attention as you
could spare from us, for I recognized my fellow beneficiaries—
you had started to cultivate *your* great garden as well; the tract
of virgin soil that, begining as a cluster of bright, fresh, sunny
and savoury patches, close about the house, as it were, was to
become that vast woodly pleasaunce of art and observation, of
appreciation and creation, in which you have laboured, without
a break or a lapse, to this day, and in which you have grown so
grand a show of—well, really of everything. Your liberal visits
to *my* plot, and your free-handed purchases there, were still

greater events when I began to see you handle, yourself, with such ease the key to our rich and inexhaustible mystery. Then the question of what you would make of your own powers began to be even more interesting than the question of what you would make of mine—all the more, I confess, as you had ended by settling this one so happily. My confidence in myself, which you had so helped me to, gave way to a fascinated impression of your own spread and growth; for you broke out so insistently and variously that it was a charm to watch and an excitement to follow you. The only drawback that I remember suffering from was that *I*, your original debtor, couldn't print or publish or pay you—which would have been a sort of ideal *re*payment and of enhanced credit; you could take care of yourself so beautifully, and I could (unless by some occasional happy chance or rare favour) scarce so much as glance at your proofs or have a glimpse of your "endings." I could only read you, full-blown and finished—and see, with the rest of the world, how you were doing it again and again.

That then was what I had with time to settle down to—the common attitude of seeing you do it again and again; keep on doing it, with your heroic consistency and your noble, genial abundance, during all the years that have seen so many apparitions come and go, so many vain flourishes attempted and achieved, so many little fortunes made and unmade, so many weaker inspirations betrayed and spent. Having myself to practise meaner economies, I have admired, from period to period, your so ample and liberal flow; wondered at your secret for doing positively a little—what do I say a little? I mean a magnificent deal!—of Everything. I seem to myself to have faltered and languished, to have missed more occasions than I have grasped, while you have piled up your monument just by remaining at your post. For you have had the advantage, after all, of breathing an air that has suited and nourished you; of sitting up to your neck, as I may say—or at least up to your waist— amid the sources of your inspiration. There and so you were at your post; there and so the spell could ever work for you, there and so your relation to all your material grow closer and stronger, your perception penetrate, your authority accumulate. They make a great array, a literature in themselves, your studies of American life, so acute, so direct, so disinterested, so preoccupied but with the fine truth of the case; and the more attaching to me, always, for their referring themselves to a time and an order when we knew together what American life *was*— or thought we did, deluded though we may have been! I don't pretend to measure the effect, or to sound the depths, if they be not the shallows, of the huge wholesale importations and so-called assimilations of this later time; I can only feel and speak for those conditions in which, as "quiet observers," as careful painters, as sincere artists, we could still, in our native, our human and social element, know more or less where we were and feel more or less what we had hold of. You knew and felt these things better than I; you had learnt them earlier and more intimately, and it was impossible, I think, to be in more instinctive and more informed possession of the general truth of your subject than you happily found yourself. The *real* affair of the American case and character, as it met your view and brushed your sensibility, that was what inspired and attached you, and, heedless of foolish flurries from other quarters, of all wild or weak slashings of the air and wavings in the void, you gave yourself to it with an incorruptible faith. You saw your field with a rare lucidity; you saw all it had to give in the way of the romance of the real and the interest and the thrill and the charm of the common, as one may put it; the character and the comedy, the point, the pathos, the tragedy, the particular home-grown humanity under your eyes and your hand and with which the life all about you was closely interknitted. Your hand reached out to these things with a fondness that was in itself a literary gift, and played with them as the artist only and always can play: freely, quaintly, incalculably, with all the assurance of his fancy and his irony, and yet with that fine taste for the truth and the pity and the meaning of the matter which keeps the temper of observation both sharp and sweet. To observe, by such an instinct and by such reflection, is to find work to one's hand and a challenge in every bush; and as the familiar American scene thus bristled about you, so, year by year, your vision more and more justly responded and swarmed. You put forth *A Modern Instance,* and *The Rise of Silas Lapham,* and *A Hazard of New Fortunes,* and *The Landlord at Lion's Head,* and *The Kentons* (that perfectly classic illustration of your spirit and your form,) after having put forth in perhaps lighter-fingered prelude *A Foregone Conclusion,* and *The Undiscovered Country,* and *The Lady of the Aroostock,* and *The Minister's Charge*—to make of a long list too short a one; with the effect, again and again, of a feeling for the human relation, as the social climate of our country qualifies, intensifies, generally conditions and colours it, which, married in perfect felicity to the expression you found for its service, constituted the originality that we want to fasten upon you, as with silver nails, to-night. Stroke by stroke and book by book your work was to become, for this exquisite notation of our whole democratic light and shade and give and take, in the highest degree *documentary;* so that none other, through all your fine long season, could approach it in value and amplitude. None, let me say too, was to approach it in essential distinction; for you had grown master, by insidious practices best known to yourself, of a method so easy and so natural, so marked with the personal element of your humor and the play, not less personal, of your sympathy, that the critic kept coming on its secret connection with the grace of letters much as Fenimore Cooper's Leather-stocking—so knowing to be able to do it!—comes, in the forest, on the subtle tracks of Indian braves. However, these things take us far, and what I wished mainly to put on record is my sense of that unfailing, testifying truth in you which will keep you from ever being neglected. The critical intelligence—if any such fitful and discredited light may still be conceived as within our sphere—has not at all begun to render you its tribute. The more inquiringly and perceivingly it shall still be projected upon the American life we used to know, the more it shall be moved by the analytic and historic spirit, the more indispensable, the more a vessel of light, will you be found. It's a great thing to have used one's genius and done one's work with such quiet and robust consistency that they fall by their own weight into that happy service. You may remember perhaps, and I like to recall, how the great and admirable Taine, in one of the fine excursions of his French curiosity, greeted you as a precious painter and a sovereign witness. But his appreciation, I want you to believe with me, will yet be carried much further, and then—though you may have argued yourself happy, in your generous way and with your incurable optimism, even while noting yourself not understood—your really beautiful time will come. Nothing so much as feeling that he may himself perhaps help a little to bring it on can give pleasure to yours all faithfully,

Henry James.

To WYTTER BYNNER

[undated   ca. 1906]

Dear Witter Bynner.

I have your graceful letter about *The Troll Garden*[1] which duly reached me some time ago (as many appealing works of fiction duly reach me); and if I brazenly confess that I not only haven't yet read it, but haven't even been meaning to (till your words about it thus arrive), I do no more than register the sacred truth. That sacred truth is that, being now almost in my 100th year,[2] with a long and weary experience of such matters behind me, promiscuous fiction has become abhorrent to me, and I find it the hardest thing in the world to read almost *any* new novel. Any is hard enough, but the hardest from the innocent hands of young females, young American females perhaps above all. This is a subject—my battered, cynical, all-too-expert outliving of such possibilities—on which I could be eloquent; but I haven't time, and I will be more vivid and complete some other day. I've only time now to say that I *will* then (in spite of these professions) do my best for Miss Cather—so as not to be shamed by your so doing yours.

Believe me,
Yours ever,
Henry James.

To HUGH WALPOLE

Rye, May 13th, 1910

Dearest, Dearest Hugh,

I have been utterly, but necessarily, silent—so much of the time lately quite too ill to write. Deeply your note touches me,

---

[1] Willa Cather's first volume of tales, *The Troll Garden,* was published in 1905.

[2] James often pictured himself as a centenarian during his last years to emphasize his sense of the great backward reach of his memory. He was at this time actually 63.

as I needn't tell you—and I would give anything to be able to have the free use of your "visible and tangible" affection—no touch of its tangibility but would be dear and helpful to me. But, alas, I am utterly unfit for visits—with the black devils of Nervousness, direst, damnedest demons, that ride me so cruelly and that I have perpetually to reckon with. I am mustering a colossal courage to try—even tomorrow—in my blest sister-in-law's company (without whom and my brother, just now in Paris, I couldn't have struggled on at all) to get away for some days by going to see a kind friend in the country—in Epping Forest. I feel it a most precarious and dangerous undertaking—but my desire and need for change of air, scene and circumstance, after so fearfully overmuch of these imprisoning objects, is so fiercely intense that I am making the push—as to save my life—at any cost. It *may* help me—even much, and the doctor intensely urges it—and if I am able, afterwards (that is if the experiment isn't disastrous,) I shall try to go to 105 Pall Mall for a little instead of coming abjectly back here. Then I shall be able to see you—but all this is fearfully contingent. Meanwhile the sense of your personal tenderness to me, dearest Hugh, is far from not doing much for me. I adore it.

I "read," in a manner, "Maradick"[1]—but there's too much to say about it, and even my weakness doesn't alter me from the grim and battered old *critical* critic—no *other* such creature among all the "reviewers" do I meanwhile behold. Your book has a great sense and love of life—but seems to me very nearly as irreflectively juvenile as the Trojans, and to have the prime defect of your having gone into a subject—i.e. the marital, sexual, bedroom relations of M. and his wife—the literary man and his wife—since these *are* the key to the whole situation—which have to be tackled and faced to mean anything. You don't

1 Walpole's *Maradick at Forty* which had been published at the end of April.

tackle and face them—you *can't.* Also the whole thing is a
monument to the abuse of voluminous dialogue, the absence of
a plan of composition, alternation, distribution, structure, and
other phases of presentation than the dialogue—so that *line*
(the only thing *I* value in a fiction etc.) is replaced by a vast
formless featherbediness—billows in which one sinks and is lost.
And yet it's all so loveable—though not so *written.* It isn't
written *at all,* darling Hugh—by which I mean you have—or,
truly, only in a few places, as in Maradick's dive—never got
expression *tight* and in close quarters (of discrimination, of
specification) with its subject. It remains loose and far. And you
have never made out, recognized, nor stuck to, *the centre of
your subject.* But can you forgive all this to your fondest old
reaching-out-his-arms-to you.

H. J.?

To T. S. PERRY

London, March 18th, 1912

My dear Thomas.

I have two bristling letters from you and your scathing exposure of the Howells dinner does me good and renews my—
well, I won't say my youth but my convictions or several of
them. One of the most irresistible, if not most cherished of these
is that the Great Country *que vous savez* has developed the
genius for vulgarity on a scale to which no other genius for anything anywhere can hold a candle. But what an awful state of
things when a quiet decent honest man like W. D. H. *has* to
think he can't under peril of life, do anything but become part
of the horror. An old friend of mine here, Lucy Clifford (W. K.'s
widow), who was there and at the "high table" and has sent me
a catalogue of the guests which I hang over in the appallment

of fascination—or the fascination of appallment; and which, as she has just returned and I am to see her tonight, she will fill out with hideous detail—though indeed she appears, by a line she wrote me, to have enjoyed, rather the weird desolation of it. I sent (though I say it who shouldn't) a quite beautiful and copious letter[1]—and I'm sorry my fine prose, my really *very* graceful tribute, meant to be read out as an attestation of my long relation with the dear man, was simply shoved aside. As he appears not to have spoken of it to you (on the occasion of your lunching with him,) I am afraid he hadn't himself even seen it. But any lapse of attention or interest is credible on the part of one who has traversed so hideous an experience.

March 21st.

I had to break off the other day, under pressure, and, under the same pressure I haven't been able to take up my pen, as we used to say, till this moment. I saw Lucy Clifford that evening, flushed with a breathless month of observation and agitation in New York (delighted with everything and everyone, and not knowing one of all these from any other,) and she, in her place of pride, took a more genial view of the banquet—though finding the speeches almost incredibly fulsome and undiscriminating, all the speakers talking so extraordinarily "tall" about our friend. Fancy deliberately *stirring up* such an exhibition—pulling with a wanton hand the string to let loose the flood of shame, otherwise for the time confined! Oh objectionable "Colonel"! But let us banish the black vision!—Not that the vision before us here isn't black enough in its different way. We are really overdarkened by the Coal Strike, by which and its consequences a couple of million of people are out of work, a number that will be hugely swelled if it goes on much longer.

---

1 See letter to Howells on p. 160.

To HUGH WALPOLE [*1912*]

But the Government is proceeding very justly, sanely and ably—don't believe anything else if you hear it said in your neighborhood. "Labour" is rising everywhere like a huge Bugaboo, and happy, or fortunate, the country that tackles him first and has it out with him to a practical issue, so far as that may be. And the Women loom monstrous beside him—they are really very wonderful here, and the end is not yet. Hitherto, however, *their* question has only *bored* me to extinction: strangely, it isn't interesting—I don't know, and can't say, why; a *priori* one would say it *would* be—everything else about them is. I give it up—and must give *this* up.

Ever your faithful old Henry James

To HUGH WALPOLE

The Reform Club
May 19th, 1912

Beloved little Hugh,

Your letter greatly moves and regales me. Fully do I enter into your joy of sequestration, and your bliss of removal from this scene of heated turmoil and dusty despair—which, however, re-awaits you! Never mind; sink up to your neck into the brimming basin of nature and peace, and teach yourself—by which I mean let your grandmother teach you—that with each revolving year you will need and make more piously these precious sacrifices to Pan and the Muses. History eternally repeats itself, and I remember well how in the old London years (of *my* old London—*this* isn't that one) I used to clutch at these chances of obscure flight and at the possession, less frustrated, of my soul, my senses and my hours. So keep it up; I miss you, little as I see you even when here (for I *feel* you more than I see you;) but I surrender you at whatever cost to the beneficent powers. Therefore I rejoice in the getting on of your work—how splendidly copious your flow; and am much interested in what you tell me of your readings and your literary emotions. These latter indeed—or some of them, as you express them, I don't think I fully share. At least when you ask me if I don't feel Dostoieffsky's "mad jumble, that flings things down in a heap," nearer truth and beauty than the picking and composing that you instance in Stevenson, I reply with emphasis that I feel nothing of the sort, and that the older I grow and the more I *go* the more sacred to me do picking and composing become—though I naturally don't limit myself to Stevenson's *kind* of the same. Don't let anyone persuade you—there are plenty of ignorant and fatuous duffers to try to do it—that strenuous selection and comparison are not the very essence of art, and that Form *is* [not] substance to that degree that there is absolutely no substance without it. Form alone *takes,* and holds and preserves, substance—saves it from the welter of helpless verbiage that we swim in as in a sea of tasteless tepid pudding, and that makes one ashamed of an art capable of such degradations. Tolstoi and D. are fluid pudding, though not tasteless, because the amount of their own minds and souls in solution in the broth gives it savour and flavour, thanks to the strong, rank quality of their genius and their experience. But there are all sorts of things to be said of them, and in particular that we see how great a vice is their lack of composition, their defiance of economy and architecture, directly they are emulated and imitated; *then,* as subjects of emulation, models, they quite give themselves away. There is nothing so deplorable as a work of art with a *leak* in its interest; and there is no such leak of interest as through commonness of form. Its opposite, the *found* (because the sought-for,) form is the absolute citadel and tabernacle of interest. But what a lecture I am reading you—though a very imper-

[171]

fect one—which you have drawn upon yourself (as moreover it was quite right you should.) But no matter—I shall go for you again—as soon as I find you in a lone corner.

You ask for news of those I "see"; but remember that I see but one person to 99 that you do. A. Bennett I've never to this day beheld—and certain *American* papers of his in *Harper,* of an inordinate platitude of journalistic cheapness, have in truth rather curtailed in me any such disposition. There he writes about what I *know,* and makes me ask myself whether his writing about what I *don't* know mayn't have, after all, that same limitation of value. Lucy Clifford gallantly flourishes—on all fine human and personal lines; Jocelyn P[ersse] continues to adorn a world that is apparently so easy for him. I lately dined and went to a play with him (*Rutherford and Co.,* or whatever, very helpless, but more decent than anything else that's going;) and he was, as ever, sympathy and fidelity incarnate. On the whole, however, I've had very little chance to talk of you. Little May Sinclair drew me to her rather desolately vast blank Albemarle Club to tea—in a dim and dumb literary circle as of pale ink-and-water; but the high tide of blankness submerged us all. *So* blank may the naiads and Ladies of the ink-and-water stream become! I've called on the little Gräfin,[1] but missed her—unconsoledly—or call it inconsolably—as yet. From the great (prose) Minstrel of the Gallery (there's Form for you!) I've had a letter —but this is an instance that I must wait to impart to you at leisure: it has *such* a harmony with—everything else! Well, dearest Hugh, love me a little better (if you can,) for this letter, for I am ever so fondly and faithfully

Yours
Henry James

[1] Gräfin Arnim, better known as "Elizabeth," author of *Elizabeth and Her German Garden.*

To HAMLIN GARLAND

January 24, 1914

Dear Hamlin Garland:

I am afraid I don't agree with you that autographed material odds and ends of writers have anything whatever to do with a "keeping up the best literary traditions," those signatured superfluities seeming to me today to be the only parts of "literature" in which the least interest is shown—surely a very sorry state of things. And yet I am with weak amiability sending you a signed photograph for your collection. I can't send you a page of MS. My stuff is done over and over, copied and recopied, till a final immaculate and inscrutable typed result is sent to the printer—with the "states" on the way to it then all consumed by fire. My publishers tell me I send them "ideal" copy. Therefore I *have* no manuscript—for the impersonal mechanic expanse, however full of my thought (which the printed page is) is wholly disconnected from my "hand." I really haven't anything (I won't say decent but) *in*decent enough for interest, and I am yours all faithfully

Henry James

P.S. The largeish photog. goes apart from this.

To HENRY ADAMS

London, March 21, 1914.

My dear Henry,

I have your melancholy outpouring of the 7th, and I know not how better to acknowledge it than by the full recognition of its unmitigated blackness. *Of course* we are lone survivors, of course the past that was our lives is at the bottom of an abyss— if the abyss *has* any bottom; of course, too, there's no use talking unless one particularly *wants* to. But the purpose, almost, of my

printed divagations[1] was to show you that one *can,* strange to
say, still want to—or at least can behave as if one did. Behold
me therefore so behaving—and apparently capable of continu-
ing to do so. I still find my consciousness interesting—under
cultivation of the interest. Cultivate it *with* me, dear Henry—
that's what I hoped to make you do—to cultivate yours for all
that it has in common with mine. *Why* mine yields an interest
I don't know that I can tell you, but I don't challenge or quarrel
with it—I encourage it with a ghastly grin. You see I still, in
presence of life (or of what you deny to be such,) have reactions
—as many as possible—and the book I sent you is a proof of
them. It's, I suppose because I am that queer monster, the artist,
an obstinate finality, an inexhaustible sensibility. Hence the
reactions—appearances, memories, many things, go on playing
upon it with consequences that I note and "enjoy" (grim word!)
noting. It all takes doing—and I *do.* I believe I shall do yet
again—it is still an act of life. But you perform them still yourself—and I don't know what keeps me from calling your letter
a charming one! There we are, and it's a blessing that you
understand—I admit indeed alone—your all-faithful

Henry James

To ANNE THACKERAY RITCHIE

London, June 30, 1914.

Dearest Anne,

Admirable old friend and illustrious confrère!

It is altogether delightful to think that this happy thought of
your likeness being 'took' by our all-responsive and all-ready
Sargent is on the way to be effectively arranged, for such a Pub-

---

[1] The second volume of James's reminiscences. *Notes of a Son and Brother,*
just published.

lic Treasure shall the work appear destined to become, if all goes well with it.

The happy thought sprang up in the breasts of the Protheros —to them alone I more than suspect belongs the grace of having first thrown it off. I doubt whether it will seem wise to invite you to take your place on the sitter's throne before the autumn —the reason of this being that all your friends of every size and shape ought to have the chance to join in the demonstration according to their ability. I have taken the liberty of urging that consideration out of the depth of my own experience—my heart was so wrung by the plaints of those who had not been notified by my two or three acting friends when Sargent turned out my simulacrum! The lament of those who had been unknowingly over-looked distressed me almost more than the pleasure of the others gratified; and I should wish for you that everyone without exception who would like to add a pebble to your cairn, shall have been communicated with; which is in course of being seen about.

I rejoice for you meanwhile that you are not sweltering with us here in the heavy Cockney heat, but sitting, I hope, in the flutter of the Porch, and getting better of the indisposition of which you speak. Porches and airy flutters do me more good than anything in the world when I (more ponderously) droop— and even as I write this I am almost hanging out of my fourth floor window into the stuffy darkness of our Thames-side, praying for a stir in the night that doesn't come. Don't exchange your headland over the deep for this sorry state without due circumspection. You have written me a most beautiful and touching note, and only this hell-broth of the great London Social Pot has kept me from thanking you for it more instantly.

Have patience with us all and believe me your stoutest and fondest old adherent.   Henry James

[175]

(ii)

The following letters reveal James in various attitudes of friendship: one letter might be titled "Advice to a Lady on Sitting for her Portrait to Mr. Sargent;" another, "Advice to a Young Frenchman Acquiring the English Tongue." They show the novelist in his devotion to Frances Anne Kemble, at whose fireside he sat for many evenings during the last fifteen years of her life, or performing elaborate gallantries in words for a life-long friend, the homely, auburn-haired American spinster, Henrietta Reubell, who had a salon in Paris and whom he had known and liked from his earliest years abroad. And we find him paying moving tribute to the dead—the dead who inspired one of the most remarkable tales of his middle years, *The Altar of the Dead.*

There was a younger generation, too, that he cultivated assiduously. He had his responsibilities as a godfather to, say, the grandson of George du Maurier, or as a kind of friendly father to young Jocelyn Persse, whose spelling he corrected but whose social gossip he relished. And we can observe him, with ponderous affection, trying to convey to a young American sculptor, Hendrik Andersen, the idea, to which he always held, that the artist must face reality and not lose himself in grandiose day-dreams.

On another level we can listen to him describing life in Ireland to Mrs. "Jack" Gardner; or advising the Duchess of Sutherland how to read *The Ambassadors.* In all these letters we discover the boundless energy of the novelist, his interest in persons, in places, in what was happening in the immediate world around him.

To HENRIETTA REUBELL

> *Avignon, Hotel de l'Europe*
> *Oct. 28th.* [*1882*]

Dear Miss Reubell.

I have a certain idea *que vous m'en voulez—que vous me tenez même rigueur*—because I didn't come and dance a hornpipe on your plage Bretonne; and it is for this reason that I put forth a little feeler before I return to Paris—an incident now on the point of occurring. I wish to approach you with a degree of tact equal to my eagerness, and to bid you *bon jour*—to begin and bid it—three hundred miles off. I smile agreeably—I bow till my nose dips into the Rhône, which is in the streets of Avignon—I hold my hat in one hand and press the other to my heart. If *toutes ces manières* don't appease your first resentment I shall have to try and think it over and *trouver encore mieux.* I know they will succeed with Mrs. Boit! I have been making a grand voyage through all the Midi de la France, on purpose to collect impressions and anecdotes to entertain you two ladies. This has been my exclusive aim, and in the pursuit of it I have not shrunk from exposing my delicate person to the severest hardships, the most uncomfortable contacts and the dirtiest table clothes. *J'ai vécu de la vie de commis-voyageur—quoi!* Today for instance I have visited the romantic Vaucluse, sometime the residence of the celebrated Petrarch, and seen the Sorgues tumbling out of a stupendous cliff surrounded with rocks painted over with the names of 10,000 contemporary beasts—who have written them themselves. All our rivers are swollen to a fearful volume dans le Midi and I have walked about this evening to see the Rhône, looking five miles wide, in a magnificent moonlight, frighten these good people with the idea that tomorrow it will be in their streets. I sincerely hope not, though if I am inundated here I shall have better entertainment than ever for you and Mrs. Boit, who will perhaps subscribe to have me rescued. If I am rescued in time I start northwards tomorrow, and shall arrive in Paris in the course of next week. *J'ai vu beaucoup de choses,* and have examined in detail the beautiful France. I am ready to describe it to you in such detail as you may desire. I suppose you are long since recocknefied and I hope to find you, when I am ushered panting into your presence, in health, in happiness, and in spirits. I greet very kindly your dear mother, and remain your tout devoué

H. James jr.

To FANNY KEMBLE

Bellosguardo, Florence.
May 20th [1887]

Beloved Mrs. Kemble,

I wonder if you could very kindly give me a sort of notion of how you expect to proceed in Switzerland during the first half of your summer: I don't mean in the least in rigid detail—but in the main outline? I am staying in this sweet country so late that I should miss you if I were to go back to London now, and nothing would induce me to do that—I mean, to miss you. Neither do I find myself easily persuadable to return at present. I am waiting for the summer—and we don't have it yet. When it comes, I shall stop a little longer to enjoy it, and then I shall cross the Alps and jump down upon you. In other words, wherever you may be I will come to you and spend as many days as possible near you. I can't say now exactly when this will be— as I go back to Venice on the 25th of this month and the length of my stay there is uncertain. When the first *very* hot weather comes I shall probably take to my heels. Florence is lovely—and all the country about—to every sense but the sudorific; by which I mean that it isn't yet half warm enough. This remark will confirm your conviction that I am a salamander—but I ain't. I am only an American. We are just emerging from nearly three *weeks* (figgery-voo!) of fêtes à propos of the completion and unveiling of the famous front of the Duomo here—in the course of which I had the fatuity to assume a quattro-cento dress (of scarlet and black) and go to a very brilliant costumed ball that was given to the King and Queen in a wonderful tapestried hall of the Palazzo Vecchio here. I wish you could have seen me— I was lovely! We had also an historical procession in which the Florentine nobles of the present day (Strozzis, Guicciardinis, Gherardescas, &c.) represented, in accurate and splendid array, their medieval ancestors. This was really magnificent and inter- esting—the dresses, horses, trappings, &c. and the figures of the actors, &c. very noble and artistic. We have also had Rhoda Broughton and Hamilton Aidé—who, however, both departed before the best of the show began. You will have seen the latter and heard his adventures. Those of Miss Broughton, here, were, I think, happy—and liking her (in spite of her roughness) already, I liked her still more for liking Florence so much. She quite came up to my standard of appreciation. All this time I haven't thanked you for your last letter—of now nearly a month ago. But it is hard to thank you for telling me your gout was at that time so bad—though I should have appreciated still less your not letting me know it. I devoutly pray you may have been better since—though I gather that there has been small comfort in the season to make you so. I saw Mrs. Lockwood[1] two or three weeks ago—she had come out here for a month, from New York (not by way of England, but by a French or German steamer) to stay in Florence or elsewhere, with a certain queer English friend of hers, Miss Bianca Light; and she gave me very recent and very happy news of Mrs. Wister.[2] She said she had *never* seen her so well, so active and so little knocked up by her activity. Write to me only at your leisure, dear Mrs. Kemble (always to 34 De Vere Gardens,) and I will conduct myself accordingly. I haven't seen Thackeray's letters—but I *do* see Mrs. Procter's own,[3] as she is so good as sometimes to write to me. What a capacity for *caring*—taking sides, resenting, &c! I don't see why, when one *minds* as much as that, one shouldn't live for ever. Yours always affectionate

Henry James

To LADY CONSTANCE LESLIE

London, March 10th [*1888*]

Dear Lady Constance,

I helped to consign our very remarkable old friend[1] to her last resting-place yesterday morning. It was fortunately mild and moist (yet without rain) and the whole long pilgrimage to Kensal Green was less lugubrious and dreary than I have sometimes seen it. I went in a carriage with Browning and there were a great many people there—almost all her old friends. It would have pleased her to know that she had a large following and that

---

1 A prominent figure in New York society and friend of Mrs. Kemble's daughter, Sarah.

2 Sarah Butler Wister, daughter of Mrs. Kemble.

3 The aged Anne Benson Procter, widow of Barry Cornwall, who had known nearly all the great English poets and novelists from Shelley to Browning.

1 On the occasion of the death of Mrs. Procter.

she passed away like a person of importance. She was buried in the Protestant Cemetery, but at a remote edge of it—where it touches the Catholic—to be near her daughter Edith. This settled the question of her faith—so far as she had any—for I had always vaguely supposed that she had quietly embraced the Catholic. But a person who knew told me that she had said almost on her deathbed that the adoration of the Virgin was, for her, an insurmountable stumbling-block and she had not that exalted idea of her sex! She was much harassed, I fear, by her infirmities and the nature of her malady, till within half an hour of the end, that is she struggled and suffered. It was a difficult physical extinction. Morally I am sure she had accepted it from the moment she saw it was really inevitable—but not before. Then when the end was definitely in view, she found out she really *was* weary (though she hadn't admitted it even to herself) and that the idea of rest was good to her. I saw her about three weeks before she died; she was very pathetic—it was such an image of defeat—almost of humiliation. I shall miss her greatly, for I saw her often and she was always fresh. I saw her often sad and bitter—but never dull, never common or commonplace. And then she was so historical. She was a kind of window in the past—now it's closed there is so much less air.

I hope Ireland is sympathetic just now; London is wet and blowy, but there is a look of spring in the light and even a feeling of it in the March wind. But bring the reality with you when you come.

Believe me, dear Lady Leslie, ever faithfully yours

Henry James

To LAURA WAGNIÈRE

London S.W.
March 10th, 1888

Dear Madame Wagnière,

I don't think I know! Your curiosity is communicative and it makes me wish immensely I did.

But that isn't part of the story[1]—what Mrs. Pallant said to the young man. It was something pretty bad of course to make him give up, but the particular thing is a secondary affair whether it were true or whether it were false. The primary affair is that she told him something, no matter what—which *did* make him give up. The primary affair is also the nature and the behaviour of the lovely and inscrutable Linda. She thought Linda a monster of secret worldliness and in a fit of exaltation and penitence over her own former shabby conduct, wished to do something heroic and sacrificial to repair her reputation with her old lover. Therefore she abused the girl affectionately to his amorous nephew, but I have no light on what she said. She may have told him that she had been not as young ladies should be, but if she did I incline to think the statement was false. Linda was too careful of her future to have sacrificed to that extent to the present, and too little likely to have got into a mess that didn't pay—of course as you suggest (so sagaciously) it *might* have paid, and they were hard up etc.—But it wouldn't have paid in comparison with keeping straight and marrying with patience— a lord or a millionaire. Yet I admit they were very hard up and that the thing *was* possible.

If it *had* happened, however, I think Mrs. P. would not, even in her exaltation have mentioned it: whereas she might have

---

[1] In James's story "Louisa Pallant," Louisa, mother of Linda Pallant, is so horrified by the calculating coldness of her daughter that she warns a suitor against her. James does not relate, however, what she said to him. Mme. Wagnière, a friend of many years, wrote to the novelist to find out.

done so if it were false. Do you understand? You see, I have in the story told you all I can for the money. I am as ignorant as you, and yet not as supposing!

It was charming to hear from you. I wish it were sight as well as sound. I shall pray for that and am ever faithfully yours

Henry James

I shall myself thank your mother for her delightful and generous letter.

To SARAH WISTER

34, De Vere Gardens, W.
Jan. 20th 1893

Dear Mrs. Wister,

I have just written to Mrs. Leigh, and she may send you my letter—but I must speak to you a direct, and very old friend's word. I stood by your mother's grave[1] this morning—a soft, kind, balmy day, with your brother-in-law and tall pale handsome Alice, and a few of those of her friends who have survived her, and were in town, and were not ill—as all the world lately has been. The number is inevitably small for of her generation she is the last, and she had made no new friends, naturally, for these last years. She was laid in the same earth as her father— and buried under a mountain of flowers—which *I* don't like— but which many people, most people do. It was all bright, somehow, and public and slightly pompous. I thought of you and Mrs. Leigh[2] "far away on the billow," as it were—and hoped you felt, with us here, the great beneficence and good fortune of

1 Fanny Kemble had died at 83 on January 15th. Shortly thereafter James published a long essay of tribute to her and included it in his *Essays in London* (1893).
2 Mrs. Leigh, like Mrs. Wister, was a daughter of Fanny Kemble.

your mother's instantaneous and painless extinction. Everything of the condition at the last, that she had longed for was there—and nothing that she had dreaded was. And the devotion of her old restored maid, Mrs. Brianzoni, appears to have been absolute—of every moment and of every hour. She stood there this morning with a very white face and her hands full of flowers. Your mother looked, after death, extraordinarily like her sister. Indeed the resemblance to Leighton's last drawing of Mrs. Sartoris[3] was *complete*. I mention these things—to bring everything a little nearer to you. I am conscious of a strange bareness and a kind of evening chill as it were in the air, as if some great object that had filled it for long had left an emptiness—from displacement—to all the senses. It seemed—this morning—her lying to rest—not but that I think, I must frankly say, the act of *burial* anything but inacceptably horrible, a hideous old imposition of the church—it seemed quite like the end of some reign or the fall of some empire. But she wanted to go—and she went when she could, at last, without a pang. She was very touching in her infirmity all these last months—and yet with her wonderful air of smoldering embers under ashes. She leaves a great image—a great memory. I have greatly regretted to hear lately that you have not been well. Please receive, dear Mrs. Wister, all my sympathy—all my participation, which though far is not faint, in everything which touches you closely—and believe me when I say that I hope you will look upon me ever as your very constant old friend

Henry James.

---

[3] The former Adelaide Kemble, Fanny's sister.

To W. MORTON FULLERTON

Ramsgate, July 14 [1893]

My dear Fullerton.

No, I'm not a brute for having failed so long to thank you for the good offices, proffered at least, of your last letter and for the touching two words you had the friendly thought of sending me when the indignity that life had heaped upon poor Maupassant found itself stayed.[1] I wanted moreover to applaud your energy and vivacity during the journées de juin and the art with which you brought internecine warfare home to us. But not till this hour, as ever is, have I been sufficiently my master to thank you for these luxuries. The detail of my servitude would not interest you; but knowing my feeble powers of resistance you will believe in the fact. I don't know what prevented my wiring you a crystalline tear to drop on Maupassant's grave. Or rather, I do. Everything prevented it, including the fact that my tears had been already wept; even though the image of that history had been too *hard* for such droppings. I have taken refuge from the abominations and over-populations of London in this refined retreat, where there is no one I know—no one but 'Arry and his female, who don't know me—or at least pretend they don't, a delicacy of which Mayfair is incapable. *J'y suis, j'y reste.* It was very good of you to offer to send me the last distillation of Bourget, and the last chunk of Zola.[2] They lie at present on my intellectual board. What won't the French write about next? Strange are the loves of a sick sexagenarian and his niece. Yet I love my Zola. Also my Fullerton, and am his ever

Henry James

1 Maupassant had died on July 6.
2 The Bourget novel was *Un Scrupule.* Zola's novel was *Le Docteur Pascal* of the Rougon-Macquart series.

To MRS. MAHLON SANDS

London [*1894*]

Dear Mrs. Sands.

I meant to delay less to answer your two interesting notes; but even now that I *am* scrawling a few lines to you I feel that my *matter* so overflows my space, and time, that abstention is almost the line most practicable. I want to give you a bushel of good advice, in short—advice about the supreme wisdom, in a situation like yours, or the policy of self-surrender to the artist—that of giving him his head and letting him utterly alone. Trust him completely and ask no questions. "Go love me not at all or all in all." From the moment one trusts him enough to ask for a portrait at all—trust him enough to leave him his ways, his variations, his mysteries and circumgyrations and idiosyncracies. You can't keep step with him and you can't assist at the process. You can't collaborate or co-operate, except by sitting still and looking beautiful, in your own portrait. You are outside of it altogether and you will—you always *must*—consult the highest interest of the result by preserving this perfectly helpless and detached attitude!! Cultivate indifference, cultivate not looking at it nor thinking about it. Don't challenge him by the way and give him a tremendous margin. It's *his* affair—yours is only to be as difficult for him as possible; and the more difficult you are the more the artist (worthy of the name), will be condemned to worry over you, repainting, revolutionizing, till he, in a rage of ambition and admiration, arrives at the thing that satisfies him and that enshrines and perpetuates you. There are as good eyes on his palette as ever were caught and yours, on Sargent's canvas, will still be the mystification of posterity, just as they often are that of yours most didactically

Henry James

To URBAIN MENGIN

London, November 27th. 1894.

Mon cher ami.

Please believe that I am touched by the really angelic generosity of your beautiful letter. I have neglected you brutally, though only by the cruelly perverse force of things—of things independent of my will; and yet your charity still has kind thoughts of me and your admirable pen beautiful accents as well as perfections more formal, even though microscopic. I have been so long silent simply because I had arrived at a crisis bringing it home to me that either I or my correspondence must perish—so I let it go to save my own life. But this same silence left me leisure to think of you, to wonder what your fortune had been and to hope it was proving in some degree congruous with your ambition.[1] Now you tell me, and though I am sorry to hear of your philosophic discouragements I rejoice in your return to our poor dear patient old language, because it brings you nearer to me again and seems to furnish me with a presumption that we shall meet once more. This time you must keep well hold of your English—you must not give it up. You will find much to do with it—only you must *live* with it if you expect it to live with you. One's own language is one's mother, but the language one adopts, as a career, as a study, is one's wife, and it is with one's wife that *on se met en ménage.* English is a very faithful and well-conducted person, but she will expect you too not to commit infidelities. On these terms

[1] Urbain Mengin, a young French scholar-poet, and friend of Paul Bourget, had called on Henry James in 1887 when at the age of twenty-three he went to England to teach French and study English. He was made welcome on many occasions at 34 De Vere Gardens. A devoted student of the Romantic poets, he later took a walking tour through Italy visiting all the scenes that had figured in the lives of Byron, Shelley and Keats and wrote his dissertation on *L'Italie des Romantiques.* When this letter was written Mengin was teaching English in the Lycée d'Albi.

she will keep your house well. I am afraid you have had some dark hours and many dismal thoughts—have been, in short through rather a cruel experience. But renouncement is the larger half of success and one's mistakes the best part of one's certitude. Read, read, read, and speak to your pupils from a full and easy mind. Know more than they want to know—for if you only knew as much you would know nothing. Work for the day when you can come back to London. It will be a much better and more fruitful visit than your last. I am glad Bourget advises and assists you. A man so intelligent and so sagacious can't *touch* you without giving you something. I can't talk to you of myself —save in a very superficial sense—I am utterly unable, always, to speak of what I am "doing"—for when I speak of it I seem to expose it to some hard profaning light; even when I speak to an ear as receptive as yours. If it were of importance you would hear of it—and you must believe in me on general grounds. To give up Greek and Greece—that must indeed have been a sorrow; but it is something—a great deal—to have loved such things enough to weep for them. Weep no more—but work and live and love, rejoice in your charming mind and your delicate soul and believe in the pleasure with which I see them reflected in what you write to me. Whenever London again becomes possible to you write a word in advance to yours, my dear Mengin, very faithfully   Henry James.

To MRS. ROBERT LOUIS STEVENSON

[*Dec. 1894*]

My dear Fanny Stevenson,

What can I say to you that will not seem cruelly irrelevant or vain? We have been sitting in darkness for nearly a fortnight,[1]

---

1 Robert Louis Stevenson had died in Samoa on December 3, 1894.

but what is *our* darkness to the extinction of your magnificent light? You will probably know in some degree what has happened to us—how the hideous news first came to us via Auckland, etc., and then how, in the newspapers, a doubt was raised about its authenticity—just enough to give one a flicker of hope; until your telegram to me via San Francisco—repeated also from other sources—converted my pessimistic convictions into the wretched knowledge. All this time my thoughts have hovered round you all, around *you* in particular, with a tenderness of which I could have wished you might have, afar-off, the divination. You are such a visible picture of desolation that I need to remind myself that courage, and patience, and fortitude are also abundantly with you. The devotion that Louis inspired —and of which all the air about you must be full—must also be much to you. Yet as I write the word, indeed, I am almost ashamed of it—as if anything could be 'much' in the presence of such an abysmal void. To have lived in the light of that splendid life, that beautiful, bountiful being—only to see it, from one moment to the other, converted into a fable as strange and romantic as one of his own, a thing that *has* been and has ended, is an anguish into which no one can enter with you fully and of which no one can drain the cup for you. You are nearest to the pain, because you were nearest the joy and the pride. But if it is anything to you to know that no woman was ever more felt *with* and that your personal grief is the intensely personal grief of innumerable hearts—know it well, my dear Fanny Stevenson, for during all these days there has been friendship for you in the very air. For myself, how shall I tell you how much poorer and shabbier the whole world seems, and how one of the closest and strongest reasons for going on, for trying and doing, for planning and dreaming of the future, has dropped in an instant out of life. I was haunted indeed with a sense that I should

never again see him—but it was one of the best things in life
that he was *there,* or that one had him—at any rate one heard
him, and felt him and awaited him and counted him into everything one most loved and lived for. He lighted up one whole
side of the globe, and was in himself a whole province of one's
imagination. We are smaller fry and meaner people without
him. I feel as if there were a certain indelicacy in saying it to
you, save that I know that there is nothing narrow or selfish in
your sense of loss—for himself, however, for his happy name
and his great visible good fortune, it strikes one as another
matter. I mean that I feel him to have been as happy in his
death (struck down that way, as by the gods, in a clear, glorious
hour) as he had been in his fame. And, with all the sad allowances in his rich full life, he had the best of it—the thick of the
fray, the loudest of the music, the freshest and finest of himself.
It isn't as if there had been no full achievement and no supreme
thing. It was all intense, all gallant, all exquisite from the first,
and the experience, the fruition, had something dramatically
complete in them. He has gone in time not to be old, early
enough to be so generously young and late enough to have
drunk deep of the cup. There have been—I think—for men of
letters few deaths more romantically right. Forgive me, I beg
you, what may sound cold-blooded in such words—or as if I
imagined there could be anything for you 'right' in the rupture
of such an affection and the loss of such a presence. I have in my
mind in that view only the rounded career and the consecrated
work. When I think of your own situation I fall into a mere
confusion of pity and wonder, with the sole sense of your being
as brave a spirit as he was (all of whose bravery you shared) to
hold on by. Of what solutions or decisions you see before you
we shall hear in time; meanwhile please believe that I am most
affectionately with you. . . . More than I can say. I hope your

first prostration and bewilderment are over, and that you are feeling your way in feeling all sorts of encompassing arms—all sorts of outstretched hands of friendship. Don't my dear Fanny Stevenson, be unconscious of *mine,* and believe me more than ever faithfully yours,

Henry James

To ISABELLA STEWART GARDNER

Royal Hospital, Dublin.
March 23d, 1895.

Dear Isabella Gardner,

Yes, I have delayed hideously to write to you, since receiving your note of many days ago. But I always delay hideously, and my shamelessness is rapidly becoming (in the matter of letter-writing) more disgraceful even than my procrastination. I brought your letter with me to Ireland more than a fortnight ago with every intention of answering it on the morrow of my arrival; but I have been leading here a strange and monstrous life of demoralization and frivolity and the fleeting hour has mocked, till today, at my languid effort to stay it, to clutch it, in its passage. I have been paying three monstrous visits in a row; and if I needed any further demonstration of the havoc such things make in my life I should find it in this sense of infidelity to a charming friendship of so many years.

I return to England to enter a monastery for the rest of my days—and crave your forgiveness before I take this step. I have been staying in this queer, shabby, sinister, sordid place (I mean Dublin), with the Lord Lieutenant (poor young Lord Houghton), for what is called (a fragment, that is, of what is called) the "Castle Season," and now I am domesticated with very kind and valued old friends, the Wolseleys—Lord W. being commander of the forces here (that is, head of the little English army of occupation in Ireland—a five-year appointment) and domiciled in this delightfully quaint and picturesque old structure, of Charles II's time—a kind of Irish Invalides or Chelsea Hospital—a retreat for superannuated veterans, out of which a commodious and stately residence has been carved. We live side by side with the 140 old red-coated cocked-hatted pensioners— but with a splendid great rococo hall separating us, in which Lady Wolseley gave the other night the most beautiful ball I have ever seen—a fancy-ball in which all the ladies were Sir Joshuas, Gainsboroughs, or Romneys, and all the men in uniform, court dress or evening hunt dress. (*I* went as—guess what! —alas, nothing smarter than the one black coat in the room.) It is a world of generals, aide-de-camps and colonels, of military colour and sentinel-mounting, which amuses for the moment and makes one reflect afresh that in England those who *have* a good time have it with a vengeance. The episode at that tarnished and ghost-haunted Castle was little to my taste, and was a very queer episode indeed—thanks to the incongruity of a vice-regal "court" (for that's what it considers itself) utterly boycotted by Irish (landlord) society—the present viceroy being the nominee of a home-rule government, and reduced to dreary importation from England to fill its gilded halls. There was a ball every night, etc., but too much standing on one's hind-legs —too much pomp and state—for nothing and nobody. On my return (two days hence) to my humble fireside I get away again as quickly as possible into the country—to a cot beside a rill, the address of which no man knoweth. There I remain for the next six months to come; and nothing of any sort whatever is to happen to me (this is all arranged,) save that you are to come down and stay a day or two with me when you come to England. There is, alas, to be no "abroad" for me this year. I rejoice with you in *your* Rome—but my Rome is in the buried past. I spent, however, last June there, and was less excruciated than I feared. Have you seen my old friend Giuseppe Primoli—a great friend, in particular, of the Bourgets? I dare say you have breakfasted deep with him. May this find you perched on new conquests. It's vain to ask you to write me, or tell me, anything. Let me only ask you therefore to believe me your very affectionate old friend, Henry James

To GUY HOYER MILLAR

Rye [*1897*]

My dear Godson Guy,[1]

I learned from your mother, by pressing her hard, some time ago that it would be a convenience to you and a great help in your career to possess an Association football—whereupon, in my desire that you should receive the precious object from no hand but mine I cast about me for the proper place to procure it. But I am living for the present in a tiny, simpleminded country town, where luxuries are few and football shops unheard of, so I was a long time getting a clue that would set me on the right road. Here at last, however, is the result of my terribly belated endeavour. It goes to you by parcel post—not, naturally, in this letter. I am awfully afraid I haven't got one of the right size: if so, and you will let me know, you shall have a better one next time. I am afraid I don't *know* much about the sorts and sizes since they've all been invented since I was of football age. I'm an awful muff, too, at games—except at times I am not a bad cyclist, I think—and I fear I am only rather decent at playing at godfather. Some day you must come down and see me here and I'll do in every way the best I can for you.

1 Guy Millar, grandson of George du Maurier.

You shall have lots of breakfast and dinner and tea—not to speak of lunch and anything you like in between—and I won't ask you a single question about a single one of your studies, but if you think that is because I can't—because I don't know enough—I *might* get up subjects on purpose.

Your most affectionate Godfather,

Henry James.

To THE DUCHESS OF SUTHERLAND

Rye, Dec. 23rd 1903

My dear Duchess,

I fear there is little chance this will reach you on Christmas Day in your remote stronghold, but let it take you none the less my warmest Christmas greetings and my lively appreciation of the kindness of your charming letter about your dear W[illiam] W[etmore] S[tory] and my effort to perform in that record, in a manner, the operation of making bricks without straw and chronicking (sometimes) rather small beer with the effect of opening champagne. Story was the dearest of men, but he wasn't massive, his artistic and literary baggage were of the slightest and the materials for a biography *nil.*—However (once I had succumbed to the amiable pressure of his children,) I had really to *invent* a book, patching the thing together and eking it out with barefaced irrelevancies—starting above all *any* hare, however small, that might lurk by the way. It is very pleasant to get from a discriminating reader the token that I have carried the trick through. But the magic is but scantly mine, and it is really that of the beloved old Italy, who always will consent to fling a glamour for you, whenever you speak her fair.

It's ill news, however, that you have been ill, though if I brightened an hour of that I shall not have laboured, as they say, in vain. I don't know that you make in Scotland as much of Christmas as we make—say, at Rye—perhaps because if you *did* make much your machinery of mirth (by which I mean your war-dances and frolic pipings generally) might bring down the vault of heaven. But I trust you are able by this time to face, bravely, whatever demonstrations the discretion of the national character permits.

Take, meanwhile pray, the *Ambassadors* very easily and gently: read five pages a day—be even as deliberate as that—but *don't break the thread.* The thread is really stretched quite scientifically tight. Keep along with it step by step—and then the full charm will come out. I *want* the charm, you see, to come out for you—so convinced am I that it's there! Besides, I find that the very most difficult thing in the art of the novelist is to give the impression and illusion of the real *lapse of time, the quantity* of time, represented by our poor few phrases and pages, and all the drawing-out the reader can contribute helps a little perhaps the production of that spell. I am delighted meanwhile to hear that you are to be in town a little later on. I go up next month—some time—to stay a goodish many weeks, and nothing will make me feel more justified of my adventure than the great pleasure of seeing you. Perhaps you will then even tell me more about the composition you have been busy with— there are literary confidences that I am capable of rejoicing in. But I shall rejoice more to know that health and strength possess you and that they dedicate you to a secure and prosperous New Year. I invoke a friendly benediction on all your house, and am, my dear Duchess,

Yours very cordially and constantly
Henry James

To JOCELYN PERSSE[1]

Very dear Jocelyn.

It breaks my heart to have had to wait a little to make you a sign of response to your note. But I have been furiously pressed finishing some work and tidying up my situation a little before making an absence here of some duration (pressed catching the American post of today really,) and as every half hour has made a difference I have been distressfully sacrificing you. My packet went off before dinner today, and though I am face to face now with 15 letters, and an imminent renewal of my job, I clutch my pen of friendship and with it in my hand, give you, very affectionately, the *accolade* for the New Year. (If you don't know what accolade—which I ought not to have underlined—means, look it up in the Dictionary!) I come up to town on Tuesday Feb. 5th—mark the Date—and hereby invoke your company for *Major Barbara* (with me) on the 7th. p.m. (No, I mean *Wednesday 6th,* p.m.) if you haven't already, or shan't have by that time, seen it too damned often. Will you let me know if you have—and keep away from it as much as possible meanwhile? It will be an old story in London by that time— must be in fact already, but I, you see, have had no opportunity of beholding it. I was in town for 48 crowded and fleeting hours on my way back from a rather outstretched and very tranquil and convenient Christmastide at Brighton. I came quickly back here to put in this very necessary interval before returning there for a longish stay. Forgive my hurling so many hard hit-

---

1 Jocelyn Persse was a Persse of Galway and a relative of the Irish dramatist, Lady Gregory. A dandy in Edwardian London, he was a great social resource to the novelist who invariably sought him out on coming up from Rye to enjoy his vivid talk and the latest social gossip of the drawing-rooms he could no longer frequent. Sir Shane Leslie, Persse's friend of many years, has called him "one of the last gentlemen."

ting little china pots at your unfortunate head, or rather at your beautiful chin; it is too absurd. But the little history was that I wanted, extremely, being in town, to put my hand on some object that I could send you as a New Year's offering (I having been, during the time precedent to Christmas, remote from the arts and the places;) but during a rapid, too hurried look round I beheld but the mere residuum, as it seemed to me, of superfluous rot; whereupon I said to myself: "Go to, I wont pick up on the run some base object that he doesn't want, but will wait till I see him, and then artfully discover if there be not some convenient accessory that he does desire and lack—which I will then most officiously thrust upon him." Such is my belated purpose still; so think it obligingly over. Meanwhile the little shaving pots are but a prosaic stopgap. So good night my dear boy. I spell it cunningly out that things are decently well with you. I hope this odious looking little 1906 announces itself, the vile brat, goodnaturedly enough to the individual Jocelyn. It is very vacant and very moist and very mild here; but I think it must be very good for me, for the weeks dash by like motor cars breaking the law (and their inmates' necks.) We will also visit the French Comedy. Go you meanwhile to see Jonathan Sturges[2] at Long's: He asked about you the other day with interest and desire; and he is wretchedly unwell there and laid up with a nurse. But he sees people at times, and the best hours are the afternoon. Try him, at any rate, and if he isn't well enough, or whatever, try again. (He *can't* go out.) I renew the accolade. Yours, my dear Jocelyn, always—and ever

Henry James.

2 Sturges, a New Yorker, graduate of Princeton, had been a cripple from childhood. Between bouts of illness he wrote essays, translated French writers, and was admired for his wit and personal charm by such friends as James, Whistler, and the French Symbolists whom he came to know through Francis Vielé-Griffin and Stuart Merrill.

To JOCELYN PERSSE

Rye, Sussex. Monday p.m.

My dear Jocelyn,

This is but a poor word, omitted three days ago, very stupidly, to say that I have written to have a copy of *The Ambassadors* sent you—every copy I have succeeded in being possessed of here having successively melted away. Don't write to 'thank' me for it—but if you are able successfully to struggle with it try to like the poor old hero, in whom you will perhaps find a vague resemblance (though not facial!) to your always

Henry James.

To HENDRIK ANDERSEN

London, April 14th. 1912

Dearest Hendrik,[1]

Not another day do I delay to answer (with such difficulty!) your long and interesting letter. I have waited these ten days or so just *because* of the difficulty: so little (as you may imagine or realize on thinking a little) is it a soft and simple matter to stagger from under such an avalanche of information and announcement as you let drop on me with this terrific story of your working so in the colossal and in the void and in the air! Brace yourself for my telling you that (*having*, these days, scrambled a little from under the avalanche) I now, staggering to my feet

---

1 Hendrik Andersen, a distant relative of Hans Christian Andersen, was raised in America, and at the turn of the century went to Rome where he became a sculptor. James met him in 1899, liked him, purchased one of his busts, and encouraged him in his artistic career. The novelist's correspondence with Andersen belongs to the same order as the letters to Jocelyn Persse and Hugh Walpole. While most of the letters to Andersen tend to be "twaddle," a few help define James's attitude toward the realities of art and the artistic career. Andersen was always designing enormous fountains and large groups of nudes for which, James kept telling him, he could never hope to find a market in any American city.

again, just simply flee before the horrific mass, lest I start the remainder (what is hanging in the air) afresh to overwhelm me. I say "brace yourself," though I don't quite see why I need, having showed you in the past, so again and again, that your mania for the colossal, the swelling or the huge, the monotonously and repeatedly huge, breaks the heart of me for you, so convinced have I been all along that it means your simply burying yourself and all your products and belongings, and everything and Every One that is yours, in the most bottomless and thankless and fatal sandbunks. There is no use or application or power of absorption or assimilation for these enormities, beloved Hendrik, anywhere on the whole surface of the practicable, or, as I should rather say, impracticable globe; and when you write me that you are now lavishing time and money on a colossal ready-made City, I simply cover my head with my mantle and turn my face to the wall, and there, dearest Hendrik, just bitterly *weep* for you—just desperately and dismally and helplessly water that dim refuge with a salt flood. I have practically said these things to you before—though perhaps never in so dreadfully straight and sore a form as today: when this culmination of your madness, to the tune of five hundred millions of tons of weight, simply squeezes it out of me. For that, dearest boy, is the Dread Delusion to warn you against—what is called in Medical Science MEGALOMANIA (look it up in the dictionary!) in French *la folie des grandeurs,* the infatuated and disproportionate love and pursuit of, and attempt at, the Big, the Bigger, the Biggest, the Immensest Immensity, with all sense of proportion, application, relation and possibility madly submerged. What am I to say to you, gentle and dearest Hendrik, *but* these things, cruel as they may seem to you, when you write me (with so little *spelling* even—though that was always your wild grace!) that you are extemporizing a World-City from top to toe, and employing forty architects to see you through with it, etc.? How can I throw myself on your side to the extent of employing to back you a single letter of the Alphabet when you break to me anything so fantastic or out of relation to any reality of any kind in all the weary world???? The idea, my dear, old friend, fills me with mere pitying dismay, the unutterable WASTE of it all makes me retire into my room and lock the door to howl! Think of me as doing so, as howling for hours on end, and as not coming out till I hear from you that you have just gone straight out on the Ripetta and chucked the total mass of your Paraphernalia, planned to that end, bravely over the parapet and well into the Tiber. As if, beloved boy, any use on all the mad earth can be found for a ready-made city, made-while-one-waits, as they say, and which is the more preposterous and the more delirious, the more elaborate and the more "complete" and the more magnificent you have made it. Cities are living organisms that grow from within and by experience and piece by piece; they are not bought all hanging together, in *any* inspired studio anywhere whatsoever, and to attempt to plank one down on its area prepared, as even just merely projected, for use is to—well, it's to go forth into the deadly Desert and talk to the winds.

Dearest Hendrik, don't ask me to *help* you and to talk—don't, don't, don't. I should be so playing to you the part of the falsest, fatalest friend. But do *this*—realize how dismally unspeakably much these cold hard, desperate words, witholding sympathy, cost your ever-affectionate, your terribly tender old friend

Henry James

V

"MERE TWADDLE OF GRACIOUSNESS"

THE letters which follow are not all "mere twaddle," but they constitute our guide to the way in which Henry James used his method of cushion-words described in detail in the Introduction to this book. The key letter is the one addressed to Sarah Orne Jewett and for this reason it has been placed at the head of this group, out of its chronological place. A quite different instance is to be found in the letter to Vernon Lee which reflects James's embarrassment at having a book dedicated to him which he disliked. The verbal subterfuges to which he resorts convey his disapproval beyond a shadow of doubt.

The method has its shortcomings and treacheries, especially since posterity is not likely to understand all the nuanced ironies and delicate word-usages employed by the writer. The letter to Margot Asquith reflects this in particular. She had allowed James to read her diaries. He pays a full measure of tribute to their documentary value while calling her archly the "Balzac of diarists" and invoking gently the name of Saint Simon. The smothering extravagances of such letters in themselves serve as an index to James's feelings in writing them. If he is forced into the position of having to offer thanks he will inundate his correspondent with verbal sentiment; and if he is asked to read the overloaded diaries of the wife of a prime minister what can he, indeed, say? The answer for him lay in being opulently gracious, and playing at the same time a game of subtle verbal duplicity.

To SARAH ORNE JEWETT

Rye, Oct. 5, 1901

Dear Miss Jewett,[1]

Let me not criminally or at all events gracelessly, delay to thank you for your charming and generous present of *The Tory Lover*. He has been but three or four days in the house, yet I have given him an earnest, a pensive, a liberal—yes, a benevolent attention, and the upshot is that I should like to write you a longer letter than I just now—(especially as it's past midnight) —see my way to doing. For it would take me some time to dis-embroil the tangle of saying to you at once how I appreciate the charming touch, tact and taste of this ingenious exercise, and how little I am in sympathy with the experiments of its general (to my sense) misguided stamp. There I am!—yet I don't do you the outrage, as a fellow craftsman and a woman of genius and courage, to suppose you not as conscious as I am myself of all that, in these questions of art and truth and sincerity, is beyond the mere twaddle of graciousness. The "historic" novel is, for me, condemned even in cases of labour as delicate as yours, to a fatal *cheapness*, for the simple reason that the difficulty of the job is inordinate and that a mere *escamotage*, in the interest of ease, and of the abysmal public *naiveté* becomes inevitable. You may multiply the little facts that can be got from pictures and documents, relics and prints as much as you like—*the* real thing is almost impossible to do and in its essence the whole effect is as nought: I mean the invention, the

---

[1] For a critical discussion of this letter see the Introduction to this volume pp. xxv-xxvii.

representation of the old *consciousness,* the soul, the sense, the horizon, the vision of individuals in whose minds half the things that make ours, that make the modern world were non-existent. You have to think with your modern apparatus a man, a woman —or rather fifty—whose own thinking was intensely otherwise conditioned, you have to simplify back by an amazing tour de force—and even then it's all humbug. But there is a shade of the (even then) humbug that *may* amuse. The childish tricks that take the place of any such conception of the real job in the flood of Tales of the Past that seems of late to have been rolling over our devoted country—these ineptitudes have, on a few recent glances, struck me as creditable to no one concerned. You, I hasten to add, seem to me to have steered very clear of them—to have seen your work very bravely and handled it firmly; but even you court disaster by composing the whole thing so much by sequences of speeches. It's when the extinct soul talks, and the earlier consciousness airs itself, that the pit-falls multiply and the "cheap" way has to serve. I speak in general, I needn't keep insisting, and I speak grossly, summarily, by rude and provisional signs, in order to suggest my sentiment at all. I don't mean to say so much without saying more, and now I have douched you with cold water when I only meant just lightly and kindly to sprinkle you as for a new baptism— that is a re-dedication to altars but briefly, I trust, forsaken. Go back to the dear country of the Pointed Firs, *come* back to the palpable present *intimate* that throbs responsive, and that wants, misses, needs you, God knows, and that suffers woefully in your absence. Then I shall feel perhaps—and do it if only *for* that—that you have magnanimously allowed for the want of gilt on the gingerbread of the but-on-this occasion *only* limited sympathy of yours very constantly,   Henry James.

P.S. My tender benediction please to Mrs. Fields.

To VERNON LEE (Violet Paget)

St. Alban's Cliff
Bournemouth
May 10th [*1885*]

My dear Miss Paget.

I take up my pen, as we used to say in our infancy; but who shall say what I can possibly do with it in such a case? The difficulty is increased by the fact that I am on my knees, prostrate, humble, abject, in the dust.[1] That is an awkward position for articulate and intelligible speech, and yet I can't hold up my head, or rise to manly stature again, till I have caught some glimpse of a hint of a hope—even from the mere tremor of one of your eyelids—that there lurks in your generous nature, some slight capacity to pardon my disgusting conduct, my odious, unmannerly and inconceivable delay in writing to you. It is more inconceivable to me than to you, I assure you, and I haven't the slightest hesitation in saying that it is the most discreditable act (if *act* it can be called!) of an otherwise tolerably decent and virtuous life. Don't judge me by it, or if so, leave room for an appeal; for I hereby declare to you that the rest of my days shall be devoted to removing from your mind the vile implication my ignoble silence must have produced upon it. I am really not a bad person to be indebted to for compensation, and compensation you shall have, my dear Miss Paget, if I leave every other future duty and pleasure unregarded. There, I shall sit up again, and even with supplicating eyes, venture to look you in the face; not because I precipitately and fatuously assume that I have been forgiven, but because I do respectfully hope that you have listened. This has been for

---

[1] Vernon Lee had dedicated her first novel to Henry James. He had intensely disliked it and accordingly delayed acknowledging it. "I am sadly put to it to know what to write to *her*," he confided to T. S. Perry. "I think I shall be brave and tell her what I think—at least a little of it. The whole would never do."

me a winter of infinite domestic worry, preoccupation and anxiety, and my correspondence and many other social duties have been woefully neglected in consequence. After I had allowed myself to be prevented a certain time from writing to you, the simple *shame* of my situation, I assure you, settled upon me like a spell and paralyzed me quite. Every week that—by a detestable fatality—I didn't write, the redemptory step became more difficult, till at last I began to feel that any interest you may have had in hearing from me had completely died out and that if I were at last to address you you would merely return my letter, as a document that had fallen below its opportunities and had no intelligible message for you. This of course is nonsense; you have tolerance for all aberrations that are not of purpose, but only of hapless and accidental form. I am down at this dull place looking after my poor sister, who is wretchedly ill, and who has been for me, these last six months, a great anxiety and occupation. She came from America just at the time. *Miss B[rown]* came out, in very bad case, and I grieve to say, has steadily been getting worse. I am remaining with her for the present, and for I know not how much longer. My preoccupations on her account have had much to do with the *demoralized* state I sank into (there is no other word than that) on this subject of writing to you.

I read *Miss B* with eagerness, of course, as soon as I received the volumes, and have lately read a large part of them over again. It is to me an imperfect, but a very interesting book. As regards the *idea* of it, the conception and presentation of the character of the heroine, I think it a very fine one. The girl is really a very noble and remarkable vision, and she is sustained with singular evenness, in the key in which you have pitched her—except, I think at the end, in regard to the last fact that you have to relate of her. Making every allowance for a kind of grand rigidity and mournful, dismal, heroism that you have attributed to her—her offering to marry Hamlin strikes me as false, really unimaginable. Besides, *he* wouldn't, I think: he must at last have been immensely afraid of her, and his fear would have been deeper than his vanity. But Anne lives in the mind (outside of that point) as a creature projected (from *your* intelligence) in all her strange, original, tragic substance and form, with real imaginative and moral superiority. The imperfection of the book seems to me to reside (apart from, occasionally, a kind of intellectualized rowdyism of style) in a certain ferocity. It will probably already have been repeated to you to satiety that you take the aesthetic business too seriously, too tragically, and above all with too great an implication of sexual motives. There is a certain want of perspective and proportion. You are really too savage with your painters and poets and dilettanti; *life* is less criminal, less obnoxious, less objectionable, less crude, more *bon enfant,* more mixed and casual, and even in its most offensive manifestations, more *pardonable,* than the unholy circle with which you have surrounded your heroine. And then you have impregnated all those people too much with the sexual, the basely erotic preoccupation: your hand was over violent, the touch of life is lighter. This however is a secondary fact, with regard to the book; the primary one (for me) is that it's after my own heart in this sense: that it is bravely and richly, and continuously psychological and that, for you, *life* seems to mean moral and intellectual and spiritual life, and not the everlasting vulgar chapters of accidents, the dead rattle and rumble, which rise from the mere surface of things. I find the *donnée* of *Miss Brown* exceedingly in the right direction—a real subject, in the full sense of the word; carrying with it the revelation of character, which is the base of all things and finding its perspective in that; appealing too to the intelligence, the moral sense and experience of the reader. You have appealed indeed too much to that sense; and too little to 2 or 3 others—the plastic, visual, formal—perhaps. You have proposed to yourself too little to make a firm, compact work—and you have been too much in a moral passion! That has put certain exaggerations, overstatements, *grossissements,* insistences wanting in tact, into your head. Cool first—write afterwards. Morality is hot—but art is icy! Excuse my dogmatic and dictatorial tone, and believe it is only an extreme indication of interest and sympathy in what you do. I regard *Miss Brown* as a most interesting and (if the word didn't sound so patronizing I should say *promising*) experiment. It has in this age of thinnest levity and claptrap the signal merit of being serious. Write another novel. You owe it to yourself, and to me—to give me a chance to show how prompt I shall be on *that* occasion! Be, in it, more piously plastic, more devoted to *composition*—and less moral: for in that last way you will seem (if you care) to your probable readers less immoral than they appear to have found *Miss B.* Dear Miss Paget—I shall write you again for my spirit is greatly friendly to you. I shall also soon send you a book. I hope you are well and are coming this summer to England. I don't venture to breathe a word of the hope of hearing from you: that would be much happiness for yours most faithfully

Henry James.

To MRS. EDWIN AUSTIN ABBEY

34 De Vere Gardens W.

Nov. 1, 1894.

Dear Mrs. Abbey,

We are very unhappy at the non-arrival of our eggs[1] and are full of delicacy, at the same time, as to inquiring about them.

---

1 The Abbeys had been providing James with eggs from the barnyard of their country home.

Is the egg crop failing? Have the animals struck? Are we and they all victims of agricultural depression? I fear it, and if the disaster is at last upon us, won't you very kindly let me know the worst? I have been wanting yet fearing to write to you? Today at last I seem to find courage just to twitch the hem of your garment. I seem also to myself to have divined that you most naturally can't be any longer bothered by the bugbear of my breakfasts. It would indeed break down the patience of the angels. Nevertheless, a still, small hope does flicker in my breast. May we at any rate have news? News would be good, but eggs would be better. I shall hope for the best, but, after one tragic sob, I shall completely enter into the worst. With love to the Master,

Yours, Mrs. Abbey, in affectionate suspense,

Henry James.

To FRANCES HODGSON BURNETT

Lamb House, Rye,
Wednesday

Noblest of Neighbors, and Most Heavenly of Women!—

Your gorgeous, glorious gift shook Lamb House to its foundations an hour or two ago—but that agitated structure, with the light of purpose rapidly kindling in its eye, recuperates even as I write, with a sense of the futility, under the circumstances of a mere, economical swoon. We *may* swoon again—it is more than likely (if you *can* swoon from excess of everything!)—but we avail ourselves of this lucid interval absolutely to *fawn* upon you with the force of our gratitude.

It's too magnificent—we don't deserve the quarter (another peach, please—yes, it *is* the 7th—and *one* more fig— it *is* as I can't deny it—the 19th!) Well, I envy you the power to make a poor, decent body so happy—and, still more, so proud. The decent body has a pair of *other* decent bodies coming to him for the week's end, from town, and—my eye! won't he swagger over his intimate friend, the Princess of Maythem, for whom these trophies are as mere lumps of sugar or grains of salt.

For once in my life I shall be as I have always yearned and fondly dreamed: I shall say, "Tompkins, hand the fruits." And Tompkins, who has a red nose and is universally hideous, will look for the occasion like the celebrated picture of Utica's daughter, with the groaning, golden salver flourished in the air.

It has its crushing side—but I shall have sufficiently rebounded, even from *that* week's work (under the grape cure) to ride over to you again and pour forth at your feet the unalterable sentiments of yours, dear Mrs. Burnett, more and more gratefully and constantly,

Henry James

P.S. I shall wire my afternoon.

To MRS. EVERARD COTES

Rye. January 26th, 1900

Dear Mrs. Cotes,

I grovel in the dust—so ashamed am I to have made no response to your so generous bounty and to have left you unthanked and unhonoured. And all the while I was (at once) so admiring your consummately clever book,[1] and so blushing to the heels and groaning to the skies over the daily paralysis of my daily intention to make you some at least (if not adequate) commonly courteous and approximately intelligible sign. And

---

1 Mrs. Cotes had sent her novel *His Honor and a Lady* to James with the suggestion that its manner in some way resembled his own.

I have absolutely no valid, no sound, excuse to make but that
I am like that!—I mean I am an abandonedly bad writer of
letters and acknowledger of kindnesses. I throw myself simply
on my confirmed (in old age) hatred of the unremunerated pen
—from which one would think I have a remunerated one!

Your book is extraordinarily keen and delicate and able.
How can I tell if it's "like me"? I don't know what "me" is
like. I can't *see* my own tricks and arts, my own effect, from
outside at all. I can only say that if it *is* like me, then I'm much
more of a *gros monsieur* than I ever dreamed. We are neither
of us dying of simplicity or common addition; that's all I can
make out; and we are both very intelligent and observant and
conscious that a work of art must make some small effort to *be*
one; must sacrifice somehow and somewhere to the exquisite, or
be an asininity altogether. So we open the door to the Devil
himself—who is nothing but the sense of beauty, of mystery,
of relations, of appearances, of abysses of the whole—*and* of
EXPRESSION! That's *all* he is; and if he is our common parent
I'm delighted to welcome you as a sister and to be your brother.
One or two things my acute critical intelligence murmured to
me as I read. I think your drama lacks a little, *line*—bony structure and palpable, as it were, tense cord—on which to string
the pearls of detail. It's the frequent fault of women's work—
and *I* like a rope (the rope of the *direction and march of the
subject,* the action) pulled, like a taut cable between a steamer
and a tug, from beginning to end. It lapses and lapses along a
trifle too liquidly—and is too *much* conceived (I think) in
dialogue—I mean considering that it isn't conceived like a play.
Another reflection the Western idiot makes is that he is a little
tormented by the modern mixture (maddening medley of our
cosmopolite age) of your India (vast, pre-conceived and ab-
sently-present,) and your subject not of Indian essence. The two

things—elements—don't somehow illustrate each other, and are juxtaposed only by the terrible globe-shrinkage. But that's not *your* fault—it's mine that I suffer from it. Go on and go on —you are full of talent; of the sense of life and the instinct of presentation; of wit and perception and resource. Voilà.

It would be much more to the point to *talk* of these things with you, and some day, again, this must indeed be. But just now I am talking with few—wintering, for many good reasons, in the excessive tranquillity of this tiny, inarticulate country town, in which I have a house really adapted to but the balmier half of the year. And there is nothing cheerful to talk of. South Africa darkens all our sky here, and I gloom and brood and have craven questions of "Finis Britanniae?" in solitude. Your Indian vision at least keeps *that* abjectness away from you. But goodnight. It's past midnight; my little heavy-headed and heavy-hearted city sleeps; the stillness ministers to fresh flights of the morbid fancy; and I am yours, dear Mrs. Cotes, most constantly,

Henry James.

To MRS. WILFRID SHERIDAN

Lamb House
October 22, 1911

Dearest Clare.[1]

You should have heard the peal of strident laughter with which I greeted—and treated—your question of whether I shall really turn up on Friday next; a question so solemnly and so sacredly settled in the affirmative, an intention so ardently cherished, a prospect so fondly caressed! The earthworm and the silkworm have had their heads together over it all day and night, by speech, by letter, by telegraph and telephone and ex-

1 Clare Frewen Sheridan, a cousin of Sir Winston Churchill.

press messenger, ever since it flushed upon our vision and swam into our ken, and no visitations of Nature nor convulsions of Society, believe me, shall avail to prevent us from crawling breathlessly (for joy—but mutually supported,) into the bower of the gentle glowworms. I am to take to Waterloo on this never-to-be-sufficiently-accelerated Friday afternoon a train for Godalming that Howard[2] will designate to me and that he will "board", as they say in America, at Woking, I believe, having proceeded thither from Windsor. He will advise you of this delicious detail—of the hour, that is, of our arrival at Godalming—whence, as I understand it, we are to be precipitated into your arms. Let *me* advise you, scarce less conveniently, that I do not in the least propose to you the charge of a servant, whom I shall not in the least require or dream of bringing (I am but too glad to get rid of him:) and I shall really complicate your beautiful case, yours and Wilfred's, or encumber your sweet scene, not a tiny grain more than you can bear. I'm a good safe stodgy mass of *tact* and you'll scarcely notice that I'm there! I *do* eat bouncing beefsteaks, than'ee—quite freely; but I *can* partake of (and even subsist by) apples and nuts and Brussels sprouts, and even, vegetable marrow—on the vegetarian side of my nature. You talk of "devouring animals" as if there were bears and tigers about; but if your allusion is to *my* devouring them then I feel that the tender creatures from whom I expect mainly to derive refreshment, without the fear of a single tough mouthful, are just you and Wilfred. Well done and with that admirable Howdie sauce, I *shall* have a feast of you! I am sending you a small storybook lately published[3]—but as to which I have literally had to wait for this 1st possession of your

2 Howard Overing Sturgis of Qu'Acre, ("Howdie" to his friends), author of *Belchamber*.
3 Apparently *The Finer Grain* (1910).

address. Don't bother to read it—only *furnish* with it: every-thing counts. I will write your name on it in the pink parlor. I am yearning and languishing up to town of Thursday—to 105 Pall Mall SW—all-devotedly and impatiently, my dear Clare, yours both

Henry James.

To MARGOT ASQUITH

London, April 9th, 1915

My dear Margot Asquith,

By what felicity of divination were you inspired to send me a few days ago that wonderful diary under its lock and key?—feeling so rightly certain, I mean, of the peculiar degree and particular *pang* of interest that I should find in it? I don't wonder, indeed, at your general presumption to that effect, but the mood, the moment, and the resolution itself conspired to-gether for me, and I have absorbed every word of every page with the liveliest appreciation, and I think I may say intelli-gence. I have read the thing intimately, and I take off my hat to you as the Balzac of diarists. It is full of life and force and color, of a remarkable instinct for getting close to your people and things and for squeezing, in the case of the resolute por-traits of certain of your eminent characters, especially the last drop of truth and sense out of them—at least as the originals affected *your* singularly searching vision. Happy, then, those who had, of this essence, the fewest secrets or crooked lives to yield up to you—for the more complicated and unimagineable some of them appear, the more you seem to me to have caught and mastered them. Then I have found myself hanging on your impression in each case with the liveliest suspense and wonder, so thrillingly does the expression keep abreast of it and really translate it. This and your extraordinary fullness of opportunity, make of the record a most valuable English document, a rare revelation of the human inwardness of political life in this country, and a picture of manners and personal characters as 'creditable' on the whole (to the country) as it is frank and acute. The beauty is that you write with such authority, that you've seen so much and lived and moved so much, and that having so much chance to observe and feel and discriminate in the light of so much high pressure, you haven't been in the least afraid, but have faced and assimilated and represented for all you're worth.

I have lived, you see, wholly out of the inner circle of political life, and yet more or less in wondering sight, for years, of many of its outer appearances, and in superficial contact—though this, indeed, pretty anciently now—with various actors and figures, standing off from them on my quite different ground and neither able nor wanting to be of the craft or mystery (preferring, so to speak, my own poor, private ones, such as they have been) and yet with all sorts of unsatisfied curiosities and yearnings and imaginings in your general, your fearful direction. Well, you take me by the hand and lead me back and in, and still in, and make things beautifully up to me—*all*—my losses and misses and exclusions and privations—and do it by having taken all the right notes, apprehended all the right values and enjoyed all the right reactions—meaning by the right ones, those that must have ministered most to interest and emotion; those that I dimly made you out while getting while I flattened my nose against the shop window and you were there within, eating the tarts, shall I say, or handing them over the counter? It's today as if you had taken all the trouble for me and left me at last all the unearned increment or fine psychological gain! I have hovered about two or three of your distinguished persons a bit longingly (in the past); but you open up the abysses, or such like, that I really missed, and the torch you play over them is often luridly illuminating. I find my experience, therefore, the experience of simply reading you (you having had all t'other) varitably romantic. But I want so to go on that I deplore your apparent arrest—St. Simon is in forty volumes—why should Margot be put in one? Your own portrait is an extraordinarily patient and detached and touch-upon-touch thing; but the book itself really constitutes an image of you by its strength of feeling and living individual tone. An admirable portrait of a lady, with no end of finish and style, is thereby projected, and if I don't stop now, I shall be calling it a regular masterpiece.[1] Please believe how truly touched I am by your confidence in your faithful, though old, friend, Henry James.

[1] Margot Asquith's own footnote to this letter was: "Out of all my diaries, I have hardly been able to quote fifty pages, for on re-reading them I find they are not only full of political matters but jerky, disjointed and dull."

VI

"OVER THE ABYSS"

THE LAST letters of Henry James, those which he wrote between the outbreak of the war in 1914 and the onset of his final illness late in 1915, are among the most eloquent of all his utterances. He imagined himself as dipping his pen in ink and finding it dripping blood; he saw the collapse of his age and his century into barbarism. An abyss had opened up in the civilization he had always prized. James inscribed his *Notes on Novelists* to his friend Edmund Gosse "Over the Abyss."

James Joyce, perhaps echoing the American novelist, was to put into Stephen Dedalus's mouth the declaration that "History is a nightmare from which I am trying to awake." If he did, he was inverting James's description of the First World War as "a nightmare from which there is no waking save by sleep." James fought the nightmare as long as he could and then, in February of 1916, after becoming a British subject and receiving the Order of Merit from George V, he found the waking for which he had waited.

Through the late reaches of the nineteenth century liberalism had inured itself to an ideal of progress and "improvement" and democracy had made such gains that the crossing of the German armies into Belgium, as James clearly put it, could represent only a relapse into barbarism. After the first shock the novelist recovered his perspective: the Old Realist could still contemplate what was happening about him for it was still life, even if it was also a negation of life, and of all that he had stood for. There were soldiers to be helped, sick to be visited, refugees to be given shelter and solace. And when a group of Americans, among them sons of old friends, organized the American Volunteer Motor Ambulance Corps in France, James gave it his fullest measure of support, becoming its chairman and using his name and his pen to publicize its works.

At the end he seemed to himself an old soldier fighting beside the young and he identified himself with Walt Whitman, who many years before had ministered to the soldiers of James's own war, the one that he had lived through during his Newport youth, but in which he had not fought beause of ill-health. And when his valet enlisted, James wrote letters to him as if he were a son who had gone off to fight the cause that he himself was prepared to defend stoutly to the end.

To RHODA BROUGHTON

Rye. August 10th, 1914

Dearest Rhoda!

It is not a figure of speech but an absolute truth that even if I had not received your very welcome and sympathetic script I should be writing to you this day. I have been on the very edge of it for the last week—so had my desire to make you a sign of remembrance and participation come to a head; and verily I must—or may—almost claim that this all but "crosses" with your own. The only blot on our unanimity is that it's such an unanimity of woe. Black and hideous to me is the tragedy that gathers, and I'm sick beyond cure to have lived on to see

it. You and I, the ornaments of our generation, should have
been spared this wreck of our belief that through the long years
we had seen civilization grow and the worst become impossible.
The tide that bore us along was then all the while moving to
this as its grand Niagara—yet what a blessing we didn't know it.
It seems to me to *undo* everything, everything that was ours, in
the most horrible retroactive way—but I avert my face from
the monstrous scene!—you can hate it and blush for it without
my help; we can each do enough of that by ourselves. The
country and the season here are of a beauty of peace, and love-
liness of light, and summer grace, that make it inconceivable
that just across the Channel, blue as *paint* today, the fields of
France and Belgium are being, or about to be, given up to
unthinkable massacre and misery. One is ashamed to admire, to
enjoy, to take any of the normal pleasure, and the huge shining
indifference of Nature strikes a chill to the heart and makes me
wonder of what abysmal mystery, or villainy indeed, such a cruel
smile is the expression. In the midst of it all at any rate we
walked, this strange Sunday afternoon (9th), my niece Peggy,
her youngest brother and I, about a mile out, across the blessed
grass mostly, to see and have tea with a genial old Irish friend
(Lady Mathew, who has a house here for the summer,) and
came away an hour later bearing with us a substantial green
volume, by an admirable eminent hand, which our hostess had
just read with such a glow of satisfaction that she overflowed
into easy lending. I congratulate you on having securely put it
forth before this great distraction was upon us—for I am utterly
pulled up in the midst of a rival effort by finding that my job
won't at all consent to be done in the face of it. The picture of
little private adventures simply fades away before the great
public. I take great comfort in the presence of my two young
companions, and above all in having caught my nephew by the

coat-tail only *just* as he was blandly starting for the continent on Aug. 1st. Poor Margaret Payson is trapped somewhere in France—she *having* then started, though not for Germany, blessedly; and we remain wholly without news of her. Peggy and Aleck have four or five near maternal relatives lost in Germany—though as Americans they may fare a little less dreadfully there than if they were English. And I have numerous friends—we all have, haven't we?—inaccessible and unimaginable there; it's becoming an anguish to think of them. Nevertheless I do believe that we shall be again gathered into a blessed little Chelsea drawing-room—it will be like the reopening of the salons, so irrepressibly, after the French revolution. So only sit tight, and invoke your heroic soul, dear Rhoda, and believe me more than ever all-faithfully yours,

Henry James

To WILLIAM ROUGHEAD

London, September 30th 1914

My dear Roughead,

We do indeed meet again in portentous, prodigious conditions—but I take all the more pleasure in our meeting. Our last seems to me to have been half-a-century ago; so utterly broken off and disconnected, and all in a night, has become every blest old fact of the happy world made for our stricken sight, as we turn it back, by the simple, or at least the single, the comprehensive circumstance of its not having been a perpetual black nightmare. However, *my* dark dream has lights, lurid, but extremely vivid; I never *wanted* to live on to see the collapse of so many fond faiths, which makes all the past, with this hideous card all the while up its sleeve, seem now a long treachery, an unthinkable humbug: and *yet* in a manner the whole business, as world-revolution, has its uplifting side, the side on which I see England (and Scotland!) as having, after too long, *found* themselves again—or found a part of themselves, a hugely vital and essential, which had seemed a good deal lost. Here it is again—magnificent! and it enormously interests, sustains and reassures me. But there is too much of all *that* to say—and meanwhile we watch, we take it all in, we *believe*—! I'm sure I speak for you there as much as for myself.

It's delightful to have had the Juridical[1] from you again to turn to—from the horrific Daily Press; which I can neither live without nor live with. Mr. Smith's is a very pretty tale, always with your fine light touch, and worth re-telling; yet would have been more worth it, one reflects, if he had only been more of a hand at his noble craft. Crimes are too apt not to be fine enough for me, nor the manner of them elegant enough; though I recognize of course that you can make your nosegay but of the flowers kindly Nature does suffer to meet your searching eye. Mr. Smith's petals are not quite of rich enough hue—he grew them too fast and too freely. Of a more pleasing tint are those of E. M. Chantrelle, the report of whose Edinburgh case (picked up off the booktable at a Club) I had very oddly indeed but just laid down—after perusal, when I came home yesterday to find your good remembrance! Root out some others of *his* baleful charm; though again even he sins by excess of the obvious. Don't cease to believe that I am always interested in whatever you produce, always sure to find a savor in it, and above all always most faithfully yours   Henry James.

---

1 William Roughead, (1870-1952) Scottish jurist, regularly sent James his chronicles of famous murder trials, much to the novelist's delight.

To EDITH WHARTON

London, December 1st, 1914.

Dearest Edith,

Walter[1] offers me kindly to carry you my word, and I don't want him to go empty-handed, though verily only the poor shrunken sediment of me is practically left after the overwhelming and *écrasant* effect of listening to him on the subject of the transcendent high pitch of Berlin. I kick myself for being so flattened out by it, and ask myself moreover why I should feel it in any degree as a revelation, when it consists really of nothing but what one has been constantly saying to one's self—one's mind's eye perpetually blinking at it, as presumably the case—all these weeks and weeks. It's the personal note of testimony that has caused it to knock me up—what has permitted this being the nature and degree of my unspeakable and abysmal sensibility where "our cause" is concerned, and the fantastic force, the prodigious passion, with which my affections are engaged in it. They grow more and more so—and my soul is in the whole connection one huge sore ache. That makes me dodge lurid lights when I ought doubtless but personally to glare back at them—as under the effect of many of my impressions here I frequently do—or almost! For the moment I am quite floored—but I suppose I shall after a while pick myself up. I dare say, for that matter, that I am down pretty often—for I find I am constantly picking myself up. So even this time I don't really despair. About Belgium Walter was so admirably and unspeakably interesting—if the word be not mean for the scale of such tragedy—which you'll have from him all for yourself. If I don't call his Berlin simply interesting and have done with it, that's because the very faculty of attention is so overstrained by it as to

[1]Walter Berry, a distinguished lawyer, and for many years a friend of Mrs. Wharton, had just passed through London on his way back to Paris from a brief trip to Berlin.

hurt. This takes you all my love. I have got back to trying to work—on one of three books begun and abandoned—at the end of some "30,000 words"—15 years ago,[2] and fished out of the depths of an old drawer at Lamb House (I sent Miss Bosanquet[3] down to hunt it up) as perhaps offering a certain defiance of subject to the law by which most things now perish in the public blight. This does seem to kind of intrinsically resist—and I have hopes. But I must rally now before getting back to it. So pray for me that I do, and invite dear Walter to kneel by my side and believe me your faithfully fond

Henry James

To RICHARD NORTON

Rye, 9.19.14

My dear Richard,

Your admirable letter quite makes me break my heart over the fact of my not having known you were in London these last three or four days, where I should at once have taken such measures to see—for I got back this afternoon from a short stay there (with Mrs. Wharton at 25 Grosvenor Place) only an hour before getting your news. I go back to town a few days hence to remain —but then you will be off on your magnificent errand of mercy for which I admire and bless you more than I can say. I supposed—or imagined—you still in America not knowing you had returned hither and still less that you had been to Paris. I wired you at once today about your trying to see Mrs. Wharton, but I quite take it for granted it will have been impossible to you— and I did so on the barest chance. She goes back to 53 Rue de Varenne herself in a very few days—she came away but about

2 *The Sense of the Past.*

3 Theodora Bosanquet, the novelist's amanuensis, during the last decade of his life.

three weeks since.—I echo with all my heart—or rather I farther extend—your sense of the enviable element in your Uncle William Darwin's closing his eyes to these horrors that men of his generation and mine had never supposed, never dreamt, we were to live on to see with the weakening chill of age upon us. I see him cover his kind head with his mantle and give it all up. So I would fain do, I confess to you! and at the same time I *care*, unutterably, that the right should now be awfully achieved and the whole Infamy rolled in the dust! Only, alas, what an amount of doing it will take!—not indeed that I doubt for a moment it will *be* done! I can't tell you how I rejoice in your splendid spirit of service, my dear Richard—it makes me proud of your acquaintance so to speak, and of our common nationality. May you indeed carry balm to the so horribly stricken! But I quite unspeakably regret not to have had sight of you—when I might. You would have had so much to tell me—and, hurried as you must have been, how kind of you to write!—Let me repeat that I shall most exceedingly miss, for old and long friendship's sake, dear W. E. D. I was exceedingly fond of him—and what a void now for Sally's and Lily's London—if they are ever to have a London again. However, of course, they will have the grange— heaven send you are able to keep it. Heaven—though a strange heaven now!—send you all furtherance every hour. Yours, my dear Dick, all affectionately,

Henry James

To FLORENCE PERTZ

London, Jan. 21st 1915

My dear Florence[1]

I *did* have a bad time on Monday night—but it's over now; and I fear the moral simply is that in these belated days I

[1]Florence Pertz, grand-daughter of Dr. J. J. Garth Wilkinson, English physician and Swedenborgian friend of the elder Henry James.

mustn't dine out at all—on any contingency whatever. The cabless void stretched away, in space and time without limit, wholly mocking at *any* amount of whistle; but the kind gentleman who had come to you from out of town with his wife, overtook me mercifully, and proceeding to the Bayswater Road with my whistle ended by bringing a taxi back to where I leaned against a railing under the extremity of an attack of angina pectoris—which *any* "upset," however small, exposes me to in this dark age. What had started it was witnessing the vanity of your bareheaded and uncovered maid's tooting in the icy blast and the unbrokenly irresponsive desert. I *had* to turn her in and then my own reiterated vain toot, and consequent despair (till I was rescued by that priceless gentleman) did the rest. But I had of course my remedial drug—nitro-glycerine—and once it had time to act, and the protective taxi gave it a chance, I began to recover and was in a much better state on getting home. But I am a very cracked vessel and really should stay on the shelf.

Yours all truly

Henry James

To BURGESS NOAKES

London, Mar 22nd, 1915

My dear Burgess.[1]

I have delayed longer than I meant to thank you for your interesting letter of the 9th. of this month—that *does* seem a good while ago. But I know Minnie has written to you (she and Joan showed me your excellent and amusing letter to them) and we have sent you certain articles of refreshment which I hope you

[1] Burgess Noakes came into Henry James's service at Lamb House in his early 'teens. He served first as house-boy in a staff that included a cook, a maid and a gardener. As he grew older he became James's personal valet and travelled with the novelist to America in 1904 and 1910. When Noakes joined the service, James wrote him a series of fatherly letters of which this one is a characteristic example.

have safely received or are in the act of receiving. I shall pack off to you some more Food and Chocolate as soon as I can get again to the Stores—I judge that that is more "comforting" to you, under your wear and tear, than anything else. But remember that if there is any particular thing you want and will mention it to us even by a simple post card you shall have it at once. The jolly plucky spirit of your letters gives me the greatest pleasure, and makes me feel that you are seeing life indeed. It is an immense adventure, truly, and one in which, if things go well with you, as I so heartily hope they will, you will always be glad and proud to have played your part. Play it up to the very notch and take all the interest in it you possibly can. I like immensely your telling me how you hold out in marches, under whatever drawbacks, when longer legs have to fall out; this does you the greatest honour. What a lot you must be seeing, feeling and above all hearing—with that terrific artillery always in your ears! Notice and observe and remember all you can—we shall want to have every scrap of it from you on your return.

We go on as quietly here as all our public anxiety and suspense allow; and it helps us greatly that we believe in you all at the Front so thoroughly and are doing all we can, very great things in fact, to make you believe in *us.* I get on personally very well with such help as Minnie can render me in the small valeting way, and I think it must be a proof of my being better of those two or three old troubles, comparatively better I mean, that I manage so fairly without much aid. George is coming up from Rye in a day or two, to be with us from Wednesday noon of this week (this is Monday) to Saturday evening next; and he will of course greatly miss you, as I think he has no great turn for finding his way about London alone. But we shall take good care of him and Minnie goes to meet him at the station. Make, by the way, very free use of that ointment we sent you—I hope you will find it a really good preventive; if you do we shall keep you supplied with it without interruption. We are having very decent and Springlike dry days, in fact weeks, here now, and I hope this weather and the wet are all much less against you at the Front, than they were for so long. Cultivate good relations with the French whenever you come in contact with them—which must be, in one way and another, pretty often; they are a wonderfully clever and intelligent, a highly civilized people when you come to know them; though of course you see them now under the most tremendous strain and burden that ever a nation had to bear. Like them, admire them and fraternise with them as much as you can; I used to see much of them in my younger time, and I take the most enormous satisfaction in their Alliance with this country. So do all you can to contribute your mite to the success of that! But goodbye now—and all good fortune to you! We shan't let you want for letters, or for anything else, if you will have a bit of patience with us; and I am yours very truly

Henry James

Oughtn't you, for your address to tell us your Brigade or Division or whatever, for locating you more easily to the postal authorities?

To PRIME MINISTER H. H. ASQUITH.
London, June 28th, 1915.
My dear Prime Minister and Illustrious Friend,[1]

I am venturing to trouble you with the mention of a fact of my personal situation, but I shall do so as briefly and considerately as possible. I desire to offer myself for naturalization in this

---

1 This letter was written by James on his return from a visit to the Prime Minister at Walmer Castle.

country, that is, to change my status from that of American cit-
izen to that of British subject. I have assiduously and happily
spent here all but 40 years, the best years of my life, and I find
my wish to testify at this crisis to the force of my attachment and
devotion to England, and to the cause for which she is fighting,
finally and completely irresistible. It brooks at least no inward
denial whatever. I can only testify by laying at her feet my
explicit, my material and spiritual allegiance, and throwing into
the scale of her fortune my all but imponderable moral weight
— 'a poor thing but mine own.' Hence this respectful appeal.
It is necessary (as you may know) that for the purpose I speak of
four honorable householders should bear witness to their kind
acquaintance with me, to my apparent respectability, and to my
speaking and writing English with an approach of propriety.
What I presume to ask of you is whether you will do me the
honour to be the pre-eminent one of that gently guaranteeing
group? Edmund Gosse has benevolently consented to join it.
The matter will entail on your part, as I understand, no expen-
diture of attention at all beyond your letting my solicitor wait
upon you with a paper for your signature—the affair of a single
moment; and the 'going through' of my application will doubtless be proportionately expedited. You will thereby consecrate
my choice and deeply touch and gratify yours all faithfully,

Henry James

INDEX

INDEX